D1534891

PRAISE FOR *BEYOND TENEBRAE*

"It's as if C. S. Lewis and Christopher Dawson were sent by God to touch the mind of Brad Birzer to communicate to the rest of us mere mortals those deeper truths about ourselves of which we constantly need reminding even though they are never quite forgotten."
— **FRANCIS J. BECKWITH**, Professor of Philosophy and Church-State Studies, Baylor University

"Over the last several decades, it has become clear that the greatest achievement of the West is its tradition of Christian humanism. In this age of forgetting, we need to be reminded yet again of the principles and fruits that come to us from that tradition, sprung from the seeds of Athens and Jerusalem, from sacred scripture and the classics. Bradley J. Birzer's new study comes just in time, giving us in one brief volume a rich account of Christian humanism's vision and its greatest disciples. May it inspire yet a new generation to become civilized."
— **JAMES MATTHEW WILSON**, Associate Professor of Humanities and Augustinian Traditions, Villanova University

"In *Beyond Tenebrae*, Brad Birzer sketches an image of the darkness of the present day — Tenebrae, the dying of the light — but gives us as well a humanist hope for what lies beyond these shadows. He explores the lives and influences of a number of 20th-century humanists, and he adds to them — frames them with — his own deep experience. Indeed, it is a deeply personal book, a genealogy of reading, starting in 1977, when Birzer first read Tolkien's *The Silmarillion* — an experience that influences to this day the way he conceives of humanism and the Christian future. This is a book of pieties, not only to great figures important in Birzer's intellectual life, such as Russell Kirk and Christopher Dawson, but to all who participate nobly in the Republic of Letters that connects us to the whole of humanity."
— **GLENN ARBERY**, President, Wyoming Catholic College

"In *Beyond Tenebrae*, Brad Birzer offers us insight into the wonder, mystery, and power of the individual — ranging from Ray Bradbury to Margaret Atwood to Ronald Reagan. In each, he finds sparks of hope and imagination, ready to set the world on fire, even in these strange times."
— **KEVIN J. ANDERSON**, New York Times bestselling co-author of *Dune: House Atreides*

"*Beyond Tenebrae* reflects the very personal ruminations of one of America's leading conservative historians on the true meaning of humanism. Bradley Birzer looks back into the past to show us how renewal and restoration of the truth about man can become real in the future. In these pages, readers will discover a Republic of Letters of great minds and proud spirits conversing with each other across the ages. They will not be disappointed."

— **SAMUEL GREGG**, Research Director, Acton Institute

"This wonderful, wide-ranging, and rollicking guide to Christian humanism is bursting with both profound insights and infectious energy, exactly what we've come to expect from the lively mind and trenchant pen of Brad Birzer."

— **CARL E. OLSON**, Editor, *Catholic World Report*

BEYOND TENEBRAE

BEYOND
Tenebræ

CHRISTIAN HUMANISM
in the
TWILIGHT OF THE WEST

BRADLEY J. BIRZER

Angelico Press

First published in the USA
by Angelico Press 2019
Copyright © Bradley J. Birzer 2019

For information, address:
Angelico Press, Ltd.
169 Monitor St.
Brooklyn, NY 11222
www.angelicopress.com

978-1-62138-497-7 pb
978-1-62138-498-4 hb
978-1-62138-499-1 ebook

Book and cover design
by Michael Schrauzer

Dedicated to my Hillsdale brethren

Lee Cole, Mark Kalthoff, John J. Miller,
Paul Moreno, Ivan Pongracic, and *Stephen Smith*

TABLE OF CONTENTS

PREFACE ix

INTRODUCTION: Beyond Tenebrae xiii

I CONSERVING CHRISTIAN HUMANISM

  1 Humanism: A Primer 3

  2 Humanism: The Corruption of a Word 7

  3 The Conservative Mind 13

  4 Burke and Tocqueville 17

  5 What to Conserve? 21

  6 Conserving Humanism 27

II PERSONALITIES AND GROUPS

  1 T. E. Hulme 37

  2 Irving Babbitt 43

  3 The Christian Humanism of Paul Elmer More 51

  4 The Order Men 61

  5 Willa Cather 69

  6 Canon B. I. Bell 77

  7 Christopher Dawson 81

  8 Nicolas Berdyaev's Unorthodoxy 97

  9 Theodor Haecker, Man of the West 103

  10 The Inklings and J. R. R. Tolkien 107

  11 Sister Madeleva Wolff 125

  12 Peacenik Prophet: Russell Kirk 129

  13 St Russell of Mecosta? 133

  14 Eric Voegelin 137

  15 Flannery O'Connor 149

  16 Clyde Kilby 153

  17 Friedrich Hayek's Intellectual Lineage 159

  18 Ray Bradbury at His End 169

19 Shirley Jackson's Haunting. 173

20 Wendelin E Basgall. 177

21 Julitta Kuhn Basgall 183

22 Ronald Reagan. 187

23 Walter Miller's Augustinian Wasteland 195

24 Alexander Solzhenitsyn as Prophet 201

25 The Ferocity of Marvin O'Connell. 205

26 The Good Humor of Ralph McInerny 209

27 The Beautiful Mess That is Margaret Atwood 213

     CONCLUSION: Confusions and Hope 221

PREFACE

THE CHRISTIAN HUMANISTS HAVE HAUNTED my imagination all of my life. When I was just aged ten, I first encountered *The Silmarillion*. Though I could make little sense of the overall story, I read and re-read—too many times to count—the introduction, essentially the story of the first chapter of Genesis if it had been written by Plato. From that moment, my understanding of the humanities was Catholic, and my understanding of Catholicism was humane. After too many nerdy teenage years reading Austrian and Chicago School economics (as well as loads of science fiction), I re-encountered Tolkien in a philosophy class as an undergraduate at the University of Notre Dame. Kevin McCormick, one of my two closest friends in college, also reintroduced me to the depths of Catholicism through many, many, many late-night discussions. I also found myself falling in love with Russell Kirk's *The Conservative Mind* in the fall of 1989, that *annus mirabilis* of all twentieth-century years. From that reading forward, my life wouldn't be the same, and the Christian humanist encounters became greater and greater. In December 1991, I read a brilliant piece on "Decadence and Christian Humanism" by Gleaves Whitney. In 1995, I met Winston Elliott, later the co-founder of one of the most important websites dealing with Christian humanism, *The Imaginative Conservative*, as well as the person with whom I most regularly discuss the ideas that matter most in the world. Only a few years later, I met *the* Gleaves Whitney (of "Decadence" fame) and Joseph Pearce, each of whom gave talks on a whole series of Christian humanists: G.K. Chesterton, Hilaire Belloc, C.S. Lewis, Christopher Dawson, Wilhelm Roepke, E.I. Watkin, and E.F. Schumacher. By 1999, Christian humanism and the Christian humanists had come to occupy almost all of my professional thoughts (such as they are). My department chair and fellow Christian humanist, Mark

Kalthoff, even offered me my own seminar on the subject, beginning in the spring of 2003. I have had the privilege of teaching
the course every other year since. I have also had the privilege
of delving into the lives of several humanists — J.R.R. Tolkien,
Christopher Dawson, and Russell Kirk, to name the three most
important to me — finding biography the most satisfying way to
explore personalism and humanism.

The book you now hold in your hands (whether tangibly or on
your Kindle) is the result of writings and thoughts and guesses
and assumptions and presumptions and prejudices and dogmas
that have never made it into any book and have resided safely, if
somewhat timidly, in my own mind and soul. If they have appeared
before, they've appeared mostly at *The Imaginative Conservative*,
Catholic World Report, *The American Conservative*, *Spirit of Cecilia*,
Stormfields, *Politico*, and *Modern Age*.

I've divided this book by ideas, and by the persons and groups
best embodying those ideas. In no way do I want to give the sug-
gestion that there was some kind of ideological unity among those
mentioned in this book. They definitely shared certain principles
and (especially) definite worries about the horrors committed by
the ideological regimes — whether fascist or communist or some
combination of the two — over the last 100 years. Some of those
discussed in this book did not personally know the others mentioned; sometimes those mentioned held fast friendships with
others mentioned; and, not infrequently, some of those mentioned
really disliked and despised others mentioned. Thus, one should
not come away from this book believing that the figures here
formed some kind of cell or party. Indeed, they were too intensely
personalist to be conformist!

Additionally, I do not want to pretend any kind of strict academic
objectivity in this book, though I am a professional historian. Each
of the humanists discussed in this book has touched me — intellectually or spiritually — in some vital way. I consider them allies,
friends, and mentors, but never mere subjects. Throughout my
adult life, I have done my best to get to know each of them. I speak
to them often, and they speak to me through their deposits and

treasures of words. This book is an attempt to introduce some great women and men to new generations, present and future, of great women and men. The Republic of Letters, after all, may rest, but it should never sleep.

Two things should be noted before diving into the book itself.

First, I have used footnoting selectively and, I hope, with common sense. Generally, if the chapter deals with only one primary work, I forgo footnoting. I do, however, try to footnote whatever is not necessarily common bibliographic knowledge. I have, for reasons that I hope are obvious, footnoted more tenaciously in Part I than I have in Part II.

Second, I have a number of folks to thank, all of whom either encouraged or helped with my own thoughts as expressed in this book: Dedra Birzer; Nathaniel Birzer; Gretchen Birzer; Steve Hayward; Francesca Murphy; David Deavel; Kevin J. Anderson; Matt Gaetano; Maria Grace Birzer; Harry Birzer; John Augustine Birzer; Veronica Rose Birzer; Allen Mendenhall; Gary Gregg; John Riess; Ulrich Lehner; Wilson Miscamble; John Zmirak; James Matthew Wilson; Mark LeBar; Carl Olson; Dave Smith; Greg Spawton; Tom Woods; Erik Heter; Tad Wert; Kevin McCormick; Winston Elliott; Steve Klugewicz; Dan McCarthy; Jim Otteson; Dave Stewart; Gleaves Whitney; Rita Feist; Kevin Birzer; Todd Birzer; Steve Horwitz; Sarah Skwire; Ingrid Gregg; Sam Gregg; Dan Hugger; Charissa Reul; Charles Alvarez; Mark Yellin; Amy Willis; Doug Denuyl; Alex Salter; Mahesh Skreekandath; Rick Krueger; Abby Blanco; Rachel Gough; Laurel Good; Jordan Wales; Mary Kate Lindsey; Anne Rolfe; Melinda Nielsen; Kelley Vlahos; Chris VanOrman; and all of the ones to whom this book is dedicated.

Bradley J. Birzer
Hillsdale, Michigan
Feast of Our Lady of Sorrows, 2019

Introduction:

BEYOND TENEBRAE

Darkness

I AM FASCINATED BY THE RECOGNITION OF Tenebrae (the hours after 3pm on Good Friday)—the moment when the world shook with the absence of grace. The extinguishing of light, candle by candle; the stripping of the altar; the beating of the books; the departure from the chapel in a deafening silence.

The state of the world, the state of our republic, and the state of Western and American culture linger in Tenebrae. Hovering, circling, peering into the abyss, too timid to jump in, not strong enough to walk away. Easter comes and goes, and Western culture seems to have missed it—its reality, its symbolism, its joy, its glimpse of all that is Good, True, and Beautiful.

This is to state the obvious: we live in a time of great troubles. When our present time of troubles began ... well, it is difficult to say, definitively. But troubled it is.

Maybe it began when Radical Islam once more asserted itself in a very bloody and tangible way; maybe it began when Presidents George H.W. Bush and Bill Clinton refused to follow-up and solidify Reagan's cold war triumphs; maybe it began when the United States deserted an ally in the spring of 1975; or when the United States acquiesced to Operation Keelhaul, forcing repatriation of Russian citizens in 1946 and 1947. Or when the Bolsheviks claimed victory in the autumn of 1917, or when an obscure Serbian terrorist killed an Austrian Archduke in 1914; or when a Russian dissident published "What is to be Done" in 1902; or, perhaps, when a terrorist struck Tsar Alexander II in 1881. "The first bomb wounded several Cossacks of the Imperial Guard. Tsar Alexander II got out of his carriage to see in person to the care of the wounded men," Whittaker Chambers described in *Cold Friday*. The Tsar "even spoke, 'not urgently' we are told, to the terrorist who had thrown the bomb, and thanked God that the damage was no greater. 'It is too early to thank God yet,' said Grinevitsky, and tossed a second bomb between the Tsar's feet. The explosion tore him apart, and killed Grinevitsky. 'Home to the Palace, to die there,' muttered the dying Tsar."[1] What other incident of the previous two centuries since the French Revolution could reveal as much regarding the divide between the old, Christian world, and the new, sterile world of terrorism and ideology?

Most likely, our time of troubles began long before any of these events. But, without question, the time of troubles has increased in violence and intensity. We continue to wallow in darkness, in Tenebrae, as citizens of Western civilization. We've flirted with the abyss for well over a century. And while as a whole, we've not stepped in — again, too entranced to walk away, too uncertain to walk in — we've watched many thrown in against their will, and we've stood by, all too often, in complete silence.

From any perspective, a look back over the recent past is messy. It's difficult to see through the limbs, the parts, the pieces, the charred flesh, the coagulated blood that once made up individual human persons, unique in origin, unique in dignity, time, and place. The field of history and our vision of it are obscured: littered with the victims, the Jewish and Christian martyrs of the twentieth and twenty-first centuries — those humans not deemed quite human enough by those wielding power in their ideological death camps and regimes throughout the world.

We also live in an age of confusions, as explored in the conclusion to this work.

A Republic of Letters

In the Western academy, many brilliant and well-meaning scholars drown in their own subjective realities. We might trace this back

---

1 Whittaker Chambers, *Cold Friday* (New York: Random House, 1964), 147.

to the most important trends and thinkers of the nineteenth and early twentieth centuries. A look at three of the most significant men of that time period reveals much about the modern world and the ultimate denigration of the human person. Though I could list more, I'll list the three most obvious: Karl Marx, Charles Darwin, and Sigmund Freud. Their ideas have had consequences. Each, in his own right, offered some serious insights on the nature of man and of the world, whether we agree with the ideas or not.

But the form of the ideas, as presented by each of these figures, is extremely important as well. Each of these men, by focusing on a particular aspect of the human person, ignored the whole of the human person. Or worse, each exaggerated the particular aspect, claiming it to define the whole person. For Marx, man is at heart economic. For Darwin, man is biological. For Freud, man is psychological. Each of these things is true. But man — a complexity and mystery even to himself — is all of these things and so much more. This is what twentieth and twenty-first century society continues to misunderstand, whether in the corrupt soul of some dictator in the East or in the labyrinth of a bureaucrat's mind in the West.

As scholars such as historian Christopher Dawson and theologian Romano Guardini have penetratingly noted, modernity compartmentalizes all things — breaking things into units, and then breaking down such units even further. When dissecting a thing, not only is the thing lost, but all connection to a universal truth and reality is lost.

> No longer does the unity of the different spheres of man's existence and of his activities seem obvious, a matter of course. Man begins to hesitate, moving from one sphere to another, from the domain of faith to that of human culture, from the field of ethics to that of aesthetics, from philosophy to politics. There is no longer found the somewhat naive ease by which criteria valid in one sphere were transferred to another, by which the results obtained in one area were taken uncritically into another. Each sphere tends to find its own roots in itself, seeking what especially sets it apart from all other spheres. Each sphere seeks its

own specific meaning and purpose, its own basic values, its authentic standards of validity and its corresponding norms by which all efforts in this sphere are determined; that is, it seeks its own, critically pure, methods.

Understanding "culture" in its broadest sense, as the embodiment of what man creates and himself becomes in his living encounter with the surrounding world, the autonomy of the various spheres of culture is at issue, an autonomy first vaguely felt, then becoming more demanding, seeking its theoretical foundation. Thus the different spheres grow apart from each other, according to their subject and mode of operating, their constitutive value and specific method. This often is accompanied by severe struggles, tainted by an attitude irreligious in fact or in appearance, breaking asunder sacred claims of order and tradition. The specific character of each domain is consistently emphasized with ever greater one-sidedness and persistence, as seems the rule with contradictory human nature.

The specific areas begin to arise. Science recognizes nothing except what arises in methodical consequence from the quest for truth within its own sphere. For art there is nothing except what serves exclusively the realization of aesthetic values, the perfection of expression and form. Politics has no other aim but to maintain and increase the power and welfare of the state. In commercial life no standard and value are acknowledged which do not lead to the maximum in production and to saturation with material goods. Ethics as a pure "doing good for the sake of good" grows without taking account of any religious or secular concerns. Each domain asserts itself so emphatically that the unifying view of the whole is lost before each domain's claim to autonomy.[2]

---

2   Romano Guardini, *Foundations of Pedagogy*, 12. This version is originally in German, translated into English. Personal copy in my possession.

The question must be asked, how do we move back toward true unity and wholeness without imposing a stifling conformity? How can we place the human person back in the order of things — fallen, but bearing the image of God? How can we bring the highest out of the person, elevating the best qualities while attenuating the worst, without remaking that person in OUR own image?

One thing must be noted, and noted repeatedly. For, I think, modernity and postmodernity have led all of us to believe, for a variety of reasons, that changes can happen quickly, that solutions come almost as quickly, and that all things are solvable. Not all things are solvable, and change that happens quickly usually only adds new problems, thus demanding new changes and new solutions. Because of the complexity of each individual person and the unfathomable complexity of existence itself, real change requires time, laborious effort, fortitude, and patience. The world cannot be fixed overnight. If we want to reform the world, we must exert the necessary effort and not look for the quick and easy fix. We must strive for victory, but we must do so with humility.

How can we dedicate ourselves to what has been given to us by thousands of years of thought and of sacrifice by men and women? From the Greek agora to the Jewish Temple to the Roman Senate; to that Good Friday at the Place of Skulls; to a seat on the shores of North Africa, watching the Vandals descend, recording what we can over 14 years in the *City of God*; to a beheading under a Friesian sky as St Boniface challenged one too many Norse gods; to an imaginary journey through hell, purgatory, and paradise; to a stage where we are "merely players"; to the commons of Lexington, deciding whether to entrench or retreat; to the Hornet's Nest of Shiloh, calling upon the tradition of Leonidas to defend and protect to the last man, preventing those who would enslave a man for the accidents of his skin color from triumphing over the U.S. Constitution; to a flight over September 2001 Pennsylvania skies, knowing that no more innocents need die that day for a heresy.

Ideologies, no matter how limiting or dangerous, continue to attract the attention of scholars "because there remains a culturally systemic misconception of four subjects: human nature, virtue, education, and tradition."³ From the ancients, however, one can find powerful alternatives to the superficiality and violence of modern ideologies. Cicero understood that the ties that hold man to man originated in the language of the gods:

> Man was endowed by the supreme god with a grand status at the time of his creation. He alone of all types and varieties of animate creatures has a share in reason and thought, which all the others lack. What is there, not just in humans, but in all heaven and earth, more divine than reason? When it has matured and come to perfection, it is properly named wisdom…. Reason forms the first bond between man and god.⁴

When man recognizes his connection to the divine through wisdom, he will be a "citizen of the whole world as if it were a single city."⁵

A man deeply rooted in the Great Tradition of the West and a follower of Cicero, Harvard's Christopher Dawson, argued for a Republic of Letters, one that recognizes that continuity of thought and dialogue and sacrifice, generation to generation. As proof of the power of the Republic of Letters, Dawson offered us this example: Without a Republic of Letters,

> there would have been two completely separate cultures in the Protestant North and the Catholic South, divided by an iron curtain of persecution and repression which would have made the two parts of Europe as alien and incomprehensible from one another as Christendom was from Islam. It was the influence of the humanist education that saved Europe from this fate…. For there were humanists in both camps from the first, and in spite of their theological opposition they remained in

---

3 Mark Kalthoff, "Contra Ideology," *Faith and Reason* 30 (2005): 222.
4 Cicero, *On the Laws*, Book 1.
5 Ibid.

substantial agreement in their educational ideals and their concept of humane learning…. [Melanchthon] establish[ed] a sound tradition of Protestant education…. Calvin himself fully appreciated the importance of education and study. Wherever the Calvinists went, from Transylvania to Massachusetts, they brought with them not only the Bible and Calvin's *Institutes*, but the Latin grammar and the study of the classics.[6]

If we are to challenge — with any degree of success — the ideological hostility toward the liberal and whole understanding of man, Dawson wrote, we — Catholics, Protestants, Orthodox, Jews, and women and men of good will — must fight as a Republic of Letters, avoiding a "civil war of rival propaganda." We must learn our lessons from history, and not just the sixteenth century.[7] "Virgil and Cicero, Ovid and Seneca, Horace and Quintilian were not merely school books, they became the seeds of a new growth of classical humanism in Western soil," Christopher Dawson wrote in 1956. "Again and again — in the eighth century as well as in the twelfth and fifteenth centuries — the higher culture of Western Europe was fertilized by renewed contacts with the literary sources of classical culture."[8]

The model, as noted elsewhere, must be St Paul in Athens. While standing on Mars Hill, he congratulated the Athenians for being religious. Specifically, he noted, he was impressed with their statue to the "unknown God." Christ, he told them in no uncertain terms, was their unknown God. All of their religion, philosophy, and culture had pointed them to Him. Paul even quoted approvingly (though sanctifying their meaning) two pagan philosophers and poets, Aratus, a Stoic, and Cleanthes: "In him we live and move and have our being" and "For we are indeed his offspring" (Acts 17:28). In this moment, St Paul sanctified the pagan, bringing meaning to its completion.

---

6 Christopher Dawson, *Crisis of Western Education* [1961] (Steubenville, OH: Franciscan University Press, 1989), 36–37.

7 Ibid., 124.

8 Dawson, "Christianity and Ideologies," *Commonweal* 14 (May 11, 1956): 141.

Our citizenship belongs not to one republic, then, but to many. Some are connected within time, others to eternity. Perhaps this is what Cicero hinted at, when he argued that all men who recognize their connection to the divine through reason are citizens of the cosmopolis. Or maybe this is what Addison's Cato meant when he told the African prince Juba that one does not have to be Roman to have a Roman soul.[9] What happens, then, when a small republic asks the world to remember what is good and true and beautiful? How can one serve as a leaven to the rest, persuading the others to remember?

The American republic, it must be remembered, was at its founding a rather smallish place with a Protestant Anglo-Saxon Celtic population hugging the north Atlantic coast. Even its closest allies doubted the efficacy of republican government and the republican spirit. One of the founding fathers, Charles Carroll of Carrollton in Maryland, whose epithet was "Last of the Romans," serves as an example of what a liberally-educated person can do in the service of the Great Republic of the West and of America. Awoken himself by the liberal spirit of education, Carroll helped awaken the republican spirit of America, which in turn helped awaken the republican spirit of the West. Carroll's father (also Charles Carroll) sent his son to study in France and England. Charles Carroll left his family in Maryland in August 1748, at the age of 12, and he did not return to Maryland until February 1765. His correspondence with his father is revealing and extensive. While in France, he studied Greek and Latin, dancing and fencing, mathematics, handwriting, and bookkeeping, while studying — intensely — the works of Homer, Virgil, Cicero, and Horace. On July 8, 1757, at the age of 19, he earned a "Master of Arts" after his exams: "I sustained universall philosophy," he proudly wrote his father (July 26, 1757). Immediately after this, he entered into the study of the law. He studied the civil law of the Roman Emperor Justinian in France and the English common law of Alfred and the Magna Carta in England. Through it all, his father reminded him, the purpose of a liberal education was to inculcate

---

9   Joseph Addison, *Cato: A Tragedy* [1713], ed. by Christine Dunn Henderson and Mark E. Yellin (Liberty Fund: Indianapolis, 2004), 82.

virtue. Virtue, his father noted in 1751, is "greater than wealth." Two years later, he told his son how proud he was of him for recognizing the "advantage of a Virtuous Education." Further, "Men of Sense do not content themselves with knowing a thing but make themselves thoroughly acquainted with the Reasons on which their knowledge is founded. I beg you will carefully observe this in your present and future Studies. Memory may fail you, but when an impression is made by Reason it will last as long [as] You retain your understanding." Three years later, he reminded his son of the most important thing. "The Beginning of wisdom is the fear of the Lord." Carroll's writings in favor of the patriot cause between 1773 and 1788 reveal a common understanding of the Western tradition among Americans of his day. Throughout his speeches, essays, and private letters, Carroll referred to Cicero, Tacitus, Horace, Milton, Jonathan Swift, David Hume, Alexander Pope, Lord Bolingbroke, and Blackstone. "After the bible," he told a priest in 1830, "and the following of Christ [the *Imitatio Christi*], give me, sir, the philosophic works of Cicero."[10] As historian Forrest McDonald reminds us, the founders were first and foremost liberally educated. When a student entered college (usually at age 14 or 15), he needed to prove fluency in Latin and Greek. He must "read and translate from the original Latin into English 'the first three of [Cicero's] Select Orations and the first three books of Virgil's Aeneid' and translate the first ten chapters of the Gospel of John from Greek into Latin, as well as be 'expert in arithmetic' and have a 'blameless moral character.'"[11] Such an education was a norm for the American Founders. Should it surprise us that they gave us the Constitutional Republic that they did?

The Light

For nearly two thousand years, Christians have passed beyond the time of great darkness, the time of Tenebrae, the hours after three

10　All quotations pertaining to Charles Carroll come from Birzer, *American Cicero: Charles Carroll of Carrollton* (Wilmington, DE: ISI Books, 2010).

11　Forrest McDonald and Ellen McDonald, *Requiem* (Lawrence, KS: University of Kansas Press, 1985), 1–2.

o'clock on Good Friday, the moment when the world shook with the absence of grace. Yet the modern world seems trapped within it: the candles are void of flame, the altar has been stripped, the books have been beaten, we have departed from the chapel. What to do? Do we peer into the abyss, into the heart of Tenebrae, do we jump in, do we walk away? And, if we walk away, with what strength and what conviction? What purpose, what will? Certainly, there are those who refuse to succumb to all the glittering trinkets of modernity, those who refuse to succumb to the easy solution of ideology, those who refuse to take that which has not been earned. "Nevertheless one may say of it that it fiddles while Rome burns," Leo Strauss once wrote. "It is excused by two facts: it does not know that it fiddles, and it does not know that Rome burns."[12]

We know that it fiddles, and we know that it burns.

Such recognition should give us hope. We cannot change the world overnight, no matter what we try, or how well we succeed in any of our endeavors. Remembering what is good, true, and beautiful; seeking reformation of what has gone wrong; calling forth that which is best within us and our neighbors and attenuating that which is corrupt and fallen requires difficult and consuming labor. It demands patience, it demands fortitude. When Plato wrote, classical Athens was crumbling around him. His preservation of the best of his time and mind has repeatedly re-awoken the world to an extent he could never have anticipated. The same could be said of Cicero, St Augustine, Thomas More, and the American Founders.

Someday, if we are blessed, the same may be said of us.

Maybe some chronicler of the early twenty-first century will one day write: In a time of troubles, they weathered the storm, they preserved the best of what had come before them, and they carried the one light, away from the abyss, and through the darkness.

---

12   "Dr. Leo Strauss, Scholar, is Dead," *New York Times* (October 21, 1973), 77.

I

Conserving
Christian
Humanism

1

Humanism:

A PRIMER

CONSIDER MYSELF A DEVOUT HUMANIST. AND, for better or worse, I do mean "devout." Depending on my mood, I would argue that I'm as taken with and as loyal to humanism as I am with my Christianity. Though I would never compare myself to St Jerome or St Augustine, I certainly understand their detour away from Christianity after reading the rhetoric of Cicero. And yes, I certainly understand, as a practicing Roman Catholic, that Socrates will not escort me into heaven.

Yet when I mention the term "humanism" among conservatives, I am almost always greeted with silence, head shaking, or actual and visible disgust. Almost all conservatives, it seems, associate humanism with secularism and atheism and radicalism. They see it (very incorrectly) as a deification of the human being.

In his own writings, Russell Kirk rather famously described anywhere from five to ten canons of conservatism. In his honor, I offer five canons of humanism.

First, humanists believe in the dignity of the human person. Each person is unique, born in a certain time and place, never to be repeated. He or she comes into the world, burdened by many flaws but also armed with unique gifts, each to be made excellences over time and usage, through community.

Second, humanists see liberal education as the most proper education for the development and nurturing of a human being. True education seeks wisdom, not mere knowledge or technical skill. It does not believe in shaping the person for the here and now, but for the eternal.

Third, contrary to so much of our current understanding, real humanism never places the human person as the highest of all things, but as in the middle of all things. Man is higher than the animals but lower than the divine. Thus, humanism sought context (Justice) and place for each person throughout all of Creation. Man possesses the spiritual nature of the divine but the material nature of the animal. He, alone among all worldly creatures, wields free will. Some humanists have written about this as an "economy of nature or grace," and Renaissance humanists explained the concept of a "great chain of being," connecting the perfect creator to even the lowest order of creation. Nothing could exist outside of this hierarchy. Even evil existed only as a corruption of the good.

Fourth, the humanist upholds citizenship in the Republic of Letters — across time — as higher than loyalty to any nation or worldly power. A Roman Catholic might refer to this as a communion of saints or as the mystical body of Christ. The great pagan, Cicero, however, spoke of this as simply "reason," the language that connects not only man to the god, but all men of good will to all other men of good will, from the beginning to the end of humanity.

Fifth, while the humanists have never exactly agreed about a god or God, the humanist understands that someTHING stands above any one person or all of humanity together. Perhaps that someTHING is the Unmoved Mover or Yahweh or the Trinitarian God or the Natural Law, but a power of some supernatural order transcends all of humanity, time, and existence.

The writing career of Russell Kirk is well worth considering here. After his grand and, frankly, unexpected and astounding success with *The Conservative Mind*, he wondered what to do next. Conservatism, he argued, did not mean "stand pat-ism." It meant conserving what is dignified, humane, good, and beautiful. It meant searching for timeless truths and making them palatable for each generation. It meant defending that which the world all too often forgets. As Kirk explained in a prize-winning essay written when he was only 17, man must cling to his "mementos," finding story and meaning within each. Kirk also noted that a physical thing has real meaning only when sanctified and given soul. The same was true with conservatism. A conservatism of the wrong, the false, and the hideous means only degradation. No one, Kirk noted several times, would want to conserve ancient Egypt or Incan Peru.

But, then, what to conserve? After much soul-searching in the summer of 1953, bewildered by his own success, the 35-year-old Kirk believed that the future of conservatism lay in defining, recapturing, and promoting humanism. Much of this was already latent (and sometimes explicit) in *The Conservative Mind*. His six canons, for example, have been quoted and repeated innumerable times since he first delineated them in 1953. What is often ignored, however, is that Kirk employed the term "canon," a specifically Catholic word meaning dogma, argument, or truth. A canon is akin to a fact, rather than a story or narrative or mythos. Kirk, in *The Conservative Mind*, sought dogmas, not systems or even narratives.

Following the lead of Paul Elmer More, Romano Guardini, Gabriel Marcel, and especially Christopher Dawson and T.S. Eliot, Kirk decided to modify humanist with "Christian." Hoping to write a sequel to equal *The Conservative Mind*, he planned on writing a massive history of humanism from the Greeks to T.S. Eliot. *The Conservative Mind* began with Burke and followed his thought. Its sequel, which Kirk tentatively called *The Age of Humanism*, would begin with Socrates and follow his thought to the present. Though he never published this book, his letters indicate that he had written a huge chunk of it by the fall of 1953. What happened to those chapters has been lost, sadly, to the biographer and to the historian.

Several of Kirk's following books, however, became explorations of various aspects of Christian humanism. The actual sequel to *The Conservative Mind*, the book *A Program for Conservatives*, might well have been entitled *A Christian Humanist Manifesto*. *Academic Freedom*, *Beyond the Dreams of Avarice*, and especially *The Intelligent Women's Guide to Conservatism* each reflects Kirk's interest in Christian humanism as well. Though Kirk never left Christian humanism behind, he did relegate the topic to the background of his post-1957 non-fiction writing career. Christian humanism pervades every aspect of his fiction, however, as much as it does the writings of Willa Cather, Walter Miller, Flannery O'Connor, and Walker Percy.

For now, it is enough to know that the best minds of the twentieth century embraced humanism, properly understood. Kirk and others added the descriptive "Christian." Were the term not so adulterated, we might very well simply write "Western humanism," as the understanding of the term includes the Greco-Roman as well as the Judeo-Christian traditions. It also includes the Germanic and especially the Anglo-Saxon and northern understandings.

Heimdahl, after all, possessed a humanist streak. He watched and waited.

And so must we.

2

Humanism:

THE CORRUPTION OF A WORD

THE TWENTIETH CENTURY WITNESSED AN
assault on a number of once fine words, often hollowing
out the traditional meanings and filling them with sheer
refuse. "Myth," in the twentieth century, became lie. "Love" became
lust. Another such word, lost in the confusion of our present whirligig of postmodern life, is humanism. Even those who would and
should be friendly to the term react strongly to every one of its
syllables. For most of us not on the left, humanism has come to
mean radicalism, atheism, arrogance, and secularism.

Frankly, this corruption of the word humanism is a tragedy
almost at the level of the loss of the traditional meaning of love. Tra-
ditionally — that is, from the earliest Greek philosophers of the fifth
century B C through the end of the nineteenth century — humanism
remained rather steady as a cherished and nurtured idea. Certainly,
like many ideas and schools of thought, it has waxed and waned.
Still, its progress, properly understood, has been adaptive rather
than revolutionary. Certain personalities, in particular, have added
to humanism, from Heraclitus to Socrates to Zeno to Cicero to
Hillel to Jesus to Seneca to St John to St Paul to St Augustine to
Alcuin to St Thomas Aquinas to Erasmus to St Thomas More to
Edmund Burke to John Henry Newman. In the twentieth century,
humanists included T.E. Hulme, Irving Babbitt, Paul Elmer More,
Christopher Dawson, Russell Kirk, Robert Nisbet, T.S. Eliot, Willa
Cather, Otto Bird, Sister Madeleva Wolff, Jacques Maritain, Eti-
enne Gilson, Flannery O'Connor, and a number of others. The years
between Cardinal Newman and T.E. Hulme, especially, saw such

a rise in the popularity of the word "humanism" that it became essentially meaningless. The form remained, but the essence became whatever an individual so desired.

In 1908, Harvard's Irving Babbitt attempted to define the shape of this corruption.

> To make a plea for humanism without explaining the word would give rise to endless misunderstanding. It is equally on the lips of the socialistic dreamer and the exponent of the latest philosophical fad. In an age of happy liberty like the present, when any one can employ almost any general term very much as he pleases, it is perhaps inevitable that the term humanism, which still has certain gracious associations lingering about it, should be appropriated by various theorists, in the hope, apparently, that the benefit of the associations may accrue to an entirely different order of ideas.... Under these circumstances our prayer, like that of Ajax, should be to fight in the light.[1]

While a number of persons and groups had sought to co-opt "humanism" for their own agendas — similar to what has happened with the employment of "republic" and "democracy" over the last one hundred years — the most prominent and conspicuous co-opter was none other than the infamous utilitarian philosopher and educationalist, John Dewey. Interestingly enough, though almost every conservative cringes at the name Dewey, we have long since forgotten exactly why he elicits such a response from us. In part, it comes down to his very corruption of the term "humanism," even as we accept the result of that very same corruption. Along with several other prominent thinkers of the first third of the last century, Dewey signed the "Humanist Manifesto" of 1933.[2]

---

1   Irving Babbitt, *Literature and the American College* [1908] (Washington, DC: National Humanities Institute, 1986), 72–73.
2   See "Humanist Manifesto: Twenty Years After," *The Humanist* (1953): 58–61.

The manifesto argued that theistic institutions should conform to the concerns of human life *qua* human life.

> Religious humanism [meaning a religion worshiping humanity] maintains that all associations and institutions exist for the fulfillment of human life. The intelligent evaluation, transformation, control, and direction of such associations and institutions with a view to the enhancement of human life is the purpose and program of humanism. Certainly religious institutions, their ritualistic forms, ecclesiastical methods, and communal activities must be reconstituted as rapidly as experience allows, in order to function effectively in the modern world.

Further, society as a unit must lose its emotionalism, as manifested in theistic religion. Science should determine all that is to come, the Deweyites argued:

> Humanism asserts that the nature of the universe depicted by modern science makes unacceptable any supernatural or cosmic guarantees of human values. Obviously humanism does not deny the possibility of realities as yet undiscovered, but it does insist that the way to determine the existence and value of any and all realities is by means of intelligent inquiry and by the assessment of their relations to human needs. Religion must formulate its hopes and plans in the light of the scientific spirit and method.

Ultimately, the thirty-four signers of the Humanist Manifesto concluded, "the time has passed for theism." Should organized religion and religious institutions continue, they must do so in a manner that speaks to problems of the twentieth century, places man at the center of existence, and employs the scientific method. Religion, they concluded, serves only a utilitarian function, a "means for realizing the highest values of life."

One of Dewey's present-day admirers and disciples, Richard Rorty, has continued the secular humanist tradition at the end of the twentieth century and into the beginning of the twenty-first century. For Rorty, America is the great democratic and liberal (hence, secular) experiment. He views the United States as a nation-state in which institutions promote "co-operation" instead of embodying "a universal and ahistorical order." Any attempt to bring God back in any form of public discourse, whether in politics or the university — or, as he puts it, to "re-enchant" the world — would be folly, a regression of the world.

While we might dismiss Rorty as simply one voice in a world of many voices, he represents much of academia and politics in the Western world. Certainly, Europe has secularized far faster than America, but no single people has secularized as quickly as the English have done over the last generation. At least no generation has secularized so rapidly since the French rebelled against crown and church in the late eighteenth century.

America, however, is not far behind. While many Americans remain religious, they are loath to take their religion into the public square. Whether they fear condemnation by an activist minority or actually believe that religion should not be a part of public discourse remains unclear.

Far from being an enemy of religion, humanism, properly understood, has been a faithful ally since St Paul visited Athens and St John appropriated the Heraclitan Logos. The liberal arts teach not atheism, but virtue. They shun loyalties to things of this world (hence, "liberal," characteristic of the free man as opposed to the slave) and point us toward citizenship in something larger. Letting the leftists hijack the term has allowed them — in many ways — to promote themselves as *the* humane path in this world. Of course, we know this is simply not true. The lineage that led to Kirkian conservatism sought the dignity of the human person well beyond mere accidents of birth. The lineage that has led to Rorty and other progressives is full of eugenicists and racists and exclusionists. They are, in and of themselves, the very antithesis of humanism, even as they embrace the term. Humanism is not only *not* the enemy of conservatism, it makes conservatism meaningful. Humanism is the thing conservatives must conserve. The term is well worth defending and reclaiming.

Based on a loose alliance of similarly-minded persons, conservatism sought to defend the Platonic good, true, and beautiful in the second half of the twentieth century, believing it necessary to promote a proper anthropology of the human person. More a way of thinking, a set of guiding principles, or a habit of being than a political philosophy or creed, conservatism generally opposes all systems and ideologies as unworkable, dangerous to liberties of individuals and communities, and, ultimately, inhumane. Conservatives, consequently, tend to make some of society's best critics while they rarely offer solutions to the specific problems of the day. This has been, for conservatism, an equal source of strength and of weakness.

3

The Conservative Mind

OST CONSERVATIVES OVER THE PAST seven decades have accepted Russell Kirk's 1953 book, *The Conservative Mind* (Regnery), as the touchstone of the modern movement. A hagiography of sorts, *The Conservative Mind* identified several seemingly disparate figures—from John Adams to Samuel Coleridge, from John Henry Cardinal Newman to Paul Elmer More—all of whom considered the great eighteenth-century Anglo-Irish political philosopher, Edmund Burke, an exemplar of ethical living and moral argumentation. Not seeking a coherent story or past, Kirk readily linked such persons as John C. Calhoun and Abraham Lincoln together as rightful heirs to the Burkean tradition. Rather than a stifling consistency, something conservatives often downplayed in human affairs, each of the thinkers appearing in *The Conservative Mind* promoted some timeless truth; that is, each manifested something true and universal across time, history, and space in his own particular life and work. Kirk's book offered both a title and a community of sorts to a large number of young scholars, all of whom generally agreed with his arguments, but who had been working in isolation one from another. Trying to understand the appeal of conservatism in the midst of the Reagan Revolution, *Washington Post* writer Sidney Blumenthal recognized *The Conservative Mind* as "crucial in establishing the cause as a valid intellectual enterprise," providing a "genealogy of conservatism."[1] Sociologist Robert Nisbet expressed it well when he first encountered Kirk's work. "As one who has labored, though more modestly, in an adjacent vineyard, I think I can write with

1 Sidney Blumenthal, *The Rise of the Counter-Establishment: From Conservative Ideology to Political Power* (New York: New York Times Books, 1986), 21.

full appreciation of your own achievement," he wrote Kirk. *The Conservative Mind* "is as penetrating in its insights as it is graceful in expression, and it is impossible for me to conceive a more timely and important piece of scholarship for the education of the American intellectual."[2] The book offered Kirk the status of celebrity, and the term "conservative" became not only palatable but also intriguing to many Americans and British in the decade following its publication.

Proclaiming conservatism the negation of ideology, as had many Christian humanists of the United Kingdom and the European continent during the interwar decades, Kirk rejected the reality of a left-right spectrum, believing that in its attempt to conserve the best of the Western tradition, conservatism transcended political and ideological differences and battles. He offered six canons as forming the basis of conservatism: 1) "Belief that a divine intent rules society as well as conscience, forging an eternal chain of right and duty which links great and obscure, living and dead"; 2) "affection for the proliferating variety and mystery of traditional life"; 3) "conviction that civilized society requires orders and classes"; 4) "persuasion that property and freedom are inexorably connected"; 5) "faith in prescription and distrust of 'sophisters and calculators'"; and 6) "recognition that change and reform are not identical." Kirk revised these tenets not only through the six following editions of *The Conservative Mind* but also through various lectures and other works. *The Conservative Mind*, especially in hindsight, falls better in the category of belle-lettres, theology, or cultural criticism than it does in the category of politics and political philosophy. In his definition of conservative, the poetic, literary, and theological superseded the political. As Kirk explained, the conservative author should "recognize the greater importance, in literature as in life, of religion, ethics, and beauty." After the first reviews began to appear, Kirk grew frustrated with the political analysis offered. Not even sympathetic reviewers had laid "stress enough upon the ethical

---

2   Robert A. Nisbet to Russell A. Kirk, May 27, 1953, in Kirk Papers, Russell Kirk Center, Mecosta, Michigan.

aspect of" *The Conservative Mind.* "Politics, I never tire of saying, is the diversion of the quarter-educated, and I do try to transcend pure politics in my book."[3]

In the 1950s and 1960s, several persons became identified with conservatism: Kirk, Nisbet, Peter Stanlis, Richard Weaver, Daniel Boorstin, Waldemar Gurian, John Lukacs, Thomas Molnar, Austin Warren, Stephen Tonsor, Stanley Parry, Leo Ward, Peter Viereck, Ross Hoffman, Felix Morley, Bernard Iddings Bell, William F. Buckley Jr., Frank Meyer, Whittaker Chambers, James Burnham, Donald Davidson, Raymond English, Francis Wilson, John Hallowell, Francis Canavan, Gerhart Niemeyer, Stanton Evans, Ernest van den Haag, Frederick Wilhelmsen, Will Herberg, Willmore Kendall, Robert Frost, W.T. Couch, Max Picard, Eliseo Vivas, George Carey, Walker Percy, Flannery O'Connor, and Ray Bradbury. Though rejecting the label "conservative," political philosophers Leo Strauss, Eric Voegelin, and Friedrich August von Hayek found themselves promoted by and allied to conservatives as well. In addition to these specific thinkers, a number of schools of thought consciously or otherwise allied themselves with the conservative movement. These included the Southern Agrarians, Catholic Distributists, and the Humanists (New/American and Christian), to name a few. In England and in Europe, one might to varying extents identify T.S. Eliot, Quentin Hogg, Jacques Maritain, Etienne Gilson, C.S. Lewis, Owen Barfield, Gabriel Marcel, Romano Guardini, Josef Pieper, Bernard Wall, Otto von Habsburg, Nicolas Berdyaev, Erik von Kuehnelt-Leddihn, Hans Urs von Balthasar, and Wilhelm Roepke. In terms of politics, most scholars include Barry Goldwater and Ronald Reagan as explicit inheritors of a Kirkian-style conservatism, though each of these figures combined various forms of libertarianism as well. The second and third generations of modern American conservatives included Pat Buchanan, David Schindler, Claes Ryn, George Nash, George Panichas, Ralph McInerny, Donald Lutz, Ellis Sandoz, M.E. Bradford, Forrest McDonald, John Hittinger, Hank Edmondson,

---

3   Kirk to Henry Regnery, May 20, 1953, in Kirk Papers, Russell Kirk Center, Mecosta, Michigan.

Walter Nicgorski, Bruce Frohnen, John Willson, Richard Gamble, Mark Kalthoff, David Whalen, James Matthew Wilson, Carl Olson, Winston Elliott, Barbara Elliott, Gleaves Whitney, Ingrid Gregg, Sam Gregg, Ulrich Lehner, Francesca Murphy, Daryll Hart, Paul Moreno, Jason Peters, Jeff Polet, and Patrick Deneen.

4

Burke and Tocqueville

UCH OF THE EFFORT OVER THE PAST six decades to define, delimit, and shape a conservatism tangible for the modern and postmodern Western world has rooted itself in the works and thoughts of Edmund Burke and Alexis de Tocqueville. Each received new attention immediately following the allied victory in World War II, and the importance of their respective thought to conservatism has yet to wane. Burke, famously, not only defended American independence and the right of Americans to possess all of the traditional rights of Englishmen, but also offered the first real opposition to the French Revolution and what it unleashed upon the Western world, the concept that would be called "ideology." In his philosophy, politics, and aesthetics, Burke's overriding concern was the upholding of the dignity of the humane, whether for the American colonials, the Irish, Asian Indians, or Roman Catholics. In a similar fashion and in the vein of Burke, Tocqueville too analyzed the Western world, especially America and France, with an eye toward the humane. As Tocqueville perceptively noted in his *Democracy in America*, no liberty has ever existed anywhere unpurchased by some sacrificial exertion. Equality comes slowly but meaningfully, while liberty appears only from time to time. Still, as Tocqueville claimed, no matter how natural or God-given a right, a person must somehow claim what is his or hers. Burke and Tocqueville each sought to pursue Justice in this world through a proper, Aristotelian form of community as natural to the greatest longings of the human person. Flawed man, according to this view, can only attain his highest gifts and ultimate end in a community. By living outside of community, each argued, a human ceases to be human.

Conservatism, though appealing to Burke and Tocqueville, also viewed them as carrying on, or perhaps best exemplifying, all that had come before them in the Western tradition. Never shy about selectively reading the past, conservatives over the past six decades have identified a lineage of ancestors dating from the pre-Socratic Heraclitus, philosopher of the Logos, forward. Others in this line of thinkers include Socrates, Plato, Aristotle, Zeno, Cleanthes, Cicero, Livy, Virgil, Seneca, St John, Marcus Aurelius, St Augustine, the Venerable Bede, Alcuin, Alfred the Great, Thomas à Becket, St Francis, St Bonaventure, St Thomas Aquinas, Petrarch, Dante, Erasmus, and St Thomas More. For many conservatives of Kirk's generation, the West had slowly developed its ideas of the humane — domestically and abroad — but civilization floundered profoundly around the time of Machiavelli. As Kirk analyzed the situation, the Socratic West ended with the writing of *The Prince* and with the acceptance of power over love as the primary motive force in world affairs. Sometime during the Renaissance, according to many conservatives, the world entered a new dark age, an age that resented tradition and, by necessity, men. The Protestant Reformation and Catholic Counter-Reformation attempted to undo the damage of the Renaissance, but failed, leading to the Enlightenment and the secularization of the West. The failures of the French and English Enlightenments led directly to the age of ideologies, a dark age within a dark age, but intensely dangerous and brutal as well. Many conservatives saw the so-called "liberalism" of the seventeenth and eighteenth centuries as a mere stage between the humane culture promoted by Christendom and the terror espoused by the Nazis and the Soviets. As T.S. Eliot put it in one of his choruses:

> But it seems that something has happened that has
>   never happened before:
> though we know not just when, or why, or how, or where.
> Men have left GOD not for other gods, they say, but for
>   no god; and this has never happened before

That men both deny gods and worship gods, professing
  first Reason,
And then Money, and Power, and what they call Life, or
  Race, or Dialectic.
The Church disowned, the tower overthrown, the bells
  upturned, what have we to do
But stand with empty hands and palms turned upwards
In an age which advances progressively backwards?[1]

In sum, Eliot asserted in 1939, "If you will not have God (and he is a jealous God), you should pay your respects to Hitler or Stalin."[2] Such was the bleak view from the few remaining and stubborn islands of civilization in the 1930s. It was this view, then, that many carried with them as they watched the U.S. government intern Americans of Japanese descent during World War II and watched the atomic annihilation of two Japanese cities in 1945. These horrors, perhaps more than any other events of the day, shaped conservatism, proving to a whole generation that the "colossal" in government, unions, and corporations would never allow for the humane.

From the perspective of many in the post-war era, Burke, Adam Smith, and Alexis de Tocqueville represented the culmination of the highest of Western thought, with everything coming after them merely a rearguard action, a rout at best. In this way, the conservatives of the twentieth century assumed that Burke, Smith, and Tocqueville represented the West, coming as they did at the end of an era or perhaps an epoch. In this same way, Socrates, Plato, and Aristotle came at the end of classical Greece, Cicero came at the end of republican Rome, St Augustine at the end of imperial Rome, and Sir Thomas More at the end of the English Catholic spring. For whatever reason, the greats of the Western tradition seem to have come at the end of their eras. In

1   T.S. Eliot, "Choruses from 'The Rock,'" in *The Complete Poems and Plays, 1909–1950* (New York: Harcourt Brace, 1980), 108.
2   T.S. Eliot, *Idea of a Christian Society* (London: Faber and Faber, 1939), 63.

the twentieth century, prior to the 1950s, those carrying on the conservative tradition were Irving Babbitt, a scholar of French literature at Harvard, Paul Elmer More, a classicist at Princeton, Albert Jay Nock, a quasi-anarchist and proponent of the liberal arts, Christopher Dawson, an English convert to Roman Catholicism, and T.S. Eliot, the Missourian turned Englishman and perhaps the greatest poet of the age.

5

What to Conserve?

THOUGH CONSERVATISM NEVER ACHIEVED (nor wanted to achieve) coherence or conformity, it is possible for the modern scholar, with some trepidation, to define it broadly by a set of principles to which most conservatives adhered. The most important question a conservative must ask is: "What is to be conserved?" Numerous traditions, of course, promoted the destruction or degradation of the human person. Institutions such as slavery, for example, must be abolished. The conservative, then, must prudently and justly judge what is to be maintained, what is to be rejected, and what is to be reformed within any society. Opposing all systems and ideologies, the conservative is always and everywhere a dogmatist in the proper sense of the term. The true dogmatist promotes a series of "good little truths" without reifying all knowledge as absolute or absolutist, recognizing the importance and humility of a partial understanding of things. One man, finite but finite in a manner different from every other finite man, sees A, B, and D. Another sees C and E. Yet, another—the poetic mind—sees the connection between D and E. Perhaps, no one has yet discovered G, but every one easily sees F. This is simply the life of a finite person (or people) at any one point in history.

The first principle of the conservative, then, is the preciousness of each individual human person, each person an unrepeatable center of dignity and freedom. Though deeply flawed—or in religious terms, fallen—each man carries some unique thing or things into the world. Each man, born in a certain time and place, bears a unique image of the infinite mind of the Creator. To the modern mind, this sounds distinctly Jewish or Christian. But the ancient

Stoics, such as Zeno and Seneca, embraced a universal Creator (the Logos) as well. By this observation, a man best knows his own place within Justice. As Burke explained in 1791:

> I may assume that the awful Author of our being is the Author of our place in the order of existence, — and that, having disposed and marshalled us by a divine tactic, not according to our will, but according to His, He has in and by that disposition virtually subjected us to act the part which belongs to the place assigned us. We have obligations to mankind at large, which are not in consequence of any special voluntary pact. They arise from the relation of man to man, and the relation of man to God, which relations are not matters of choice.[1]

The second principle of the conservative is the necessity of communities. Communities may be extremely small (such as a family unit), medium sized (such as a college), or large (such as a polis). At any moment in life, an individual belongs to a number of communities, some overlapping in intent and purpose and some not. Women and men of good will also belong to a community of the civilized that transcends any particular moment in time. Cicero named the transcendent city the "cosmopolis," while St Augustine labeled it the "City of God." For the conservatives of the second half of the twentieth century, such as Dawson, Eliot, and Kirk, all who seek truth in an academic and scholarly fashion belong to a Republic of Letters bound by neither space nor time. The citizens of this Republic of Letters have a duty, through the virtues of fortitude and charity, to maintain the few truths that have been revealed in this world. Whether the truth is immediately applicable to the problems of an individual society or not, the citizen of the Republic of Letters bears the responsibility of carrying on and preserving those truths for the future — even if that future be 2,500 years distant.

---

1   Edmund Burke, *Further Reflections on the Revolution in France*, ed. by Daniel Ritchie (Indianapolis: Liberty Fund, 1992), 160.

The third principle of the conservative is the need to preserve and defend liberal education. Properly understood, all real education is liberal and is neither civic nor vocational. A liberal education introduces each student to the Great Conversation that began when the Creator spoke the universe into existence and will end when the Creator so ends it. By engaging the minds and ideas of the past, the student becomes liberated from immersion in or enslavement to the things of this world — the things of the immediate moment, problem, or generation. A liberal education thus inspires its students. "A crassly modern education, over weighted with economics, may educate us to be good clerks; only a curriculum in the broad humanities can educate us to be good human beings," Peter Viereck wrote in the late 1940s. "By harmonizing head and heart, Apollo and Dionysus, the Athenian classics train the complete man rather than the fragmentary man."[2]

The fourth principle of the conservative is the recognition that the most important knowledge is poetic knowledge. In 1977, Kirk wrote:

> Images are representations of mysteries, necessarily; for mere words are tools that break in the hand, and it has not pleased God that man should be saved by logic, abstract reason, alone.... The image, I repeat, can raise us on high, as did Dante's high dream; also it can draw us down to the abyss.... It is imagery, rather than some narrowly deductive and inductive process, which gives us great poetry and scientific insights.... And it is true of great philosophy, before Plato and since him, that the enduring philosopher sees things in images initially.[3]

Owen Barfield, one of the most important of twentieth-century thinkers, explored similar themes in his 1928 book, *Poetic Diction*:

---

2   Peter Viereck, *Conservatism Revisited* [1949] (New Brunswick, NJ: Transaction Press, 2005), 71.

3   Russell Kirk, *Renewal and Decadence in Higher Education* (Chicago: Regnery, 1978), 229, 231.

Our sophistication, like Odin's, has cost us an eye; and
now it is the language of poets, in so far as they create
true metaphors, which must restore this unity concep-
tually, after it has been lost from perception. Thus, the
"before-unapprehended" relationships of which Shel-
ley spoke, are in a sense "forgotten" relationships. For
though they were never yet apprehended, they were at
one time seen. And imagination can see them again.4

Through such Stoic and Christian insights, a person can recognize
truth dogmatically, rather than systematically. These ideas also
allow us to know our place in the order of existence. As J.R.R.
Tolkien wrote to his former student, famed poet W.H. Auden:
Each person is "an allegory...each embodying in a particular tale
and clothed in the garments of time and place, universal truth
and everlasting life."5

The fifth principle conservatives uphold is an embracing of the
classical and Christian virtues: prudence, justice, temperance, fortitude, faith, hope, and charity. Plato wrote of the first four, the
classical virtues, in his dialogue *The Symposium*, and Jewish culture
adopted them in the deuterocanonical Book of Wisdom. St Paul
added the latter three in his first letter to the Christians of Corinth.
These virtues, along with allied ones, form the strongest character
of a person and thus serve as the surest guide to order, in the soul
and in the commonwealth. The conservative, therefore, never views
history as progressive but as revelatory. That is, history reveals when
and where the virtues have become manifest, and where the vices
have predominated. With human nature as a constant, mankind
neither becomes better nor becomes worse. He merely restrains or
not, creates or not, embraces the virtues or does not. In his highest
capacity, man embraces the greatest virtue, love — the willingness
to surrender himself for the good of another.

4   Owen Barfield, *Poetic Diction* (London: Faber and Gwyer, 1928), 72–73.
5   Tolkien to W.H. Auden, June 7, 1955, in *Letters of J.R.R. Tolkien* (Boston:
Houghton Mifflin, 1981), Letter 163.

Finally, the conservative tends to distrust all large organizations and concentrations of power — corporate, educational, labor, bureaucratic, and political — as being hostile to the dignity of the individual person. While rejecting an abstract and atomized individualism, conservatism does demand a non-conformist society of talented and eccentric persons, each contributing his particular gifts and talents to the various communities to which he belongs. A person understands himself best through community, conforming to the Natural Law (though not necessarily to man's law). In this way, the conservative seeks long-term change through the slow and deliberate arts of literature, religion, education, and culture. Politics at best sustains a community, protecting it from immediate disorders, but rarely can it do more than restrain the evil within man. When politics attempts to shape, it almost always fails, creating distortions in human persons and communities. While this is true of all large power structures, such corruption empirically seems particularly dangerous in political organizations and bodies.

Conservatism's future

Though the classical liberals/libertarians and the Kirkian-style traditionalists often allied during the 1950s and 1960s, they went separate ways after a dispute within the activist political organization Young Americans for Freedom (formed at William F. Buckley's home in Sharon, Connecticut, in 1960). The dispute concerned the state of the American draft and came after the formation of the Libertarian Party in the early 1970s. Additionally, with the rise of the leftish counter-culture of the 1960s and the attempt by the Yippies and SDS to take over the Democratic Party in 1968, many war hawks and nationalists departed their party, rebranding themselves "neo-conservatives." Though they held little in common with the traditionalists of the Kirk variety, they secured for themselves a number of important federal positions in several presidential administrations over the next forty years. In significant contrast to mainstream conservatism, the neo-conservatives defined nearly everything through the lens of politics and of American exceptionalism. Generally advocates of American empire, they have unceasingly supported extensive growth in government at home and abroad.

The current state of conservatism is rich, as a younger generation begins to assert its influence: *The Imaginative Conservative* (Winston Elliott and Steve Klugewicz), *Modern Age* (Dan McCarthy), Ignatius Press (Carl Olson and Mark Brumley), *New Oxford Review* (Pieter Vree), *Front Porch Republic* (Patrick Deneen and Jeff Polet), *Law and Liberty* (Richard Reinsch), and *University Bookman* (Gerald Russello) have offered new understandings of traditional conservatism. Outside of traditional conservatism, the best exponents of classical liberalism are James Otteson (Wake Forrest University), Tom Woods (LibertyClassroom), Larry Reed (FEE), Sarah Skwire (Liberty Fund), and Steve Horwitz (Ball State University). Of a non-violent anarchism, one can turn to Aeon Skoble (Bridgewater State) and Robert Higgs (Independent Institute). And, of Straussianism and neo-conservatism, the best is Steven Hayward (UC-Berkeley).

6

Conserving Humanism

"I HAPPEN TO BELIEVE THAT YOU CAN'T STUDY men; you can only get to know them." So spoke C.S. Lewis's William Hingest in *That Hideous Strength* (1945). The fascists murder this doomed curmudgeon only a few pages later. Hingest, of course, is correct. We really cannot study men. We can only get to know them. This is as true of those closest to us as it is of ourselves. The farther away from our own daily reach, the harder the person becomes to understand. Equally important, even the wisest and most introspective among us barely know themselves. Here's a thought experiment: try to recreate everything you've done since you started reading this chapter. Every thought, every distraction, every movement, every feeling. Have you wanted some coffee? Have you thought about turning the page? Have you scratched that itch on the side of your head? Have you wondered if you should call the kids today? Have you thought about what you'll do for lunch? Now, take each of these things that we can barely reconstruct from the shortest moments of our lives—the impulses, the questions, the longings, the satisfactions—and multiply them by the minutes of the day, the days of the year, and the years of our lives. Then, multiply that again by seven billion distinct persons walking this world in any 24-hour period. Where to start? The possibilities, the decisions, the desires, and the frustrations are unaccountable and uncountable. No graph, no data set, and no equation can incorporate all of the complexities and nuances of a single human person, let alone seven billion of them.

We know names and dates and facts, and we often create a narrative to connect these varied and various things. Yet we surprise ourselves as much as we surprise others in our daily moments.

Some of us are just better at hiding this surprise behind a practiced veneer. This mystery of the human person is as it should be. Every single person is vastly complex, perhaps known only to his Creator, and — as J.R.R. Tolkien once mused — possibly to his guardian angel.

Though the Left has made a mockery of diversity, real diversity is always stunning and often glorious. Indeed, one of the most beautiful things about life is our individual ability to create, to imagine, to tinker, to innovate, to improve, and to see across the bounds of time itself. In *The Histories*, that first grand story ever written about the Western tradition, Herodotus notes that every person lives only about 26,250 days, "and any one of these days brings with it something completely unlike any other." Account for the shortenings and lengthenings of lifespan dependent on available technology and standards of living, and Herodotus' statement is as apt in the first third of the twenty-first century as it was in the fifth century B C.

In all the genres of literature and in all the schools of scholarship, the non-fiction writer who best understands the human condition is arguably the biographer. Pick up three separate biographies — say, by David McCulloch, Joseph Pearce, and Robert Utley — and read them with delight. Even the most cursory examination of the subjects reveals just how infinitely complex, nuanced, and subtle the human person can be. At the moment we believe we understand man's motivations, we find that he is capable of even higher highs and even lower lows. Man can paint the Sistine Chapel one moment and mow down his fellows in concentration camps the next.

The art of a biographer is a high one. She has the duty of honoring a person's life by taking the subject seriously (for good or ill), and by judging it according not only to the standards of the time but also to the standards of the ages. She must be faithful to every name, date, and fact of a person's life without becoming a mere antiquarian, a slave to the information. The subject may have kept extraordinary diaries during his late teens — a young man full of anxiety, full of passion, and full of life — but left no records for the next twenty years. How does the biographer faithfully render judgment, knowing that few women or men escape their youth without some mischievousness? Or perhaps the subject behaves charitably to ninety-nine folks but treats just one with seething contempt. Do we dismiss the 99 because of the evidence of the one? If a subject expresses one view at age 30 but another at age 60, do we merely overlook one, or privilege one, or mock one? Who casts the first stone?

Because of the sheer complexities of each person—subject as well as writer—the biographer must always and everywhere be poetic, connecting things that are seen with those that are unseen. When we read a great biography, we instinctively know it to be such. Why? Because we have met the subject as well as the biographer in the work. They each make themselves known to us (at least to the extent they are capable), in all their excellences and failings, in the spaces they left blank out of humility and in those they connected through imagination.

The biographer makes the fact the story, and, along the way, the story becomes the fact. What, then, is the key to a good biography? I believe the only truly good biographer (or autobiographer, as I believe they employ the same gifts and talents) is the one who is endowed with the ability and the will to entertain serious imagination. That is, we assume a competent biographer knows the FACTS of a person's life. And with these facts available to him (assuming a reasonable degree of writing competency), a merely adequate biographer will effectively draw for us a picture of an individual. But the truly good biographer, I believe, is able to make sense of the facts and to see them in context (not only within the context of the person's life, but within all life and frankly, within all humanity). The truly good biographer sees not only A, B, C, D, E, and F, but, very importantly, connects A to B, and (where necessary) A to F. He also humbly realizes and acknowledges where he cannot make the necessary connections in writing of another's life. In the end, the good biographer draws us a picture not just of an individual, but of a person—deeply flawed, but made in God's image; sinful, yet endowed with many gifts. Above all, each person emerges as a temple of the Holy Spirit.

To do this, the biographer must enter the mind of his subject and perhaps enter his soul (these things, I believe, are equally true in autobiography). He must be distanced enough to be objective about the facts, but he must also be willing to jump into his person's mind and life. Ultimately, he must try to think and feel and believe the way his subject thought, felt, and believed.

In a sense, all true history is biography — that is, good history recognizes the human person and human cultures, and it recognizes the essence in the matters of the world. But history and humanity are, we should acknowledge, almost unfathomable in their complexity. Every minute of every day, the seven billion plus humans of the world make numerous decisions based on whim, emotion, faith, and logic. Their choices, of course, are not unlimited. All live in polities and cultures constrained by authority and power and in economies marked by regulations and scarce resources. The sum of these billions of decisions makes local, regional, national, continental, and global history. As individuals, we ourselves are often unsure of our actions. We are even less certain of others' actions. Though it may be overwhelming, by recognizing the intricacies of life, we will be better able to study the world in all its wonder and perplexity.

With all the above in mind, I recall several amazing and excellent recent biographers (some well-known, some not).

David McCullough's biography of John Adams clearly reveals the necessity of sacrifice for the formation and continuation of a republic.

Richard Brookhiser's biography of George Washington offers us the image of a man — perhaps the greatest American — steeped and immersed in the classical traditions of virtue.

In a different vein, William F. Buckley's last book, *The Reagan I Knew* (2008), published posthumously, shows us a singularly imaginative, witty, and principled man, through the memoirs of his friendship with President Reagan and Nancy Reagan.

Robert Utley, in his *The Lance and the Shield: The Life and Times of Sitting Bull*, provides modern Americans with a glimpse of one of the most complex and virtuous men of the late nineteenth century — a Lakota Sioux medicine man who did everything in his power to preserve the traditions of his community.

One of my favorite current biographers is Joseph Pearce, who has written biographies of G. K. Chesterton, Alexander Solzhenitsyn, Hilaire Belloc, Oscar Wilde, J. R. R. Tolkien, Roy Campbell, and William Shakespeare. Pearce is sometimes criticized for attempting too much; this seems especially true when Pearce "invades" his critics' academic domain (read "turf"). I'm sure he makes errors here and there (as we all do) because he's willing to take chances and explore new areas, areas unfamiliar to him before he begins his research. But I know of no other modern writer who can so easily and readily enter the mind of his subject. As I wrote of one of his books:

> Joseph Pearce has produced yet another masterpiece with *The Quest for Shakespeare*. With a profound grasp of Shakespeare's impressive life and the disturbing dangers and culture of Elizabethan England, Pearce writes with historical insight in one hand and poetic imagination in the other. Perhaps our greatest living biographer, Pearce has the uncanny ability to get into the minds, hopes, fears, and motivations of his subjects. Equally impressive, we the readers experience true greatness, as Pearce will still be read, remembered, and studied centuries from now as one of the most important Catholics of our day.

This is no less true for me today than it was when I wrote it. Nothing Pearce writes — in terms of topic or style — is unimportant.

In my own work, I've had the privilege of writing several biographies.

I wrote my first one (intermixed with a lot of unpublished fiction) on Jean-Baptiste Richardville, a Frenchman who controlled much of the trade of the Western Great Lakes during the American Revolution by serving as a chief for the Miami Indians. He was a diplomat and entrepreneur (almost certainly one of the ten wealthiest North Americans by the time of the War of 1812). I think I understood Richardville's uncle and his mother quite well — but I never understood Richardville and I failed, I think, to write a good biography of him. He remains to this day alien to me.

After Richardville, I stuck with the theme of the frontier, believing it offered the best glimpse of American identity. But I turned to the New York frontier and to its great literary genius, James Fenimore Cooper. While I never wrote a formal biography of the creator of Leatherstocking, I think I was able (at least at some level) to get into his mind and understand his motivations, his republicanism, and his Christian faith.

With the dissertation out of the way, I turned to my favorite writer, the Oxford don and mythmaker J.R.R. Tolkien — a man who had been a part of my life since I turned 10. Writing on Tolkien felt more like a privilege and calling than a challenge, and I remember those writing sessions fondly.

While working on Tolkien, I stumbled on one of his friends and fellow parishioners, Christopher Dawson. An Oxford-trained scholar of undoubted brilliance, Dawson approached history with the mind of a poet. True history, according to Dawson, is ultimately poetic: "The mastery of" professional historical methods and "techniques will not produce great history, any more than a mastery of metrical technique will produce great poetry," he wrote.

Between 2007 and 2010, I wrote a biography of Charles Carroll of Carrollton, one of the signers of the Declaration and possibly the most liberally educated of the American founders. Again, I found myself able to enter the mind of this devout republican and patriot, though not completely. Something in his aristocratic manner eluded me and remains to this day incomprehensible to me.

After getting to meet one of my literary heroes, Kevin J. Anderson, I decided to write a biography of the notoriously private and immensely talented Canadian drummer Neil Peart of the rock band *Rush*. I had been thinking about Peart and his lyrics since March 1981, and I think I captured him and his ideas relatively well. Additionally, I have experienced some of the same family tragedies as has he, thus making an identification even stronger.

Sometime in 2009 or 2010, Annette Kirk graciously opened up her husband's private papers to me. Russell Kirk had been a serious part of my life since the fall of 1989, and I had been reading and thinking about him and his ideas for twenty years when Annette opened the archives to me. Studying Kirk has proven one of the most glorious tasks of my professional career.

Most recently, I have had the chance — much to my surprise and never my intention — to write a biography of the controversial seventh president of the United States, Andrew Jackson. While many in our contemporary culture consider him the demon of all demons in early American history, I found him to be as refreshingly honest as he was brutally violent.

When dealing with biography, we should also deal, I think, with autobiography, itself intimately related to biography. By its very nature and by almost any measure, an autobiography is self-indulgent, and this probably explains why so few autobiographies are successful in conveying a larger message. They do remain endlessly fascinating, however, because the human person is endlessly fascinating and because each new person is a unique and finite reflection of the infinite and loving face of God. In our follies and in our achievements, we each have something to offer. Some things we offer for good, and some we offer for ill.

A good biographer or autobiographer understands what makes a person human. We can summarize this understanding in three points.

1. The good biographer and autobiographer recognizes what is best in a person and what is worst. Consciously or unconsciously, he views each person as made in the image of the Divine and as a unique reflection of what is universally true.

2. The good biographer also recognizes that while each person is a reflection of the infinite, he is very much a part of the finite — an incarnate soul, born into a certain time and in a certain place.

3. The good biographer also recognizes that his subject has many relations and can best be understood in light of those relations — to grandparents, parents, children, teachers, ministers, priests, professors. He understands that a man has duties as well as rights — duties to his family, to his faith, to his friends, and to his country.

II

Personalities
and Groups

1

T.E. Hulme:

FIRST CONSERVATIVE OF THE TWENTIETH CENTURY

I'VE COME ACROSS THE NAME AND IDEAS OF
T.E. Hulme (1883–1917) a number of times in the last two
decades, but I've only recently had time to examine his life
and ideas in any detail.

As I dug around, I must admit I was rather astounded by the
ideas I found, as well as by the importance conferred upon him by
his generation. History should never have forgotten him, and we
would do well to remember him and to remember what he wrote.
Indeed, the German shell that took his life in the early autumn of
1917 may have changed a considerable part of the twentieth century
by removing Hulme from it. Our whole "Time of Troubles," as Kirk
defined it, might have been attenuated by the presence, personality,
and witness of this man.

T.S. Eliot, certainly one of the greatest of twentieth-century men,
understood the importance of Hulme in 1924. Eliot saw him as the
new man, that is, as the *twentieth-century man*. In April 1924, he wrote:

> When Hulme was killed in Flanders in 1917 ... he was
> known to a few people as a brilliant talker, a brilliant
> amateur of metaphysics, and the author of two or three
> of the most beautiful short poems in the language. In this
> volume [the posthumous *Speculations*, edited by Herbert
> Read] he appears as the forerunner of a new attitude of
> mind, which should be the twentieth-century mind,
> if the twentieth century is to have a mind of its own.

Hulme, Eliot continued, is

> classical, reactionary, and revolutionary; he is the antip-
> odes of the eclectic, tolerant, and democratic mind of
> the end of the last century.... A new classical age will
> be reached when the dogma ... of the critic is so mod-
> ified by contact with creative writing, and when the
> creative writers are so permeated by the new dogma,
> that a state of equilibrium is reached. For what is meant
> by a classical moment in literature is surely a moment
> of *stasis*, when the creative impulse finds a form which
> satisfies the best intellect of the time, a moment when
> a type is produced.

Eliot continued to praise Hulme in his private letters. In one, he
stated bluntly to Allen Tate: "Hulme has influenced me enormously."
In another, Eliot claimed Hulme to be "the most remarkable theologian of my generation."

Historian Christopher Dawson believed that Hulme, almost
alone in his generation, understood the dangers of progressivism:

> The essentially transitory character of the humanist
> culture has been obscured by the dominance of the belief
> in Progress and by the shallow and dogmatic optimism
> which characterized nineteenth-century Liberalism. It
> was only an exceptionally original mind, like that of the
> late T.E. Hulme, that could free itself from the influence
> of Liberal dogma and recognize *the sign of the times* — the
> passing of the ideals that had dominated European civi-
> lization for four centuries, and the dawn of a new order.

In hindsight, praise of such magnitude from both Eliot and Dawson should give any twenty-first-century conservative pause. Who
was this man who profoundly shaped the thought of two of the
most recognized conservatives of the last century? Unfortunately,
the name "Hulme" no longer rolls off the tongue when we think

of our lineage. We might think of Godkin, Babbitt, More, Nock, Eliot, Dawson, Kirk... but rarely does a conservative mention the name of Hulme.

Yet, at one time, few would have questioned that he shaped a movement. In 1948, the Jesuit periodical *America* proclaimed Hulme the model — mostly in thought, if not in person — for a literary revival. The English poet offered a "charter" (as the author put it) of Catholic arts and literature. A writer in the *New York Times* in 1960 summed up Hulme's influence nicely: "T. E. Hulme had modified the consciousness of his age in such a way that by 1939 his name had become part of a myth." It is a myth that we would do well to revive.

Hulme, from all accounts, possessed a rather powerful personality, able to form communities of thought and art around himself. As just mentioned, he might well serve as a model for our own conservatism, especially as we strive to rebuild what two decades have torn apart (in terms of our coherence as an intellectual movement) and what centuries have deconstructed (in terms of culture and the rise of Leviathan and Demos).

If Hulme is remembered, he's best remembered as a poet of influence. Most credit Hulme with founding Imagist poetry. Imagism connected the horizon and the sky, the vertical and horizontal, time and eternity. In the May 1, 1915 issue of *The Egoist*, F. S. Flint, a companion of Hulme's, remembered the actual creation of the Imagist movement in 1908:

> Somewhere in the gloom of the year 1908, Mr T. E. Hulme, now in the trenches of Ypres, but excited then by the propinquity, at a half-a-crown dance, of the other sex (if, as Remy de Gourmont avers, the passage from the aesthetic to the sexual emotion, *n'est qu'un pas*, the reverse is surely also true), proposed to a companion that they should found a Poets' Club. The thing was done, there and then. The Club began to dine; and its members to read their verses. At the end of the year they published a small plaquette of them, called "For Christmas MDCCCCVIII."

Hulme's poem "Autumn" also appeared in the same issue.

> A touch of cold in the Autumn night —
> I walked abroad,
> And saw the ruddy moon lean over a hedge
> Like a red-faced farmer.
> I did not stop to speak, but nodded,
> And round about were the wistful stars
> With white faces like town children.

While this poem's theme doesn't strike the modern reader as anything profound, I can readily understand its influence on the work of Eliot. Could Eliot have produced *The Wasteland*, *The Hollow Men*, or the *Four Quartets* without the influence of Hulme and the school of poetry he founded? *The Four Quartets* is arguably the greatest work of art of the twentieth century. If for no other reason, I'm truly thankful Hulme contributed what he did, simply in offering this new form of poetry.

Like Eliot, Hulme adopted and accepted modernist forms of art while rejecting the meaning and essence of modernity. In one of his most powerful essays, defining the nature of humanism, Hulme argued that all scholarship and art must begin with the premise (fact) of original sin.

> What is important is what nobody seems to realise — the dogmas like that of Original Sin, which are the closest expression of the categories of the religious attitude. That man is in no sense perfect but a wretched creature who can yet apprehend perfection.

Rousseauian/Enlightenment thinking had moved society away from an understanding of this fundamental truth of the human person. As Hulme saw it, Rousseauianism is a "heresy, a mistaken adoption of false conceptions." By focusing on feelings and individual desires and blind lusts (and by glorifying them), it attempts to allow man to become a God — and as a result "creates a bastard

conception of *Personality.*" The human person overcomes his deprav-
ity only though heroic virtue, Hulme argued:

> From the pessimistic conception of man comes naturally
> the heroic task requiring heroic qualities…virtues which
> are not likely to flourish on the soil of a rational and
> skeptical ethic. This regeneration can, on the contrary,
> only be brought about and only be maintained by actions
> springing from an ethic which from the narrow rational-
> ist standpoint is irrational, being not *relative,* but absolute.

When Hulme received a commission in the British Army during
the Great War, he embraced what he had preached, and gave his life
as a patriot of Western civilization.

Even in the trenches, before his death, Hulme continued to shape
his contemporaries.

> In all this [group of poets] Hulme was ringleader. He
> insisted too on absolutely accurate presentation and
> no verbiage; and he and F. W. Tancred, a poet too lit-
> tle known, perhaps because his production is precious
> and small, used to spend hours each day in the search
> for the right phrase. Tancred does it still; while Hulme
> reads German philosophy in the trenches, waiting for
> the general advance.[1]

Hulme published a series of war notes from France. In one, he
attempted to explain to the liberals that their version of history
rested on dubious assumptions.

> Similarly our Liberal friends may be reminded that
> the lines now making a map of Europe are the result
> in every instance of local circumstances governable by
> men; and as they were determined by men they can
> be changed by men. Europe, in short, is a creation, not

---

1 *The Egoist* (May 1, 1915).

a blind evolutionary product; and nothing connected with its mental features is any more fixed than the present relations, as expressed in the trench-lines, between the Allies and the enemy.

Another prevalent Liberal assumption, hostile to a proper appreciation of the significance of the war, is that progress is both inevitable and of necessity in one direction. That change, like the girl in the play, may of itself or by the intention of those who bring it about, take the wrong turning seems never to enter the heads of some of our most popular doctrinaires. All that is not Liberal in Europe or elsewhere is in their opinion not even fundamentally anti-Liberal or other-than-Liberal, — it is merely an arrested development of an evolution which in any case must needs be Liberal in the end, or a reaction against, but still upon the line of Liberalism. This, I need not say after stating it, is not only an error, but a particularly insular error. In the first place, evolution in our sense of the word — that is, evolution towards democracy — is not only not inevitable, but it is the most precarious, difficult, and exigent task political man has ever conceived. And, in the second place, far from it being the predestined path of every nation and race, only one or two nations have attempted to pursue it, while the rest deliberately and even, we might say, intelligently, pursue another path altogether as if that were progress, and are thus sincerely hostile to our own.[2]

If only Hulme's mind — per Eliot's wishful thinking in 1924 — had become the "twentieth-century mind," we might very well have avoided a "progressive" world, immersed in ideological terror on one side and in flabby citizens demanding unearned health care and subsidies for big businesses — so-called "stimulus packages" — on the other.

2   Quoted from Karen Csengeri, ed., *The Collected Writings of T. E. Hulme* (Oxford: Clarendon Press, 1994), 333.

2

Irving Babbitt

AT ROUGHLY THE SAME TIME THAT HULME was formulating a pre-Renaissance humanism in the United Kingdom, Harvard University's Irving Babbitt was formulating what would come to be known as the "New Humanism" or "American Humanism." To almost the same degree that Hulme inspired an entire generation of the best men and women of letters in the United Kingdom, Babbitt inspired at least one of his closest friends, Paul Elmer More. He also inspired generations of students to follow his teachings. Each of these students became reminders of what had been lost or mocked throughout Western and world thought. One student remembered Babbitt's undergraduate seminar at Harvard:

> At that time he had very small classes — meeting around a table. He came in with a bag bursting full of books, and took out a handful of notes which he arranged around him. — Began to sway in his chair, then leaped out upon one of them and poured a barrage of criticism upon some doctrine or some line of poetry, — "to cast o'er erring words and deeds a heavenly show" — Buddha, Aristotle, Plato, Horace, Dante, Montaigne, Pascal, Milton, etc., etc. He deluged you with wisdom of the world; his thoughts were unpacked and poured out so fast you couldn't keep up with them. You didn't know what he was talking about, but you felt that he was extremely in earnest, that it was tremendously important, that some time it would count; that he was uttering dogmatically things that cut into your beliefs, disposed derisively of what

you adored, driving you into a reconstruction of your
entire intellectual system. He was at you day after day
like a battering ram, knocking down your illusions. He
was building up a system of ideas. You never felt for a
moment that he was a pedagogue teaching pupils. You
felt that he was a Coleridge, a Carlyle, a Buddha, pouring
out the full-stuffed cornucopia of the world upon your
head. You were no longer in the elementary class. You
were with a man who was seeking through literature for
illustrations of his philosophy of life. You were dealing
with questions on the answer to which the welfare of
nations and civilizations depended. He himself seemed to
know the right answer and was building a thoroughfare
of ideas from the Greeks to our own day. You went out
of the room laden down with general ideas that he had
made seem tremendously important.... He related for
you a multitude of separate and apparently disconnected
tendencies to the great central currents of thought. You
carried away also a sense of the need for immense reading. He had given you theses about literature, about life,
which you would spend a lifetime in verifying.[1]

Of his first generation of followers, none was more important
than T.S. Eliot. Other followers included G.R. Elliott, Austin Warren, Gordon Keith Chalmers, Louis Mercier, Hoffman Nickerson,
Norman Foerster, and Frank Jewett Mather, Jr. Later, his admirers
included Ray Bradbury, Milton Hindus, Robert Nisbet, Russell Kirk,
George Panichas, and Claes Ryn.[2] Kirk, the founder of post-World
War II conservatism, described Babbitt glowingly as "one of the

---

1   "Chronicle and Comment," *The Bookman* (November 1929): 293.
2   See Austin Warren, "The 'New Humanism' Twenty Years After," *Modern Age*
3 (Winter 1958–1959); G.R. Elliott, *Humanism and Imagination* (Chapel Hill: University of North Carolina Press, 1938); Frederick Manchester and Odell Shepard,
eds., *Irving Babbitt: Man and Teacher* [1941] (New York: Greenwood Press, 1969); and
George A. Panichas and Claes G. Ryn, eds., *Irving Babbitt in Our Time* (Washington,
DC: Catholic University of America Press, 1986).

sages of antiquity, along with Longinus and Quintilian."[3] He was certainly not alone in such praise. Lynn Harold Hough labeled him one of the five greatest thinkers of Western civilization, along with Aristotle, Cicero, Erasmus, and Babbitt's closest friend, Paul Elmer More.[4]

Even those opposed to Babbitt—sometimes virulently opposed—made for impressive company: Dorothy Thompson, Albert Jay Nock, Lewis Mumford, Ernest Hemingway, Sinclair Lewis, Granville Hicks, and H.L. Mencken. Dorothy Thompson (who by the 1930s would become one of the most famous journalists in the world) once commented "when she was in the hospital at the time her baby was born" that reading an article by a humanist "was worse than having the baby."[5] Nock claimed that the humanists emphasized human will at the expense of human passion. Additionally, Nock believed, the humanists gave too much credence to the power of culture and possessed too much faith in a natural aristocracy.[6]

Like Hulme, Irving Babbitt worried that the nineteenth century (in its material culture and spiritual makeup) had merely mechanized all of humanity, creating a burden which would become crushing. "One sometimes asks one's self, in moments of despondency," he noted in his first published piece, "whether the main achievement of the nineteenth century will not have been to accumulate a mass of machinery that will break the twentieth century's back."[7] Though each thought was brilliant in and of itself, the predominant thought(s) of the century had moved toward an increased understanding of particularisms, separating each field,

3 Kirk, "The Enduring Influence of Irving Babbitt," in *Irving Babbitt in Our Time*, 20.

4 Lynn Harold Hough, *Great Humanists* (New York: Abingdon-Cokesbury Press, 1952).

5 Seward Collins to Paul Elmer More, 17 December 1930, in Box 24, Folder 3, P.E. More Papers (C0054), Princeton University. See also C. Hartley Grattan, ed., *The Critique of Humanism: A Symposium* (New York: Brewer and Warren, 1930).

6 Michael Wreszin, *The Superfluous Anarchist: Albert Jay Nock* (Providence, RI: Brown University Press, 1971), 87.

7 Irving Babbitt, "The Rational Study of the Classics," *The Atlantic* (March 1897): 356.

idea, and person from the whole. Whether a Darwin, a Marx, or soon (in America) a Freud, each thinker narrowed and narrowed his field of understanding while deepening his understanding of that particular field in isolation from all others. Not surprisingly, muddled thinking about the whole also lowered the quality of writing, adding confusion to confusion. "The nineteenth century witnessed the greatest debauch of descriptive writing the world has ever known," Babbitt claimed in his 1910 book, *The New Laokoon*.[8]

Babbitt believed Western scholars and writers had lost a "sense of proportion" as well as imagination, thus upending all that the medievals had achieved in the grand synthesis of Dante.[9] "By the overemphasis on sympathy the humanitarian shows that he has no sense of proportion," Babbitt wrote in 1915, "whereas the sense of proportion is the very essence and breath of life and humanism."[10] The predominant trajectory of post-Burkean thought had been toward "the accumulation" of knowledge (rather than its assimilation), as well as toward an unfortunate embracing of the most emotional aspects of the romantic period.[11] Like Hulme, Babbitt understood this change in the Western mind and character to be one that ultimately prepared the ground for widespread violence of particularism against particularism. Unlike Hulme, however, Babbitt believed it necessary, not to return to the "religious attitude" of the ancient and medieval worlds, but rather to bring the Western liberal tradition of education as a whole — and even that of Oriental thinkers — to bear upon all modern thought, thus embracing inheritance rather than separation or revolution.

At every level, Babbitt saw himself as a reformer, not a radical. The true goal of the humanist, he wrote, was not to encourage impulse but to resist and restrain it, harnessing it for use with a higher or moral imagination.[12] As such, he hoped, the philosopher would

---

8   Babbitt, *The New Laokoon* (Boston: Houghton Mifflin, 1910), viii–ix.

9   Babbitt, "The Rational Study of the Classics," 357.

10   Babbitt, "Humanists and Humanitarians," *The Nation* (September 2, 1915): 289.

11   Babbitt, "The Rational Study of the Classics," 359, 363.

12   Babbitt, "Humanists and Humanitarians," 289.

become literary, and the men of letters must "become to the best of their ability philosophical."[13]

Armed with strong reservations about American nationalism, and with an overt opposition to any form of progressivism, Babbitt called for a reclamation of the word humanist from the romantic sentimentalists who had hijacked it.

Though one often equates humanism with the West, its American founder in the modern era, Babbitt, considered an understanding of Asian philosophy and theology critical to one's education. Against Jean-Jacques Rousseau, Babbitt embraced the inherent Stoic qualities not only of the ancient Western world, but of high ancient Asian culture as well. "The greatest of vices according to Buddha is the lazy yielding to the impulses of temperament," More explained, quoting a footnote from Babbitt's *Literature and the American College*. Conversely, "the greatest virtue is the opposite of this, the awakening from sloth and lethargy of the senses, the constant exercise of the active will. The last words of the dying Buddha to his disciples were an exhortation to practise this virtue unremittingly."[14]

While Babbitt did not consider the Buddha to be perfect, he did believe that he possessed more Stoic virtues than had the actual Western Stoics. In particular, Babbitt appreciated that Buddha was "extraordinarily insistent upon the fact of sin," whereas Occidental Stoics ultimately embraced a form of extraordinary and supernatural optimism. The Buddha, never self-satisfied, looked only to what was eternal as essential. All things of this world would pass, thus demanding the well-centered human person to look beyond, beneath, around, and above them.[15] This contemplation should not result in complacency, the Buddha argued. Viewing himself as a medical doctor or psychologist of the soul and will, the Buddha instead demanded action. "A man may possess the noble truths,"

13 Babbitt, "Bergson and Rousseau," *The Nation* (November 14, 1912): 453.

14 Paul Elmer More, "Irving Babbitt," *American Review* (1934): 30.

15 Babbitt, "Buddha and the Occident," in *The Dhammapada* [1936] (New York: New Directions, 1965), 82–83.

he argued, "and so escapes from sorrow only by acting upon them." The well-centered man, noble in thought, must act through faith by embracing a "path" leading to "quiescence, knowledge, supreme wisdom, and Nirvana."[16]

Such actions were not necessarily equivalent to a Christian understanding of good works or of participation in the divine liturgy — each of which, Babbitt feared, might easily mislead a man (noble or ignoble). For the Buddha, "the man who is outwardly idle may be at once more strenuously and more profitably employed than the man who is outwardly active."[17] The real work (*Karma*) — what in the West might be properly called leisure or contemplation — "is a sort of fate, but a fate of which man is himself the author and which is not at any particular moment entirely subversive of moral freedom."[18] Again, Babbitt stressed, the teachings of the Buddha led neither to a religion nor to a philosophy, but to a "path."[19] In the West, according to Babbitt, St Francis of Assisi came closest to living a Buddhist life (though Francis, of course, had no contact with any element of the East and developed Stoic charity according to his own lights).[20] In this, St Francis was unique.

According to Babbitt, the West had created a dreadful world — "a world of frenzied producers" and a "world of frenzied consumers."[21] Only the most cultivated and most uncultivated had escaped the desires of consumerist passions. Most Western and American men had been trained well, but only partially educated. Rather than giving them control over the self, their education had created insatiable longings. The average man, only half-educated and almost certainly not liberally educated, has rejected all the restraint that tradition, mores, and norms enjoined on him. Partially formed, modern man was not "critical enough to achieve new" restraints, his education

---

16 Ibid., 86–87. "Nirvana" means, importantly, not nihilism as Western culture has understood it, but as the ability to move beyond one's emotions and desires.

17 Ibid., 92.

18 Ibid., 92–93.

19 Ibid., 94–95.

20 Ibid., 100–1.

21 Ibid., 110.

having led to the "proneness, namely to harbor desires that are
not only numerous but often incompatible." The Reformation had
played a vital role in the decline of the world as well, as Babbitt
understood it. While the Roman Catholic Church had offered only
an imperfect restraint upon the will and the appetites of man, it had
necessarily created an aura of mystery and reverence for the venerable and awful. Protestantism, especially Calvinism, had loosed all
real restraints, Babbitt concluded, making religion utilitarian rather
than graceful and poetic. Consequently, the desire for material
comfort had long replaced the desire for spiritual comfort. Further,
though Protestants had in theory separated the sphere of religion
from politics, in practice, it had done the opposite. "Practically
both the Lutheran and the Calvinistic state tend to run together
the things of God and the things of Caesar," Babbitt argued. Consequently, Protestantism nullified any "refuge from the secular power."
Without restraint, the secular city ultimately glorified itself in the
name of modern nationalism.[22]

---

22   See Babbitt, "Buddha and the Occident," in *The Dhammapada*, 112–14; and
Babbitt, *Democracy and Leadership*, 76.

3

The Christian Humanism of Paul Elmer More

AUL ELMER MORE'S FINAL STATEMENT—A religious one—as offered in his grand and moving book, *Pages from an Oxford Diary*, is one of the great short works of the last century.[1] If offers a profound statement of faith from a man who spent most of his life in skepticism regarding Christianity. Though he consented to Christian truth later in his life, it remains unknown whether or not he ever received communion, even on his death bed.

Though few now remember Paul Elmer More (1864–1937), he once stood with his closest friend, Irving Babbitt, as the leader of the so-called "New Humanist" movement. An editor of *The Nation* and a classicist at Princeton University, More influenced many of the greats of the 20th century — especially through his friendships. Among his closest friends were T. S. Eliot and C. S. Lewis. His correspondence with Eliot, now housed in the Princeton University archives, is nothing short of beautiful. In a rather typical letter, T. S. Eliot teased More about his supposed lack of Christian orthodoxy:

> But having refused this, how much else of orthodox theology do you refuse? What about the Angels and Archangels and the Saints and the Patriarchs? And devotions of Our Lady? And I do not forget that an eminent friend of ours has called you a binitarian contra mundum. No,

---

1 Unless footnoted, all quotations are taken from Paul Elmer More's *Pages from an Oxford Diary* (Princeton, NJ: Princeton University Press, 1937). Strangely, the original printing of the book possesses no page numbers.

sir, I call upon you to demonstrate your orthodoxy; or
alternatively, to demonstrate that you are the only Catholic living. What are your views now on the Marriage at
Cana, and the Loaves and Fishes?[2]

More took the teasing well, offering back to Eliot as much as he
received.

C.S. Lewis acknowledged his profound debt to More several
years after More's death.

I once told Paul Elmer More that while it would be an
exaggeration to call him my spiritual father, I might
call him my spiritual uncle. By this I meant, in the first
place, that one had in his presence that sense of comfort
and security and well being which a child has in the
presence of a grown-up relative whom it likes. I began
to feel it almost at once. It was something I am not sure
one would gather from his books — a real homeliness,
almost an affectionateness, the very reverse of that rar-
ified quality which some people may associate with
American "humanism." In the second place, I meant that
quality which the child would resent if it came from
the father. In our own first conversation he corrected a
fake … accent and the misuse of a scientific term, which
I had … in print, in a way which ought to be common
among old men but is actually quite rare. On the one
hand it was so done that even the vainest young author
could not have objected to it; on the other, there was no
nonsense about all being in the same boat, or "you don't
mind my mentioning it" or anything of that kind. It was
quite definitely and undisguisedly the ripe speaking to
the unripe — authority without egoism. At this distance
of time I cannot remember much of our conversation.

---

2   T.S. Eliot, London, to Paul Elmer More, 30 August 1930, in Box 3, Folder 3,
Paul Elmer More Papers (C0054), Princeton University.

He found that I agreed with him about the futility of much academic 'research' and this led him to tell with great humour, and also great tenderness, the story of a young woman he knows who refused to marry a man she loved because the "work" (a thesis on some unspeakably obscure poet) "must come first..." He talked also of the "fundamentalism" to which, in his opinion, the Church of Rome was committed. But most of our time together was spent in close argument. You saw at once he was the sort of man who welcomed attacks on his favorite beliefs and who was ready to give his whole attention to what you said without any irrelevant consideration of who you were. He was very fair and patient in discussion and talked for truth not victory. And all the time, however abstract the theme, the homely and human quality — sometimes manifested in the choice of an illustration, sometimes in the mere twinkle of his eye — was always in evidence, making one quite sure that his philosophy had roots in the earth. It is not, I think, what I should have expected. My impression is that the man was bigger than his books. There was more of him. Anything less like the popular idea of a "don" or a "philosopher" would be hard to find. Perhaps the extremely rich and flexible voice (he spoke from the chest) had something to do with it. With renewed apologies for the inconvenience I must have caused you by my delay.

Yours faithfully, C.S. Lewis.[3]

Even Babbitt (rather more skeptical about Christianity than More) teased More about his faith. More remembered the following conversation, along North Avenue in Cambridge, England. The two were talking fervently to one another "when suddenly" Babbitt "stopped short, faced about upon me, and, with both hands rigidly

---

3 C.S. Lewis, Magdalen College, Oxford, to Mr. Dakin, 3 August 1941, in Paul Elmer More Papers, Princeton University.

clenched, ejaculated: 'Good God, man, are you a Jesuit in disguise?'"4
More failed to recall the exact topic of conversation — and he may
merely have been Jesuitical in his argumentation — but the comment reveals much about More and about how others perceived
him. Concerning the question raised by Babbitt, More only wrote:
"I have never been able to answer the question satisfactorily."5

Maybe he was a Jesuit after all.

Still, More ultimately rejected Babbitt's understanding of a more
skeptical humanism, because it never fully reconciled itself to religion. Christianity for More provided ultimate purpose for all of life.
He saw Christianity as an anchor to all that the humanists desired
and as the only proper end of humanism.

> That is the dilemma that faces the humanist — the
> intuition of free will; free will exercised for a purpose;
> purpose directed to clothe human life with value; value
> measured by happiness — the chain is perfect, link by
> link, only at the end it seems to be attached to noth-
> ing. And so I ask myself, reluctantly, almost wishing my
> answer were mistaken, whether those who advocate
> humanism, as an isolated movement, are not doomed
> to disappointment. It is not that the direction in itself
> is wrong; every step in the program is right, and only
> by this path can we escape from the waste land of nat-
> uralism. But can we stop here in security? For purpose
> that will not end in bitter defeat; for values that will
> not mock us like empty masks, must we not look for a
> happiness based on something beyond the swaying tides
> of mortal success and failure? Will not the humanist,
> unless he adds to his creed the faith and the hope of

4   Paul Elmer More, *On Being Human* (Princeton, NJ: Princeton University
Press, 1936), 27.

5   Ibid. As to More's orthodoxy or heterodoxy, see the excellent correspondence between More and T. S. Eliot, dated Shrove Tuesday, 1928, through January
11, 1937, in the Paul Elmer More Collection (C0054), Box 3, Folder 3, Princeton
University.

religion, find himself at the last, despite his protests, dragged back into the camp of the naturalist?[6]

Reading through Paul Elmer More's many works, one apprehends a singularly honest man — a man full of integrity, ready to follow the Truth wherever it may lead.

In his autobiographical *Pages from an Oxford Diary,* More explored the role of faith, in culture and in the self. He labeled the book "a kind of informal prayer." He claimed that as a young man he was very taken with the idea of a materialist "New Philosophy, which should prove once for all that the world and men are the product of a fatalistic Law of Chance and Probability." More discarded this idea when he discovered that such materialism leads to the conclusion that men are merely machines and automatons, incapable of free will. At the same moment in his life, he also deeply resented the idea that he needed redemption through accepting grace. To reconcile these two positions, More turned to reading published letters, autobiographies, and biographies, searching for the key to a successful life. After extensive reading, More came to believe that almost all such successful lives were still empty, still devoid of something. "Almost invariably in the correspondence of writers and scholars and men of affairs the last letters are filled with open or ill-concealed despondency." Ultimately, and perhaps finally (though not completely), More settled upon Plato's understanding of the "True, the Good, and the Beautiful." He writes: "I can say simply and without reservation that to this goal I attained, and that I shall end my days a conscious, as I was born an unconscious, Platonist."

Still, something nagged at More's soul. "But here, I could not rest," More recorded, echoing the words of St Augustine. "Is that realm of Ideas a cold vacuum of inanimate images?…what I still needed was God." After all, he admitted to himself, "long ago Jehovah rebuked Job for his presumption: 'Shalt thou by reasoning find out God?'"

---

6   See More, "A Revival of Humanism" in *On Being Human* (Princeton, NJ: Princeton University Press, 1935), 19–20.

More concluded:

> We reason properly from facts, not towards them. The
> question of a God must be answered by direct experi-
> ence, or by the sort of inference which is rightly called
> faith.... For many years the existence of the Ideal world
> has been as real to me as these visible phenomena of
> the material world, more real since in the sphere of
> Ideas illusion would have no part. Only slowly did the
> incompetence of such a belief, in itself with no con-
> necting link between the two realms, dawn upon me.
> It was just the perception of purpose in the evolution
> of the world, as something above and beyond the static
> imitation of Ideas, that finally led me to the quest of
> a dynamic, personal agent at work. That made me a
> better as well as a more complete Platonist, and it set
> me again on the road to Christianity. Now, the thought
> of a naked soul journeying forever on and on through
> inanimate Ideas, with no personal guide or consoler,
> with no glimpse of the majestic Spirit whose eternal
> home is there, — the thought of such a journey sends a
> shudder and a chill through me. I cry out: Lord, I believe,
> help thou mine unbelief!

As More finally decided, the gift of free will allows a man to choose
grace rather than pride. Typically, though, a person chooses pride:

> And we, slothful servants, unworthy allies, treacherous
> children, ignoble friends, have wrought confusion and
> in our little blind egotism have added to the evil of the
> world, to the misery of ourselves, and — so the tragedy
> of the Incarnation would tell us — to the burden of
> the Creator.

The argument, in less personal terms, is strictly Christian humanist — that is, it is based upon More's conviction that the ideas of the

best of the Greek pagans flow into Christian theology and culture. "Greek literature, philosophic and religious, pagan and Christian, from Plato to St Chrysostom and beyond that to the Council of Chalcedon in 451 A D, is essentially a unit and follows at the centre a straight line."7

As More understood matters, the priest has the primary role of liberating man from a servile existence. For this liberation to occur, one needs leisure for the contemplative life. The schools (led by priests) should provide the fundamental vehicle for true leisure and for the advancement and preservation of culture. Hence we arrive at the title of More's religious memoir, *Pages from an Oxford Diary*. In the beginning of the book, More demonstrated a deep love for the venerable English university:

> Oxford is the creation of the Church, and her beauty witnesses to the excellence of religion. The mark was put upon her once for all, wonderful city; and why should men seek to erase it? There are other places aplenty where laboratories may be erected and secular science may flourish; why not leave this fair domicile amidst her wandering rivers and her girdle of hills, why not leave it as a home for those who choose to 'flee for the presse' and to set their hearts on God's peace? They should repay the world for all the world gave them. The signature of the Church is legible enough on the houses and streets of Oxford, but when one turns to the men who dwell in them and walk among them, one feels something like a shock. From the same cause can effects so unequal flow? Often I ask myself how it can be that dead stones and mortar should speak more eloquently of the divine presence than does the living face of man, made in the likeness of his Creator. Pass by the secular scholars, the philologians [sic], scientists,

---

7   More, quoted in "Introduction" to Lambert, ed., *The Essential Paul Elmer More* (New Rochelle, NY: Arlington House, 1972), 19.

historians, economists, and their kind. But what of the
men whose special calling it is to search out and pro-
claim the sacred revelation, whose profession is the
Church? I should like to see Oxford still more under
the domination of the priest. He has made it; the city
is his. However it may be with his own soul, he is the
custodian of the ancient tradition of the spirit; he is the
only security we have against the complete invasion of
a devastating materialism.

For the mind to be empowered through leisure and true education, More argued, it must possess imagination, harnessed and
honed. Imagination (as he understood it) allows one to see past
the immediate; to see beyond to the long line of ancestors, all
of whom contributed something to the order and justice of the
world. "The imagination in its power of grasping in a single firm
vision, so to speak," he explained in his ninth book of Shelburne
Essays, *Aristocracy and Justice*, allows one to see "the long course
of human history and of distinguishing what is essential therein
from what is ephemeral."

In More's explanation, one cannot fail to see not only echoes
of Edmund Burke, but also an anticipation of the ideas of More's
most important student, Russell Kirk. Indeed, imagination serves
as the basis of all true conservatism:

> The instinctive distrust of uncontrolled human nature
> and the instinctive reliance on the imagination are the
> very roots of the conservative temper, as their contraries
> are the roots of the liberal and radical temper, the lack
> of imagination, if any distinction is to be made, being
> the chief factor of liberalism and confidence in human
> nature being the main impulse of radicalism.[8]

That which inspires the imagination most — the Incarnate Word,

---

8   More, quoted in Byron C. Lambert, ed., *The Essential Paul Elmer More*, 25.

the Second Person of the Most Blessed Trinity — reigns from (and above) the very center of history.

1. God, by becoming fully human, while remaining fully divine, breaks down any pretense of a divide between eternity and time. The "raw conjectures about the absolute and the infinite and the unconditioned vanish away, and God appears before me simply as one who from the beginning has cherished a purpose; now brings it to fulfillment."

2. God reveals Himself fully as the Orderer of All Things. For the Incarnation proves the purpose of God — that He will bring order to the chaos we created.

3. God reveals the need to destroy the dark Necessity (evil): "We know that in some way evil and involuntary pain are bound together, and we seem to see that in some way also evil must be redeemed by voluntary suffering."

In these points, More rejected the harsher teaching of John Calvin (learned in his youth in St Louis), and proclaimed the doctrine of predestination nothing less than effeminate, as it denied men the choice to suppress their pride. By proclaiming grace so irresistible, More argued, Calvin destroyed the very notion of grace. The theology of the Reformation, which so magnified divine grace as to destroy human freedom, in this matter is false, as are all absolutes. We cannot escape the ultimate responsibility for choosing our path, and no true man would wish to do so. But to know that we have a great Friend at our side who voluntarily shares with us the consequences of our faults, who will not abandon us though we err seventy times seven, who shows us that the evil we do is a breach of trust between person and person — to know that is to gain a new insight into life and death, and to be inspired with new hopes; it may mean rebirth from above. O Lamb of God, that takest away the sins of the world.

And, to conclude, here is More, his autobiography finished only days before his own passing from this world:

And so I sit and wait, in patience and serenity — for the end which is no end. I turn over in my mind the various possibilities of the long journey, amusing myself with fancies that I trust are not purely fanciful. Only of this I am assured, that some time and in some way, spirit to spirit, face to face, I shall meet the great Lord of life, and, falling before Him, tell my gratitude for all He has done, and implore pardon for all I have left undone.

Amen.

4

The Order Men

ALMOST NO ONE REMEMBERS THE short-lived journal *Order* anymore. It only lasted four issues, but it set off a chain of events that, in hindsight, can be described as the true beginning of the "Catholic Literary Revival" of the twentieth century. Of course, it had a lot of help, but *Order* as a periodical served as a catalyst for connecting English-speaking Roman Catholics to their European counterparts (West and East). Its story, though brief, reveals much about the absolute necessity of a Catholic Republic of Letters, especially in an age of terror and ideology.

Literary groups and clubs sprang up throughout the United Kingdom in the first third of the twentieth century. There was the Bloomsbury Group, which included Leonard and Virginia Wolff, T.S. Eliot, and John Maynard Keynes. There was the Moot, which included not only T.S. Eliot but also Owen Barfield. Barfield belonged to an even more obscure group (yet one destined to become more famous) — The Inklings. This last group, intensely artistic and ecumenical, included C.S. Lewis, J.R.R. Tolkien, and Lord David Cecil. These groups knew of one another and, as just indicated, often had overlapping membership, but never did these groups — as wholes — interact with one another. Rather, the individual members came and went while the communities remained autonomous. Groups such as Bloomsbury remained adamantly secular, while the Inklings embraced various forms of Christianity, though mostly Catholic ones.

During the interwar years, artists and poets had to find their bearings again, as the First World War had turned the Western world upside down. As the Blessed Virgin Mary had warned the three Portuguese children of Fatima, the twentieth century would prove brutal and inhumane. True to her word, kingdoms fell, while empires and ideological regimes emerged to offer a New World Order, one built on the blood and disembodied remains of its countless victims.

As did so many interwar movements, these various literary and social groups sought to understand the world, to better it, and to prevent— obviously without success — a second world war. Even the more radical elements of the Bloomsbury group, though committed to anti-social and asocial norms, sought a form of human dignity lacking in all ideological regimes, be they nationalist or socialist.

Tom Burns (who is now remembered chiefly for his editorship of the English Catholic newspaper *The Tablet*) had been disgusted by his older brother's participation in the Bloomsbury Group. Their claims to social radicalism, he believed, were mere bizarre theatrics that led the Western world away from real progress, not toward it. Only by reclaiming traditional and timeless ethics and morality, the young man believed, could the West be saved in the aftermath of the First World War. As though intending to mock Bloomsbury, Tom Burns began what many considered a "never-ending party" at his Chelsea apartment. Naming itself "Order Men," Burns's group included historian and philosopher Christopher Dawson, Jesuit Martin D'Arcy, actor Robert Speaight, BBC radio personality Harman Grisewood, poet W.H. Auden, journalist Bernard Wall, artist Eric Gill, and poet David Jones. An impressive group to be sure, with Dawson and D'Arcy being the seniors (though each was only in his late 20s). Still, the other members deferred to the two men, as though they were older by much more than half a decade or so.

Indeed, more than being one of the senior members, Dawson also served (along with the writings of the absent Neo-Thomist Jacques Maritain) as the true intellectual touchstone of the group. Given his odd mixture of sheer brilliance and social awkwardness, Dawson was playfully known to the other members of the group as "Tiger." They never called him this to his face, however, preferring instead the informal "Kit."

Though they never formed a corporate mind, the Order Men did hold several beliefs in common. First, as just noted, they admired the work of Maritain and Dawson. Though Dawson would not publish his first book, *The Age of the Gods*, until 1928, the year *Order* began as a journal, he was already well known in English academic and literary circles through his numerous penetrating essays, which were published in a variety of leading journals of every discipline. No less a man than T.S. Eliot had noted that Dawson was much on the move by 1930. Maritain held equal intellectual weight in the group, though he resided in France and never visited them in London. Almost every single conversation at Burns's apartment began with some question raised by Maritain's 1924 *Art and Scholasticism*. From there, the conversation could and would range in any direction, but the group firmly embraced orthodox Roman Catholicism no matter where the logic led them.

Second, and equally important, the Order Men declared themselves enemies of every sort of utilitarianism. The human person (individually as well as in community) was sacrosanct. He was a being endowed with free will, lower than the angels but higher than the animals — unrepeatable, and made in the Image of Christ. No calculation, no matter how nuanced or how motivated, could ever understand or do justice to the complexity of human existence. Grisewood once joked that if forced to sit with soldiers who killed or liberals who organized, he would prefer the former, for they do less damage in the long run. When he stated this, he spoke for the entire group.

Third, the Order Men sought to harmonize the thought of Sts Augustine and Aquinas, believing the two offered the post-Great War world (and frankly, all times and places) a necessary understanding of the hierarchy, nature, and being of Creation itself. Augustine and Aquinas were astounding not merely for their gifts, but for their surrender of those gifts to the Christian republic. As a necessary corollary of this point, however, it must be noted that the Order Men believed the current state of Western civilization (and especially the English Roman Catholic Church) to be anything but orderly. Each had compromised and each had lost its way. As Burns put it privately to the group, they would "ridicule" compromising Catholicism until it "burst" into nothingness. As Burns claimed, serious Roman Catholics had more in common with serious Anglo-Catholics than with compromising members of their own branch. Quoting Cato the Elder's famous dictum against Carthage, Burns actually cried "delenda est" against the effete of his own church.

Fourth and finally, the Order Men dedicated themselves to the promotion of Edmund Burke's idea of the moral imagination — the use of art and creativity to leaven the world rather than seek art's conformity to some ideal or ideology.

By 1928, the men had enough confidence and bravado to begin their own journal, using it as an organ to express their ideas. For a brief but intense moment, *Order* became the rage among London intellectuals. As one member of the group remembered, *Order* "was a bombshell — as it was meant to be." Its first issue ran out immediately, and the group decided to reprint it, with some editorial changes. No doubt the brazenness of the journal, its layout, and its woodcuts by David Jones did much to make it attractive. It's equally true that English intellectual society of the interwar period loved good, intense, and humane argumentation. Despite representing a distinct minority and a religion often condemned for its foreign ruler and its association with terrorists like Guy Fawkes, *Order* provided arguments with real verve.

As a means to focus on the argument rather than the arguer, *Order* refused to give credit to any individual author. However well this anonymity worked for the authors and the journal, it remains a frustration for historians. Still, by looking at the writing style and exploring letters and diaries of the members of the group, it is possible to identify the authorship of several of the articles across its four issues. The editorship of Burns and the intellectual touchstone of Dawson overhang every aspect of the journal's brief run. Dawson, not surprisingly, wrote for the journal consistently, and his style is unmistakable. His articles dealt with the fundamental natures of civilization and cultures, sexuality, and psychology. Dawson's best article appeared in the second issue. Entitled simply, "Civilisation and Order," it could have served as the journal's deeply Catholic and Stoic manifesto. "Civilisation is not due to the birth of absolutely new faculties or qualities; it is a higher order, a more spiritual and profound harmony of every element in human life from the lowest to the highest." Real progress came from justly recognizing the individual talents of the human person within community. Utility and equality (at least as understood in the post-war West) could only lead to decline, distortion, and degeneration. Nature makes nothing in vain, as Aristotle noted. But Aquinas completed the thought: Only grace perfects nature.

Other articles in the journal — written by a number of the Order Men and their allies — dealt with beauty, family, agrarianism, Chesterbellocism, and education. Given the ages of the authors at the time, the journal was, and remains, astonishingly erudite.

Though *Order* only lasted four issues as a journal, it evolved into something else rather than dying. Though the exact details of what transpired remain unknown, the results are plain. In 1926, Burns began to work for the new Catholic publishing firm of Sheed and Ward. In 1928 he and Dawson began *Order*, and a year later Dawson published his first book with Sheed and Ward (his second book overall), *Religion and Progress*. While Frank Sheed had liked Burns personally, he found Dawson's mind overwhelmingly attractive and saw him (rightly) as the lynchpin to the success of any Catholic literary movement. With Sheed on their side, Burns and Dawson proposed a book to the firm — a book that would extend the ideas of *Order* to the European continent. They also solicited a number of essays to commemorate the 1,500th anniversary of the death of St Augustine. Sheed gladly accepted. The end product, *A Monument to St Augustine*, published in 1930, is nothing short of astounding. It was reprinted in 1945 and has recently been reprinted by Wipf & Stock; it remains as relevant now, just after the five hundredth anniversary of the Reformation, as it was in 1930.[1]

---

1   As a happy side note, my personal copy was owned by the once famous American mystery writer, Christopher Morley, and contains his insightful notes and marginalia.

For all intents and purposes, *A Monument* is a "Who's Who" for the Christian humanist movement of the last century. Impressively, Christopher Dawson, C.C. Martindale, E.I. Watkin, Martin D'Arcy, Jacques Maritain, Erich Przywara, Etienne Gilson, and Maurice Blondel each contributed to it. As Burns wrote in the "compiler's note," the book represented not just a commemoration but a fundamental "personal sympathy" for the fifth-century saint.

Critically well-received and selling successfully, *A Monument* further convinced Sheed of Dawson's importance. Dawson and Burns then proposed making *Order* something more than a journal. They would transform it into a series of books, written by Roman Catholics from all parts of the Western world and seeking a harmony of faith through the humanities. Again, Sheed responded enthusiastically, and his firm created the sixteen-volume series *Essays in Order*. Each book (as envisioned by Dawson, Burns, and Sheed) would be intellectually valuable but written for the intelligent reading public. None of the books, no matter how well-written or profound, should take more than an evening or two to read. The books should be small and light enough to fit in the pocket of a sports coat. Thus, each book should be longer than a journal but shorter than a proper book, roughly 15,000–20,000 words in length. Maritain agreed to write the first volume, *Religion and Culture*, but Burns convinced Dawson to write a massive introduction to it, thus benefitting from the French philosopher's celebrity but attenuating his influence on the series as a whole. True to original intent, however, Dawson recruited French Catholics, German Catholics (soon to be overrun by the Nazis), English Catholics, and even one Russian Orthodox, Nicolas Berdyaev, to write essays for the series. He invited others, among them G.K. Chesterton (who never completed his manuscript). Of the sixteen volumes of *Essays in Order*, Dawson's *Christianity and the New Age* and *The Modern Dilemma*, and Theodor Haecker's *Virgil: Father of the West* (discussed later in this book) were the best written, but all volumes received critical acclaim and sold relatively well to both Catholic and non-Catholic audiences.

Nearly a century later, it would be difficult to exaggerate the importance of *Order*. From a "never-ending party" to a short-lived journal to *A Monument to St Augustine* to a sixteen-volume series, *Order* undoubtedly served as one of the most important intellectual movements in twentieth-century Catholicism. If nothing else, it continued the Republic of Letters that had begun with Heraclitus and the other first philosophers at Miletus and had run continuously — well, mostly continuously — through to Edmund Burke and beyond.

No less a scholar than the grand Dominican priest Aidan Nichols has noted that *Essays in Order* served as the opening Catholic shot in a war to regenerate Western culture. Certainly Burns, Dawson, and Sheed viewed the series as a means by which the Holy Spirit would continue to sanctify the Western intellectual and philosophical tradition.

Just as the French Revolution disrupted the old West in Burke's time, however, so the rise of fascism, national socialism, and communism disrupted the West in the interwar period. Whatever Dawson and Burns had created in the 1920s could not sustain itself in the 1930s, when the world succumbed to totalitarianism, and soon, to a second world war.

In his memoirs, an older and somewhat jaded Harmon Grisewood captured the movement best:

> The world was soon to be set on a course that was proletarian and ruthless; the fire of war was soon to devastate the green shoots that showed above ground in T. S. Eliot's *Criterion*, in Tom Burns' *Essays in Order*, in the Neo-Thomism of Maritain. The bitter frosts that followed the war were to finish the job. Scientific humanism at a crude level trampled the ground which had been leveled and seeded by philosophers of another sort. Politics ate up the autonomy which the arts had won. None of this did I foresee at the time; but I did see that a turning point had been reached, and I knew that for me personally the turn things took was now for the worse. The kind of people who were now to be in the ascendancy would not be the sort of people we liked. We

would be, culturally, in opposition. In the middle ages
we would have been into exile with the King.[2]

Sadly, Grisewood's assessment has proven correct. No Thomis-
tic king awaits in exile. Truly, the opening "progressivism" of the
twentieth century, the devastation of the world wars, and the rise
of governments perpetuated not by ideals but by the blood of the
Gulag, the Killing Fields, and the Holocaust camps had torn apart
a world. The Catholic Church remains a safe yet besieged haven
as we continue recklessly into a world of fundamentalisms, terror,
and ideology. No Aragorn awaits, but possibly a second Christopher Dawson, a Frank Sheed reborn, a new Tom Burns, quietly and
patiently wait for their time. They wait to connect us to the greats,
to the voices of wisdom and of the past, allowing us to preserve
the best of now for those who are yet to come.

---

2   Harman Grisewood, *One Thing at a Time: An Autobiography* (London: Hutchin-
son, 1968), 105.

5

Willa Cather

I am amused that so many of the reviews of this book begin with the statement: "This book is hard to classify." Then why bother?

Willa Cather, 1927[1]

ILLA CATHER'S NOVEL *DEATH COMES FOR the Archbishop* (or "narrative" in the style of legend, as she preferred) is not only the greatest book ever written about American Catholicism, it might also very well be *the* "Great American Novel." Huge claims, I know, but solid possibilities nonetheless.

At the beginning of *Death Comes*, the reader meets the titular character, Father Jean-Marie Latour.

> "Mais, c'est fantastique!" he muttered, closing his eyes to rest them from the intrusive omnipresence of the triangle. When he opened his eyes again, his glance immediately fell upon one juniper which differed in shape from the others. It was not a thick-growing cone, but a naked, twisted trunk, perhaps ten feet high, and at the top it parted into two lateral, flat-lying branches, with a little crest of green in the centre, just above the

---

1 For this chapter, I have relied on the following sources: L. Brent Bohlke, ed., *Willa Cather in Person: Interviews, Speeches, and Letters* (Lincoln: University of Nebraska Press, 1990); the various novels of Cather; Cather, Open Letter to *Commonweal*, November 23, 1927; and Andrew Jewell and Janis Stout, eds., *The Selected Letters of Willa Cather* (New York: Alfred A. Knopf, 2013).

cleavage. Living vegetation could not present more faithfully the form of the Cross. The traveller dismounted,
drew from his pocket a much worn book, and baring
his head, knelt at the foot of the cruciform tree. Under
his buckskin riding-coat he wore a black vest and the
cravat and collar of a churchman. A young priest, at
his devotions; and a priest in a thousand, one knew at
a glance. His bowed head was not that of an ordinary
man, — it was built for the seat of a fine intelligence.
His brow was open, generous, reflective, his features
handsome and somewhat severe. There was a singular
elegance about the hands below the fringed cuffs of the
buckskin jacket. Everything showed him to be a man of
gentle birth — brave, sensitive, courteous. His manners,
even when he was alone in the desert, were distinguished.
He had a kind of courtesy toward himself, toward his
beasts, toward the juniper tree before which he knelt,
and the God whom he was addressing.

It would be hard (not to mention foolish) to miss Cather's appreciation of her subject, a fictional protagonist based on the real-life
figure Archbishop Jean-Baptist Lamy. It would also be hard to claim
that Latour did not represent the best of the Catholic Church in
Cather's mind. Yet in the previous chapter she describes several
of the highest members of the Church, meeting in the Vatican in
the tumultuous year of 1848, with no pretense of delicacy. Her
descriptions of these clergy paint them as nothing short of profoundly despicable. The Vatican officials are soft, effete, disordered,
arrogant, and ignorant. In short, they could not achieve a higher
state of decadence if they tried. The Church, Cather seems to be
arguing in strict Augustinian fashion, survives through small and
generally unrecognized acts of holiness, not through its corrupt
and powerful offices and bureaucracies. Cather focuses on the heart
and soul of the Church, not its physical body per se.

Though *Death Comes* is Cather's best Catholic novel, it is not
her only one. She also wrote *Shadows on the Rock* (1931), the story

of a pre-teen Catholic girl in Quebec in 1697 and 1698. In her best-known and best-regarded novels — such as *O Pioneers* (1913), *My Ántonia* (1918), and, especially, *The Professor's House* (1925) — Cather favorably and accurately depicts the drama, the struggles, and the successes of Catholic immigrants in the New World. Prolific as a fiction writer over roughly two decades, she also penned *Alexander's Bridge* (1912); *The Song of the Lark* (1915); *Youth and the Bright Medusa* (1920); *One of Ours* (1922; for this she won the Pulitzer Prize); *A Lost Lady* (1923); *My Mortal Enemy* (1926); *Obscure Destinies* (1932); and *Lucy Gayheart* (1935).

Despite all of her rather profound and intense Catholic artistry, Cather was not a Roman Catholic, nor was she ever tempted to become one. Understandably, many during her own lifetime presumed that she was a practicing Roman Catholic. How else could she have grasped the essence of the faith — in all of its beauties and in all of its failings — so majestically?

"No, I am not a Catholic, and I do not think I shall become one," she responded to a faithful reader in October, 1931. Yet, she continued, she viewed the Church as much more than a mere tool for her stories. The Church, she believed, was good and wholesome in itself, regardless of what she did or did not write regarding it.

> If the external form and ceremonial of that Church happens to be more beautiful than that of other churches, it certainly corresponds to some beautiful vision within. It is sacred, if for no other reason than that it is the faith that has been most loved by human creatures, and loved over the greatest stretch of centuries.

A year later she wrote another reader, noting: "I am a Protestant, but not a narrow minded one." Could any institution but the Catholic Church "have brought the beliefs of the early church across to us through the anarchy and brutality that followed the fall of the Roman Empire," down to the age of Martin Luther? Several years later, in a somewhat humorous vein, she expressed frustration to her sister that one could not enter a Protestant church late at night for prayer and peace. "The Catholics seem to be the only people who realize that in this world grief goes on all night."

After the release of *Death Comes for the Archbishop* in 1927, the interest among American Roman Catholics about Cather's religious views and about the sources for her story became so intense that she decided to write an open letter to the then young and burgeoning Catholic periodical, *Commonweal*. Simply put, she could not possibly have answered individually all of the letters that flooded her and her publisher's offices after the success of the book. Her open response to *Commonweal* is revealing, both in terms of what Cather had to offer the world of art, and in terms of what art should mean to Catholics and the Catholic Church.

Over fifteen years of traveling to and through the Southwest (even before the availability of accessible transit and roads), Cather began to feel that Catholicism permeated the very landscape itself. Of all the peoples, individuals, cultures, and institutions present in the region, she found herself drawn to the stories of the Catholic Church as the most interesting and the most moving. In some strange way, the Church had captured the spirit of the land. It had baptized the culture of its native and itinerant peoples.

> The old mission churches, even those which were abandoned and in ruins, had a moving reality about them; the hand-carved beams and joists, the utterly unconventional frescoes, the countless fanciful figures of the saints, no two of them alike, seemed a direct expression of some very real and lively human feeling. They were all fresh, individual, first-hand. Almost every one of those many remote little adobe churches in the mountains or in the desert had something lovely that was its own. In lonely, sombre villages in the mountains the church decorations were sombre, the martyrdoms bloodier, the grief of the Virgin more agonized, the figure of Death more terrifying.

The Church in the American Southwest, Cather believed, told its history in images rather than in mere words. A hand-carved pillar might very well reveal far more love of the infinite than a European import. Hand-crafted furniture, for example, as well as the intricate woodwork on the support beams, stood as tangible and sacramental realities in that desert world.

As inroads and "progress" continued in the region, the new priests, Cather feared, were conforming to East Coast standards, unwittingly diminishing and even dismantling the unique culture of the Church in the region. They substituted the cold and manufactured for the humane and particular. In large part, Cather hoped, *Death Comes* would capture and preserve that original spirit, now becoming somewhat ephemeral in her day and age. It might well prove a literary act of preservation, an Augustinian response to loss.

All of Cather's ideas about the mystery of the Southwest remained unfocused until she encountered the statue of the very French and very aristocratic Archbishop Lamy, situated near the cathedral in Santa Fe. How could someone so noble and civilized come to such a rustic and dusty region?

After devouring a number of published letters on Catholic life in the Southwest, Cather decided to write "legend" rather than fiction. Inspired by the European frescoes she had loved in earlier days, she decided to do for prose what frescoes had done for painting. Further, she wanted to echo the traditional hagiographies, which never privileged the deaths of martyrs but rather "dwelt upon ... the trivial incidents of their lives." Rather than research too intensely into the history of the Catholic Church in the Southwest, Cather talked to a priest friend and rehearsed the narrative in her mind innumerable times before, as she put it, joyously writing the book — letting it all flow through her rather than from her. "It was like going back and playing the early composers after a surfeit of modern music." Instead of immersing herself in myriad information — which "often makes one pompous" — Cather imagined the spirit of Catholicism. The result, she admitted, was first, "a vacation from life," and, second, the "paying an old debt of gratitude to the valiant men whose life and work had given me so many hours of pleasant reflection." In addition to her fictional Latour, Cather also created Father Joseph, a bull of a priest, based upon Lamy's closest companion. At the completion of *Death Comes*, Cather believed that the two main subjects of the book had become her intimate companions.

In *Death Comes* as in all of Cather's fiction, a straightforward simplicity of style hides depths beyond depths of thought and spiritual intent. Just as the American Southwest serves as a theater for the great drama of the passion of the Church, so it also represents the evil that lingers after centuries of brutal paganism. In one of the most powerful scenes in the narrative — perhaps one of the finest scenes in American literature — an incoming storm forces Latour and his native guide, Jacinto, into a cave, known to the local Indians as the Stone Lips. As he enters the shelter, giving thanks for protection from the storm, Latour at first imagines the cave's opening as the opening to a Gothic Cathedral, as grace perfecting nature. The smell and feel of the place, however, promptly shock him and reveal something quite different to his soul. Here is evil, palpable, tangible, and fetid. Noticing that the priest is growing physically ill, Jacinto apologizes, noting that his own ancestors have done horrific things here, all in the name of rituals to their gods. A fire of local piñon slightly purifies the air, but Latour continues to sicken.

Jacinto leads Latour deeper into the cave, allowing the priest to listen to some continual noises, to a flowing river of sorts.

> Father Latour lay with his ear to this crack for a long while, despite the cold that arose from it. He told himself he was listening to one of the oldest voices of the earth. What he heard was the sound of a great underground river, flowing through a resounding cavern. The water was far, far below, perhaps as deep as the foot of the mountain, a flood moving in utter blackness under ribs of antediluvian rock. It was not a rushing noise, but the sound of a great flood moving with majesty and power.
> "It is terrible," he said at last, as he rose.
> "Si, Padre." Jacinto began spitting on the clay he had gouged out of the seam, and plastered it up again.

Here, the reader learns as Latour does that Jacinto's ancestors had sacrificed untold numbers of their children to their bloodthirsty gods, dropping the broken bodies into the crack.

To honor the traditions of Jacinto and his people, Latour never speaks to anyone of his experiences in the cave. What has happened has happened, and it is no longer a part of the traditions of these peoples, now baptized as Catholics. Still, the horror of the cave haunts Latour for the remainder of his life. Just as the martyrdom of a saint sanctifies the land upon which their blood spills, so too, the evils committed on a land defile that land, allowing the foul deeds to linger for time immemorial. What Latour experienced in the cave was pure and simple hell.

In his own exploration of American Catholic culture, Thomist philosopher Ralph McInerny brilliantly argued that Cather was so very Catholic in her writing that American Catholics would do well to count her among their number.

Even a single reading of *Death Comes* proves McInerny, once again, correct.

6

Canon B.I. Bell

S ADLY, VERY FEW AMERICANS REMEMBER
Canon Bernard Iddings Bell (1886–1958), despite the excellent work done by Cicero Bruce and Lee Cheek in his name.
In his own day and age, Bell served as one of the leading scholars
of what would eventually be called conservatism. He relentlessly
defended the Western canon and the liberal arts, as well as Dawson's ideas of Christian culture and the thought and reputation of
his fellow iconoclast Albert Jay Nock. Bell wrote some of the most
penetrating and trenchant cultural criticism produced on American
soil. He was also — arguably — the first American to recognize the
existence of postmodernism. Indeed, one of Bell's books is entitled
Postmodernism and Other Essays (1926), and it is listed in one history
of postmodernism as the first work to employ that term. The OED
lists only one earlier mention of the term, in the English theological
periodical *The Hibbert Journal* (1914).

Not bad for a conservative writer almost nobody remembers.

In 2001, in a healthy attempt to resurrect Bell, ISI Books wisely
republished one of his classic works: *Crowd Culture: An Examination
of the American Way of Life*. Originally published by Harper and Row
in 1952, the book brought together four lectures Canon Bell had
delivered on April 22 of that year at Ohio Wesleyan University. The
lectures were entitled "The Picture," "The School," "The Church,"
and "The Rebels." Bell would pass away only six years later, and,
consequently, these lectures serve as an excellent summary of his
own thought as developed during his adult years.

"The chief threat to America comes from within America." With
this line, Bell opens his book. Given the success of the United States
against Japan and Germany in the Second World War, and the Cold

War with the Soviet Union, this is a rather astounding statement. In many ways, it completely obliterates standard histories of post-1945 conservatism, which stress the anti-Communism of the era as the main bridge across all non-leftist thought (whether variations of conservatism or libertarianism). How else, these scholars argue, could such a figure as Joe McCarthy arise? Didn't everyone on the political and cultural right seek out sameness in order to fight the dread communists?

Canon Bell argued that the most serious danger to the American character came not from the terrorist ideologies reigning abroad but from our failure to distinguish personalities and individual persons at home. Americans as a whole had exchanged their individuality for mass conformity in the false belief that such a crowd culture would provide security. They exchanged purpose for purposelessness and critical thinking for tapioca mediocrity. In our desire for security and shiny things, we would gladly become slaves through our industry and politics, selling our very humanity to the most corrupt.

Throughout *Crowd Culture*, Canon Bell reminded his readers that real success and true excellence always come from the individual human person resisting the trends, never from a committee. True patriotism and honor demand individuality, he argued repeatedly. The cry to help the common man had become merely a call for the superficiality of the masses and for rapacious power to be placed in the hands of the few.

This reveals itself rather clearly in the reading trends of the late 1940s and early 1950s:

> In former days a liberally educated minority bought books and read them; the rest, if not enlightened by letters, were not corrupt in respect to them. They did not extol trash, and worse than trash, as reputable literature. Nowadays Demos, having learned to read, reveals an infantile taste by what he reads, the greater part of it rubbish and not a little of it garbage.

Mickey Spillane shocked Bell as no other author of his day possibly could. How could the sensationalism of sex and violence sell so well? In *I, The Jury*, the "exceptionally low creature" is nothing but a "pander," the joy of the "Common Man." Here Bell reads very much like Richard Weaver in his grand rhetorician's attack on the supposed cacophonic banality of jazz. Bell made similar arguments against college and professional sports, seeing each as nothing more than our modern re-working of Roman bread and circuses.

Whether one agrees or disagrees with Bell and Weaver on the specifics, the argument remains important. Have we traded our own individual tastes for those of the PR-men, the Ad-men, the marketers, the sellers of ready-made standardization, the promoters of the new and improved rather than the good and the true? Have the corporations become our new gods? "Happiness, which is what all men desire," Bell wrote, "cannot be purchased; it is an elusive something not for sale."

It must be noted that Bell was not alone in arguing against conformity. Other prominent figures on the American right, such as Russell Kirk, Ray Bradbury, Robert Heinlein, and Robert Nisbet, argued no less persuasively that personality mattered. On the left, such figures as C. Wright Mills had similar fears, influencing even serious country club golfers and moderates like President Eisenhower.

Probably no one more clearly expressed the fear of crowd culture than did the eccentric father of modern conservatism, Russell Kirk. Armed with his typewriter, Kirk wrote from his converted Dutch barn in Michigan and traveled the world equipped with a sword cane, a revolver, and a three-piece tweed suit. Citing Bell as a friend and an authority in his works of the 1950s, Kirk praised the Anglican man of the cloth repeatedly. Much of his very language — such as his embrace of the term "Demos" — originated with Bell. Kirk's fiercest attack on conformity came in his magisterial 1954 book, *A Program for Conservatives*. "This, in essence, is the future which 'capitalists' and 'socialists' and 'communists' all are arranging for us. It may be an efficient program. It is not a human program."

As the world of conservatism continues to sink into sectarian squabbles, media yelling matches, and the playthings of the salesmen, we would do well to remember that the founding fathers of American conservatism despised all such things. They desired not sameness but excellence. In the words of Bell: "the whole cult of comfort is petty, ignoble, unworthy of human nature, absurd." To chase it, he argued, is to chase the unnatural. Rather than elevating us, it will ultimately only degrade. Rather than embracing our humanity, we will sink into subhumanity. We will circle the abyss without even knowing that our footing is insecure.

7

Christopher Dawson

O N OCTOBER 12, 1889, MARY LOUISA AND Henry Philip Dawson gave birth to a son, Henry Christopher. Descended from a long line of Celtic aristocracy, Dawson was born in the Welsh Hay Castle — an immense structure believed in myth to have been built in a single night.

His mother's family possessed great standing in the region, and Dawson remembered "a sort of Anglican theocracy" as "the landowners were largely clergymen and the clergy were either landowners or brothers of landowners, so that there was a complete unification of political, religious, economic and social authority and influence."[1] They also tended to be very high church Anglo-Catholics.

At Hay Castle, Dawson felt

> the immense age of everything, and in the house, the continuity of the present with the remote past, and the feeling was reinforced by the fact that nothing had changed since my mother had been a child in the same house and that all the family relations existed in duplicate, so that alongside of my parents, my nurse, and my uncles and aunts, I saw my mother's parents and her nurse and her uncles and aunts.[2]

His father's side came from York, and most of the men had served in the military. His father was a relatively famous explorer, having

---

1 Christopher Dawson, *Tradition and Inheritance* (privately published by John J. Mulloy, 1970), 11. See also, Birzer, *Sanctifying the World: The Augustinian Life and Mind of Christopher Dawson* (Front Royal, VA: Christendom College Press, 2007).
2 Dawson, *Tradition and Inheritance*, 12.

traveled to South America when it was still treacherous and unde-
veloped, and having served as the lead British officer in the famous
1882–1883 International Circum-Polar Expedition.[3]

From his mother's side, he learned the significance of family,
myth, the saints, and tradition, which all seemed to Dawson to be
bound together as one thing. "From the time that I was thirteen
or fourteen, I had come to know the lives of the Catholic saints
and the writings of the medieval Catholic mystics," wrote Dawson.
"They made so strong an impression on my mind that I felt that
there must be something lacking in any theory of life which left
no room for these higher types of character and experience."[4]

From his father's side, he learned a deeply-held patriotism for
Western civilization, especially as understood through Dante's
Divine Comedy.

As a young boy and a teenager, Dawson received a private education. He devoured every book he could get his hands on. Importantly, he also explored the Welsh countryside whenever possible.
The vast rural landscapes and countryside — especially its churches
and shrines — shaped Dawson as much as did his voluminous
reading. Indeed, Dawson claimed to have learned more "during
my school days from my visits to the Cathedral at Winchester
than I did from the hours of religious instruction in school."[5] The
countryside came alive for him, as the mythic Celtic past seemed
to weave itself through the land, the faith, and the books. "What
David Jones called his 'Celticity,'" Dawson's close friend Harmon
Grisewood remembered, "gave Christopher insights and a poetic
appreciation both of nature and history which is often lacking in
one whose ancestry is wholly English."[6] He credited the Celtic

---

3 E.I. Watkin, Part I of "Christopher Dawson, 1889–1970," *Proceedings of the
British Academy* (1971): 439–40; and Christopher Dawson, Devonshire, to Mr
Sheward Hagerty, London, 30 April 1958, in Box 15, Folder 72, Department of Special
Collections, University of St Thomas, St Paul, Minnesota (hereafter UST/CDC).

4 Dawson, "Why I am a Catholic," *Catholic Times*, 11.

5 Dawson, "Education and the Crisis of Christian Cultures," *Lumen Vitae* 1
(1946): 208.

6 Harmon Grisewood, "Face to Faith: The Ideas of a Catholic Tiger," *London
Guardian* (October 16, 1989).

countryside with his real education. "I got nothing from school, little from Oxford, and less than nothing from the new post-Victorian urban culture," Dawson wrote in the 1920s. "All my 'culture' and my personal happiness came from that much-derided Victorian rural home life."[7]

Dawson, already much taken with Roman Catholicism (having received the theology from the Anglo-Catholics and the poetry from Dante), had a profound religious experience while visiting Rome at Easter, 1909. The visit served "as a revelation ... to a whole new world of religion and culture," his daughter Christina wrote.[8] On that day, while standing at the Ara Coeli, Dawson experienced nothing less than a mystical revelation. There, his daughter wrote, "he first conceived the idea of writing a history of culture" and "had great light on the way it may be carried out," as he confided to his diary. "However unfit I may be," Dawson wrote after his experience in Rome, "I believe it is God's will I should attempt it."[9]

As Dawson put it in his 1926 autobiographical reflections on conversion,

> It opened out a new world of religion and culture. I realised for the first time that Catholic civilisation did not stop with the Middle Ages, and that contemporary with our own national Protestant development there was the wonderful flowering of the Baroque culture.[10]

In the fall of 1913, Dawson intellectually and spiritually assented to Catholicism. He entered the Church formally on Epiphany, 1914, at St Aloysius in Oxford. The "doctrine of Sanctifying Grace" found in the New Testament and the writings of Sts Augustine and Aquinas "removed all my difficulties and uncertainties and carried complete conviction to my mind," Dawson explained

7   Watkin, Part I of "Christopher Dawson, 1889–1970," *Proceedings*, 440.

8   Christina Scott, *A Historian and His World: A Life of Christopher Dawson* [1984] (New Brunswick, NJ: Transaction, 1992), 47.

9   Scott, *A Historian and His World*, 49.

10   Dawson, "Why I am a Catholic," *Catholic Times*, 11.

twelve years later. "It was no longer possible to hesitate, difficult though it was to separate myself from earlier associations and traditional ties."[11]

Equally important, Dawson "realised that the Incarnation, the Sacraments, the external order of the Church and the internal working of Sanctifying Grace were all parts of one organic unity, a living tree, whose roots are in the Divine Nature and whose fruit is the perfection of the saints."[12]

Additionally, Dawson did not consider the saints "a few highly gifted individuals." Instead, he saw them as "the perfect manifestation of the supernatural life which exists in every individual Christian, the first fruits of that new humanity which it is the work of the Church to create."[13]

Preparation to fight modernity

Too sickly to fight in the Great War, Christopher Dawson volunteered for civilian duty and spent roughly fourteen years reading and drawing up ideas in preparation for a career in writing. As mentioned above, he had received a profound mystical vision while visiting Rome at Easter 1909. In that vision, the nineteen-year-old Anglo-Welshman believed God had commanded him to record the entire history of the world, revealing to him all times and all peoples at once. Determined to live up to God's call, he began to build upon his already solid liberal education.

During these years, he kept extensive notes and journals. These notes contain influential writings from the significant historians, anthropologists, and thinkers of his day. He generally took notes in the same language as the original texts, delving deeply into Plato's *Laws* as well as the various writings of Aristotle, Xenophon, and Heraclitus. From these journals (which now reside at the University of St Thomas in St Paul), the reader can vividly observe how readily

11   Ibid.
12   Ibid.
13   Ibid.

Dawson moved through a variety of languages including English, French, Greek, and Latin.[14]

In the same notebook (presumably after reading the above authors), Dawson concluded tellingly: "All the events of the last years have convinced me what a fragile thing civilization is and how near we are to losing the whole inheritance which our age might have acquired [sic] enjoyed."

In addition to his voluminous academic and scholarly reading, he also devoured the works of Jane Austen, Henry David Thoreau, P.J. Wodehouse, Hilaire Belloc, G.K. Chesterton, H.G. Wells, R.H. Benson, and Arthur Conan Doyle, as well as a wide selection of science fiction, historical fiction, American westerns, and English detective stories.[15] G.K. Chesterton particularly influenced Dawson, who regarded him as "one of the greatest champions of Christian culture in our time."[16] The work of Chesterton's that most influenced Dawson was his epic poem, *The Ballad of the White Horse*. This poem, perhaps the most significant call to arms for twentieth-century Christian humanists, equally inspired C.S. Lewis, J R R. Tolkien, and Russell Kirk.

Dawson also read a number of daily newspapers and listened to a variety of radio stations — both English and foreign-language — in order to stay informed about the rapidly changing world situation.[17]

After nearly a decade and a half of reading and thinking, Dawson finally published his first book, *The Age of the Gods*, in 1928. In it, he conducted an in-depth study of primitive cultures, employing complex analyses with the aid of archeology, history, sociology, and anthropology. Twenty more books followed, including *Progress and Religion, Christianity and the New Age, Medieval Essays, The Making of Europe*, and *Dynamics of World History*.

14   Dawson, "Notebook 18" dated 1922-25, in Box 9, Folder 18, UST/CDC.

15   Dawson, "Frank Sheed Talks with Christopher Dawson," *The Sign* (December 1958): 34; and Christina Scott, "The Meaning of the Millennium: The Ideas of Christopher Dawson," *Logos* 2 (1999): 79.

16   Dawson to Mulloy, July 1, 1954, in Box 1, Folder 16, Notre Dame, Christopher Dawson Papers (hereafter, ND/CDAW) (University of Notre Dame, Notre Dame, IN).

17   Scott, "The Meaning of the Millennium: The Ideas of Christopher Dawson," 79.

Though a serious scholar, Dawson targeted a well-read, intelligent, yet general audience rather than an academic one. In a conversation with his close friend, the poet David Jones, Dawson explained: "I don't care what that wretched dean said about me — it's the kind of people who read the *Daily Mirror* I would like to be read by."[18] He rarely sought academic appointments, wishing to avoid the pressure of academic publishing. Instead, he believed that his writing should be directed toward the well-educated, intellectually curious, yet non-academic public. "It is to this middle public that I have always directed my own work," Dawson admitted. "In fact I deliberately renounced any attempt to pursue [university] research in order to cultivate this field which seems to me to be the area in which vital decisions will be reached."[19] With the exception of a few briefly held academic positions at smaller colleges in England, and a four-year stint at Harvard in America (1958–1962), Dawson lived most of his adult life as a private, freelance historian and scholar.

In this vein, Dawson sought to publish his work wherever possible, rarely seeking a profit from his writing. "An agent inevitably thinks in terms of dollars, whereas what I am concerned about is teaching the right audience," Dawson explained, "and often this means publishing in small reviews that do not pay well."[20]

In the end, Dawson wrote over twenty books, most of which are coming back into print. All of this work he directed toward one end: the fulfillment of what God had commanded him in 1909. Like his patron saint Augustine, who looked across the Mediterranean and watched the Goths sack Rome, Dawson looked across the English Channel and watched the new barbarians — the National Socialists, the Fascists, and the Communists — invade what was left of Christendom. Confronted with the ideologies of modernity, Dawson argued forcefully, each true person must act as both prophet and saint: "The only remedy is to be found in that spiritual force by which the humility of God conquers the pride of the evil one," he

---

18   Dawson quoted in Scott, *A Historian and His World*, 128.
19   Dawson, Devon, to Mulloy, 17 May 1954, in Box 1, Folder 4, ND/CDAW; and Dawson, "Memorandum," dated June 1955, in Box 1, Folder 15, ND/CDAW.
20   Dawson, Boars Hill, to Mulloy, October 3, 1953, in Box 1, Folder 4, ND/CDAW.

wrote. The majority of men will fight against the prophet or saint, and "he must be prepared to stand alone like Ezekiel" and Jeremiah. The world may very well shun or abuse the saint and prophet. Therefore, "he must take as his example St Augustine besieged by the Vandals at Hippo, or St Gregory preaching at Rome with the Lombards at the gates." Taking his argument from the Beatitudes, Dawson reminded his audience that Christ's words remain timeless. "For the true helpers of the world are the poor in spirit, the men who bear the sign of the cross on their foreheads, who refused to be overcome by the triumph of injustice and put their sole trust in the salvation of God."[21]

Dawson's most ardent views may be summarized in several points.

1. *We must promote art, not propaganda.* One of the great concerns of the Christian humanists in general (and Dawson in particular) was the politicization of culture during the 1930s and the remainder of the century. This seemed especially true in art and in journals. To gain an understanding of propaganda, one has only to leaf through the scholarly writings and the short stories (especially "Leaf by Niggle") of J.R.R. Tolkien. Art is deep, meaningful, and often of universal application; propaganda is simplistic, "in your face," and ultimately offensive to our very humanity.

In August 1946, Dawson wrote, "One has to face the fact that there had been a kind of slump in ideas during the past 10 years." Instead of thinking creatively, intelligent men had turned to realism, science, and politics to explain everything. "There is not only a positive lack of new ideas but also a subjective loss of interest in ideas as such."[22] A few weeks later, Dawson wrote on the same topic, lamenting the rise of politics in all areas of thought. "There is a terrible dearth of writers and of ideas at present, and even in France, things are not too good, judging from the little I have seen." He continued: "Politics seem to be swamping everything and the non-political writer becomes increasingly uprooted and helpless." Nothing in the world can improve if writers focus only on the

21   Dawson, *Religion and the Rise of Western Culture* [1948] (New York: Image Books, 1991), 124.

22   Dawson, Oxford, to Bernard Wall, London, 26 August 1946, in Box 15, Folder 174, UST/CDC.

sterile subject of politics, Dawson argued. The world "won't improve without new blood and new ideas and I don't see at present where these are to be found."[23]

2. *We must avoid all pure materialisms.* The rise of capitalism attempts to make man "a subordinate part of the great mechanical system that his scientific genius has created."[24] Everywhere — in science, culture, and politics — the machine ruled, and humans had become merely cogs within it. To make matters worse, the materialistic states (capitalism and communism) created "the new bureaucratic state, that 'coldest of monsters.'"[25] Finally, while the "Communists may have deified mechanism in theory," Dawson wrote, "it is the Americans who have realised it in practice."[26]

3. *Propaganda and materialism have always and inevitably led to boredom.* "The ordinary man will never stand for nihilism: it is against all his healthier instincts," Dawson wrote in 1955.[27] To find a substitute for nihilism, man turns to utopianism, drugs, and cults, "leaving the enemy in possession of the field."[28] The only effective counter to modernity (and postmodernity) is the grace of imagination.

Dawson and the Liberal Arts

Christopher Dawson worried deeply about the ideological, political, and cultural crises of the Western world during the entirety of his adult life. The root of the problem, Dawson had come to believe between the two World Wars, was the fundamental decline in the significance, love, and cultivation of ideas and in respect for the faculty of imagination.

For nearly a century, Dawson feared, despite all its technological and scientific "progress," the Western world had simplified its

23   CD, Oxford, to Bernard Wall, London, 9 September 1946, in Box 15, Folder 174, in UST/CDC.

24   Dawson, *Christianity and the New Age* (New York: Sheed and Ward, 1931), 161.

25   Ibid., 162.

26   Ibid., 167.

27   Dawson, Devon, to Father Leo Ward, Notre Dame, Ind., 20 February 1955, CD/ND; and Dawson, "The Victorian Background," *Tablet* (September 23, 1950): 246.

28   Dawson, *Christianity and the New Age*, 158.

understanding of the immense complexity of man. As discussed previously, the great intellects of the nineteenth century — men such as Karl Marx, Charles Darwin, and Sigmund Freud — had narrowed the understanding of what motivates a man, limiting those complex motives either to economics, biological adaptation, or misunderstood sexual longings at a young age. While any one of these motives may be valid, it is far more likely that *each* is valid, along with millions of other complicated and complicating factors. Man, Dawson knew, could not be understood in simplistic, materialist terms. By his very nature as a bearer of the infinite *imago Dei*, finite man carried a genuine and irreplaceable uniqueness within him — no matter how hidden such gifts might be to the person himself.

By the 1930s, ideological regimes — democratic as well as fascist and socialist — were centralizing, collectivizing, and mechanizing. One had only to cast a glance at the ideological armies, unfurling flags of red (communist), blue (liberal/capitalist), pink (socialist), black (conservative), and brown (national socialists) to see how ridiculous things had become. As if any person or idea worth anything could be symbolized by a color! The narrowing of ideas that began in the nineteenth century had become a narrowing of reality by the twentieth. Propaganda had replaced art, the pamphlet had replaced literature, and the greats of Western civilization were dismissed as elitist and irrelevant to a modern world. How wrong this all was, Christopher Dawson clearly knew. Such propaganda demeaned the human person, appealing to the lowest parts of him — his emotions, his passions, and his instincts. Dawson lamented: "The economic process, which led to the exploitation of the world by man and the vast increase of his material resources, ends in the subjection of man to the rule of the machine and the mechanisation of human life."

To follow the course of the ideologues, Dawson averred, would only end in the "mechanical monster" and in the regulation and de-personalization of every aspect of life. Such mechanization would homogenize human persons and individual cultures into one cosmopolitan, bland mess. Already, modernity had brought about horrible mechanization. Even something as seemingly innocuous as the automobile, meant only to make life more convenient, had done nothing but

> bring mutilation and death to large numbers of harmless people. We see [mechanization] on a large scale in the way that the modern industrial system, which exists to serve human needs, nevertheless reduces the countryside to smoking desolation and involves whole populations in periodic troughs of depression and scarcity. But we see it in its most extreme and devilish form in modern warfare which has a nightmare quality about it and is hardly reconcilable with a human origin or purpose.

Mass society will lead to the destruction of true individuality, and society will "dissolve into a human herd without personality."

The result of such conformity, Dawson argued, would be "the Kingdom of Anti-Christ." After all, the new ideological states are "inevitably contaminated with all sorts of impure elements and open to the influence of evil and demonic forces." The situation was as bleak as could be imagined:

> For the first time in the world's history the Kingdom of the Anti-Christ has acquired political form and social substance, and stands over against the Kingdom of God as a counter-church with its own creed and its own moral ideals, ruled by a centralized hierarchy and inspired by an intense will for world conquest.

In these fears and beliefs, Dawson was not alone. A number of humanist and Christian humanist thinkers — Irving Babbitt, Paul Elmer More, T.S. Eliot, C.S. Lewis, Jacques Maritain, and Romano Guardini, to name a few — had made similar arguments.

The decline, as noted above, had begun at the start of the 1930s and had only worsened by the mid-1940s. Mars had hastened the growth of Leviathan. "We are still living much under the shadow of war and the uncertainty of the future of Europe is unfavourable to creative work," Dawson wrote in a private letter on September 9, 1946. Ideological limitations and propaganda were quickly pervading thought, art, and music in the various Christian churches, both Catholic and Protestant. "The modern theologians in ceasing to be poets have also ceased to be philosophers" (Dawson, private letter, July 28, 1946).

Between 1946 and 1962, in a series of books and articles, Dawson argued that, while the reconstruction of Christendom would prove exceedingly difficult (should it even be possible), it must begin with a proper understanding of the liberal arts and the Western tradition. The two were intimately related, one to another. "Virgil and Cicero, Ovid and Seneca, Horace and Quintilian were not merely school books, they became the seeds of a new growth of classical humanism in Western soil," Dawson wrote in 1956. "Again and again — in the eighth century as well as in the twelfth and fifteenth centuries — the higher culture of Western Europe was fertilized by renewed contacts with the literary sources of classical culture."

The liberal arts must also embrace and engage the faculty of imagination at a fundamental level. Only the imagination would preserve the understanding of the world and of the human person from a narrowing decay. Indeed, the imagination should not only allow a person to place himself within the created order and to realize his relations with God and other men (a play on the classical definition of justice, to "give each man his due"); it should also reveal to the human person just how extraordinarily complicated the world is. Consequently, the liberal arts simultaneously humble and elevate the human person, connecting him to both time and eternity.

During the sixteen years prior to the series of strokes that forced him into retirement, Christopher Dawson offered a number of suggestions as to how the liberal arts might be revived. The English Roman Catholic developed a four-year curriculum for Catholic colleges, began to edit a series of works on the lives of the saints (the real movers of history, from Dawson's perspective), and undertook the formation of a new religious order dedicated to the Christian intellect. Unfortunately, poor health, poor administrative skills, and poor fundraising abilities hindered Dawson in all of these endeavors.

Still, Dawson never ceases to remind us of the necessity of the liberal arts, for citizens of the West and of Christendom. His words are a challenge to each one of us:

> Western man has not been faithful to his Christian tradition. He has abandoned it not once, but again and again. For since Christianity depends on a living faith and not merely on social tradition, Christendom must be renewed every fresh generation, and every generation is faced by the responsibility of making decisions, each of which may be an act of Christian faith or an act of apostasy.

The Gray Eminence of Dawson

To put it bluntly, Christopher Dawson was one of the greatest historians of the twentieth century. He was certainly one of its greatest men of letters and perhaps one of the most respected Catholic scholars in the English-speaking world. I would even go so far as to claim that Dawson was *the* historian of the past 100 years. While most Americans — Catholic or otherwise — no longer remember him, they often do remember with affection those he profoundly (one might say indelibly) influenced. The list includes well-known personalities such as T. S. Eliot, Thomas Merton, J. R. R. Tolkien, and C. S. Lewis.

In the twentieth-century world of humane learning and scholarship, Dawson was a sort of John Coltrane. Just as few non-musicians listen to Coltrane but every serious musician does, so it was with Dawson in the intellectual realm. Yet, like Coltrane, Dawson did enjoy long periods of widespread popularity and support in his own lifetime. "For Dawson is more like a movement than a man," his publisher and friend, Frank Sheed, wrote of him in 1938. "His influence with the non-Catholic world is of a kind that no modern Catholic has yet had, both for the great number of fields in which it is felt and for the intellectual quality of those who feel it."[29] There

---

29   F. J. Sheed, "Christopher Dawson," *The Sign* (June 1938): 661.

was much evidence that Sheed could cite. By the early 1930s (while Dawson was still in his early 40s), American Catholic colleges began teaching courses on his thought, tying him to the larger Catholic literary movement of the day.[30] In 1933, the American Catholic journal *Commonweal* stated that "the writings of Christopher Dawson demand the thoughtful attention of all educated men."[31] Six years later, the Jesuit journal *The Month* claimed that to "commend Mr Dawson's work is unnecessary; nothing that he writes could be unimportant."[32] In 1949, Waldemar Gurian, a refugee from the Nazis and a professor at the University of Notre Dame, wrote that Dawson's "very ability to make brilliant understatements and to display without pride, as something self-evident, his extraordinary broad knowledge makes his synthesis particularly impressive."[33] In 1950, the English Dominican journal *Blackfriars* claimed "that Mr Dawson is an educator; perhaps the greatest that Heaven has sent us English Catholics since Newman."[34]

Maisie Ward, the famous biographer and co-founder of the Sheed and Ward publishing house, admitted to Dawson in 1961: "You were, as I said on Sunday, truly the spear-head of our publishing venture."[35] Ward put it in larger context in her autobiography, *Unfinished Business*: "Looking back at the beginnings of such intellectual life as I have had, I feel indebted to three men of genius: Browning, Newman, and Chesterton," she wrote. "But in my middle age, while we owed much as publishers to many men and women, foreign and English, the most powerful influence on the thinking of both myself and my husband was certainly Christopher Dawson."[36] Even among the clergy, none held the reputation that Dawson held by the 1950s.

---

30   Arnold Sparr, *To Promote, Defend, and Redeem: The Catholic Literary Revival and the Cultural Transformation of American Catholicism, 1920–1960* (New York: Greenwood Press, 1990), 24, 103.

31   T. Lawrason Riggs, "A Voice of Power," *Commonweal* (August 4, 1933): 330.

32   Thomas Corbishly, "Our Present Discontents," *The Month* 173 (1939): 440.

33   Waldemar Gurian, "Dawson's Leitmotif," *Commonweal* (June 3, 1949).

34   Kenelm Foster, O.P., "Mr Dawson and Christendom," *Blackfriars* 31 (1950): 423.

35   Maisie Ward, New York, to Dawson, Harvard, 1961, in the Christopher H. Dawson Collection, Box 11, Folder 25, "Frank Sheed 1960," in UST/CDC.

36   Maisie Ward, *Unfinished Business* (New York: Sheed and Ward, 1964), 117.

Again, as Ward noted rather bluntly in a letter to Dawson, "There is no question in my mind that no priest exists at the moment whose name carries anything like the weight in or outside the church that yours does."[37] This is an impressive claim, especially when one recalls the intellect and influence of a Martin D'Arcy, a John Courtney Murray, or a Fulton J. Sheen.

Neo-Thomist historian and philosopher Etienne Gilson also acknowledged his profound admiration for Dawson in a 1950 letter to Frank Sheed. Gilson especially appreciated Dawson's *Making of Europe* (1932) and *Religion and the Rise of Western Culture* (1950).[38] The latter "provided me with what I had needed during forty years without being able to find it anywhere: an intelligent and reliable background for a history of mediaeval philosophy," Gilson admitted. "Had I been fortunate in having such a book before writing my [*Spirit of the Middle Ages*], my own work would have been other and better than it is."[39] High praise, indeed.

American author and Trappist monk Thomas Merton claimed to have discovered his purpose in life while reading Dawson's 1952 book, *Understanding Europe*. "Whether or not [Dawson] came too late, who can say?" Merton worried.

> In any case I have a clear obligation to participate, as long as I can, and to the extent of my abilities, in every effort to help a spiritual and cultural renewal of our time. This is the task that has been given me, and hitherto I have not been clear about it, in all its aspects and dimensions.[40]

37   Maisie Sheed, London, to Dawson, October 1953, Box 11, Folder 18, "Frank Sheed 1953" in UST/CDC.

38   Sheed to Dawson, 1936, in Box 11 (Sheed and Ward Papers), Folder 2, "Frank Sheed, 1936," in UST/CDC.

39   Etienne Gilson to Frank Sheed, 22 August 1950, in Box 11, Folder 16 "Frank Sheed 1950," in UST/CDC.

40   Thomas Merton, journal entry for August 22, 1961, *Turning Toward the World: The Pivotal Year*, ed. by Victor A. Kramer (San Francisco: HarperSanFrancisco, 1995), 155. See also Thomas Merton, *Conjectures of a Guilty Bystander* (New York: Image Books, 1966), 55, 194–95; and Patrick Hart and Jonathan Montaldo, eds., *The Intimate Merton: His Life from His Journals* (San Francisco: HarperSanFrancisco, 1999), 190.

As T.S. Eliot's best biographer, Russell Kirk, wrote, "Of social thinkers in his own time, none influenced Eliot more than Dawson."[41] For three decades, Eliot was quite taken with Dawson's views, and it would be difficult (if not impossible) to find a scholar who influenced Eliot more. In the early 1930s, Eliot told an American audience that Dawson was the foremost thinker of his generation in England.[42] He explicitly acknowledged his debt to Dawson in the introductions to his two most politically- and culturally-oriented books, *The Idea of a Christian Society* and *Notes Towards the Definition of Culture*.[43] One may also discern Dawson's influence in two of Eliot's most important writings about the moral imagination, *Murder in the Cathedral* and *The Four Quartets*.[44] Eliot continued to acknowledge his debt to Dawson after World War II. In a speech to the London Conservative Union in 1955, Eliot told his fellow conservatives that they should understand conservatism as Dawson does — that is, as ante-political and anti-ideological. Only then, Eliot argued, could English conservatives truly and effectively shape society.[45]

One cannot imagine C.S. Lewis's *The Abolition of Man* without the existence of Dawson's 1929 book, *Progress and Religion*. The same holds true of J.R.R. Tolkien's best academic essay, "On Fairie-Stories," delivered at the University of St Andrews in 1939. While the essay in its thought is purely Tolkienian, the English philologist and fantasist relies very openly on the scholarship of Dawson. All three knew each other well, and Tolkien and Dawson even attended the same parish in Oxford.

There are so many lessons here. First, we should never take the influence of Christopher Dawson for granted. Second, this story

---

41 Russell Kirk, *Eliot and His Age: T.S. Eliot's Moral Imagination in the Twentieth Century* (Peru, IL: Sherwood Sugden, 1988), 300. On Dawson's influence on Eliot, see also Bernard Wall, "Giant Individualists and Orthodoxy," *Twentieth Century* (January 1954): 59.

42 Christina Scott, *A Historian and His World*, 210.

43 The two have been republished together as T.S. Eliot, *Christianity and Culture* (San Diego: Harvest, 1967).

44 Kirk, *Eliot and His Age*, 231–32, 299–300; and Joseph Schwartz, "The Theology of History in T.S. Eliot's *Four Quartets*," *Logos* 2 (Winter 1999): 34.

45 T.S. Eliot, "The Literature of Politics," *Time and Tide* (23 April 1955): 524.

should give us hope. We must, of course, do our best in whatever we do. What others do with it is beyond our will, but we put it out there nonetheless, and we hope. Dawson's story — at least this aspect of it — reminds us that we can play a vital role in the times, even if our own individual egos have not been soothed.

8

Nicolas Berdyaev's Unorthodoxy

S WITH SO MANY FIGURES DISCUSSED IN
this book, Nicolas Berdyaev (1874–1948) has been sadly
neglected since his death. Not surprisingly, he was connected to many Christian humanists of his day. He knew the Mar-
itains well, and while C.S. Lewis mostly dismissed Berdyaev's work
as a sideline show, Christopher Dawson considered his thought
central to the restoration of the 20th-century West.

The trump card here, though, comes from a fellow Russian. A
figure no less important or heroic than Alexander Solzhenitsyn
discussed Berdyaev briefly in volumes II and III of *The Gulag*. He
was, Solzhenitsyn wrote, offering perhaps the highest praise possible — "a man." In volume II, Solzhenitsyn described Berdyaev as
the ultimate person to reject Soviet terror:

> So what is the answer? How can you stand your ground
> when you are weak and sensitive to pain, when people
> you love are still alive, when you are unprepared? What
> do you need to make you stronger than the interroga-
> tor and the whole trap? From the moment you go to
> prison you must put your cozy past firmly behind you.
> At the very threshold, you must say to yourself: "My
> life is over, a little early to be sure, but there's nothing
> to be done about it. I shall never return to freedom. I
> am condemned to die — now or a little later. But later
> on, in truth, it will be even harder, and so the sooner
> the better. I no longer have any property whatsoever.

For me those I love have died, and for them I have died.
From today on, my body is useless and alien to me.
Only my spirit and my conscience remain precious
and important to me." Confronted by such a prisoner,
the interrogation will tremble. Only the man who has
renounced everything can win that victory. But how
can one turn one's body to stone? Well, they managed
to turn some individuals from the Berdyayev [sic] circle
into puppets for a trial, but they didn't succeed with
Berdyayev. They wanted to drag him into an open trial;
they arrested him twice; and (in 1922) he was subjected
to a night interrogation by Dzerzhinsky himself. Kame-
nev was there too (which means that he, too, was not
averse to using the Cheka in ideological conflict). But
Berdyayev did not humiliate himself. He did not beg
or plead. He set forth firmly those religious and moral
principles which had led him to refuse to accept the
political authority established in Russia. And not only
did they come to the conclusion that he would be useless for a trial, but they liberated him. A human being
has a point of view!

In volume 3 of *The Gulag*, Solzhenitsyn wrote simply: Berdyaev
was a "philosopher, essayist, brilliant defender of human freedom
against ideology." Exiled from Russia in 1922 after surviving three
Soviet trials against him, Berdyaev settled in Paris and lived there
until his death in 1948.

While in Paris, Berdyaev became an integral part of the Jacques
and Raïssa Maritain circle. Indeed, as Berdyaev remembers it in
his fine autobiography, *Dream and Reality*, he and Jacques served as
equal poles in the creation and perpetuation of the group. Though
Maritain's extreme Thomism struck Berdyaev as a form of Catholic
ideology, he respected the French philosopher immensely. He did
joke, however, that Maritain's fear and rejection of Protestantism
and Protestants comprised a strange element in the convert and
implied a certain irrationality.

When he and Tom Burns first formed the Order group in Chelsea, London, seeking to unify all humanists of British and European backgrounds, Christopher Dawson sought out Maritain and Berdyaev immediately. Both men contributed to one of the best book series of the last century, the sixteen-volume *Essays in Order*. As it turned out, *Essays in Order* served as the single attempt of the twentieth century to bring all Christian humanists together into a unified Republic of Letters.

When *Essays in Order* folded, Dawson continued the same project with a second friend, Bernard Wall, this time publishing a journal (*Colosseum*). Once again, Dawson and Wall sought and received both contributions and acclaim from Berdyaev and Maritain.

One of Berdyaev's most interesting books — and presumably the reason Dawson respected him so highly — was his *The End of Our Time*, written between 1919 and 1923 (and published for the first time in English in 1933 by Sheed and Ward). Though clearly a Russian and an adherent of Eastern Orthodoxy, Berdyaev anticipated the major arguments of the English-Welsh Roman Catholic Dawson. In particular, Berdyaev stressed the primacy of cultural and theological issues over politics and economics, believing the former to be truer forms of reality. Almost the entire Western world, Berdyaev argued, had embraced some form of materialism after the collapse of Christendom. This embracing of materialism moved the world rapidly toward unreality. "We must begin to make our Christianity effectively real," Berdyaev wrote, "by a return to the life of the spirit." Economic matters, he continued, "must be subordinated to that which is spiritual, [and] politics must be again confined within their proper limits."

As did Dawson, Lewis, and others, Berdyaev feared that the new states of the twentieth century — regardless of whether they were democratic or vicious — would become totalitarian. This was a new threat to the world. St Paul did not anticipate these emerging states of the twentieth century when he wrote Romans 13. Rather, these states resembled what St John envisioned but could never explain beyond a dream-like mysticism. These new states would render all to Caesar, establishing themselves as religious bodies and entities.

The result: a "New Leviathan. And all the ends and real values of life are swallowed up in this malignant and terrifying collectivism, all spiritual culture is wiped out. Such a monster has not got a human soul, for it has got no soul... at all."

Only when society has realigned itself "towards divine objects" — individual by individual and community by community, through free will and persuasion — can humanity save itself. I emphasize "through free will and persuasion" because Berdyaev rejected all forms of statist coercion (whether that coercion should arise through outright socialism or through some form of state-capitalism or capitalistic cronyism). Berdyaev wrote of humanity's restoration in terms reminiscent of Dawson and other post-French Revolution quasi-mystics:

> The substance of life can only be religious. It is an entering into the life of God, that is, into true Being. The will of the people, the proletarian will, is a sinful will; it therefore pertains to not-being and can bring about only a kingdom of not-being.

One reads hints of Burke, Novalis, Maistre, and Tocqueville in Berdyaev's criticisms of the new ideological states, the so-called left and right. One also observes elements of Berdyaev's mysticism in his claim that the Russian people, by freely choosing "comradeship in Anti-Christ," have now (as of 1917) provided incontrovertible proof of evil in the world and have demonstrated to the world what the loss of Christendom really means.

A century earlier, Tocqueville had professed that Americans had a choice between a democracy of excellence and a democracy of mediocrity. Berdyaev believed that the same choice lay before the twentieth-century West. Tocqueville had feared the Americans would choose poorly; Berdyaev feared that the West would do the same.

At the conclusion of *The End of Our Time*, Berdyaev once again stressed the unreality of politics. He saw politics as a hindrance and distraction from that which really matters — from the order of the human soul toward the highest things and especially its order toward God and eternity. As Berdyaev put it, politics attempts to remove us from "the interior life."

For the Christian to assume victory over the next century would be sheer folly. Throughout the West, under every type of regime (free and unfree), Berdyaev feared ruin. Far from calling us to establish a century of progress, God was calling Christians back into "the catacombs, and from there to conquer the world anew." As Christians (of whatever stripe), "we are entering an epoch of ill-omened revelations and we must fearlessly face up to realities. And there is found the meaning of our unhappy joyless age."

Reading Nicolas Berdyaev is not uplifting, but it is truly (in the best sense of this distorted word) enlightening. Certainly, looking back 90 years after Berdyaev wrote these words, one would be hard pressed to miss not only the mystic but also, perhaps even more importantly, the prophet.

9

Theodor Haecker,
Man of the West

*I*F THEODOR HAECKER (1879–1945) IS REMEM-
bered today, he is remembered for two things: his translations
of Cardinal Newman's works into German and subsequent
conversion to Roman Catholicism, and his unwavering dissent in
Nazi Germany as recorded in his beautifully tragic confessional,
Journal in the Night, published five years after his 1945 death in
Munich. He should also be remembered, however, for writing *Virgil:
Father of the West*, one of the finest books of the twentieth century.
Given the nature of Sheed and Ward's *Essays in Order* and its attempt
to unify a generation of Roman Catholic intellectuals through the
entirety of the Western tradition, a translation of Haecker's book
found an appropriate place as volume 14 in the first series.

Though the book sold only marginally well when it first appeared,
it was profoundly influential and remains so to this day. In what
many consider his best or second-best work, *The Roots of American
Order* (1974), Russell Kirk spends a considerable time exploring,
teasing out, and promoting the virtues of the Roman Republican (at
least as the last generation of republicans understood them). Kirk
stressed the great trilogy of Roman virtues: fate, piety, and labor.
The footnotes reveal that Kirk drew upon T. S. Eliot's seminal 1953
article, "Virgil and the Christian World." This article was published
in the venerable *Sewanee Review* and then reprinted in the poet's
1957 volume of essays, *On Poetry and Poets*. Eliot himself had first
given the essay as a talk for the BBC in 1951. Even a cursory glance
at Eliot's talk/essay reveals that he borrowed extensively from *Virgil: Father of the West*. Aside from this tidbit of intellectual history,

Haecker's book is well worth reading for its own sake, regardless of whom it has influenced.

As he admitted at the beginning of his book on the Roman poet, Haecker intended not only to analyze the life of a great Roman, but that of a great man. He intended to show that Virgil was a true human being, one who understood the dignity of all human persons as well as their follies. In other words, in true humanist fashion, Haecker hoped to consider not only Virgil, but the very essence of all men. One can understand the essence of man only if he recognizes that all of life fits into a divine "*ordo* as the spiritual nature of the universe" (x). In the current world, intellectual, political, and theological thought has radically separated the universal from the particular, with Western civilization approaching a new Tower of Babel. The totalitarians care only about the universal, while the individualists care only about the particular. Yet, even the individualist had gone out of fashion by the 1930s, its liberalism as dead as John Stuart Mill. Even at its height, Haecker claimed, was not liberalism merely a lesser devil challenging *the* devil?

The job of the patriot of Western civilization, and especially of the Roman Catholic, is to remind the human person of his universal qualities as well as to leverage his particular gifts, abilities, and excellences. The balance, even in the best of times, is a precarious one. "No human type," he argued, "is outside the universally human. There is no human note or sound or merest whisper or simple cry but may be brought within the unity of a single primordial symphony" (7). Man, therefore, can do nothing other than stand in a relationship to all other men — past, present, and future — as well as in relationship to all things in creation, from the highest to the lowest.

Attempting to walk a fine line between what he knows must be true objectively and what he knows to be true immediately and particularly, man must (somewhat paradoxically) gravitate toward the eternal nature of existence in order to become fully human. Therefore, the person who adamantly denies the objective, as well as the man who fully embraces his particular beliefs as objective truths (which is immediately a failure, as it would imply that man equaled God), merely reveals the worst incompetence of the human person (13).

At this point (in the book as well as in my review of it), one might reasonably ask: Fine and good, but what does this have to do with Virgil? Though a pagan, Haecker argued, Virgil was the ultimate pagan—the equivalent in the pagan world to John the Baptist in the Christian one. Haecker's argument here not only reveals his brilliance as a thinker but his excellence as a writer. "A few short years before the Advent Virgil lived, that the foreseen measure of ancient paganism might be fulfilled; and he so fulfilled it that not so much as one drop overflowed. In the last hour before the fullness of time he fulfilled the measure of what was good in the ancient paganism, as others had fulfilled the measure of its evil" (13–14). Far more than the abstract Plato, Virgil thought and lived as the best of the pagans. While Plato's Greece had its accomplishments, Haecker believed, it is remembered mostly for its chaos. Virgil's Rome will always be remembered for its order.

For the pagan, "the loftiest ideal and reality of the ancient world was the hero," but for the Christian living "after the Incarnation, the loftiest ideal and reality is the saint, the ultimate motivation of whose being is the glory of God." If Virgil best understood the grace of will, St John the Beloved best understood the will of grace.

Significantly, Virgil came into the world in 70 BC, thus witnessing the collapse of the republic and the rise of the empire. In each of his three greatest works, *The Georgics, The Eclogues,* and *The Aeneid,* Virgil offered an idealized, nostalgic paean to the republican past. The monument that sits atop Virgil's grave best explains him, Haecker wrote. "I sang of shepherds, farmers, and statesmen."

True imagination and creativity, argued the greatest of Roman poets, comes not from the heart of man but from his receptive soul, from the image implanted in him by the divine. "The great creative man is first and foremost boundlessly receptive; his purity consists not in receiving nothing, but in receiving all that there is to receive. Only thus will he be able to procreate" (23). Thus the creative man must, in duty bound, offer gratitude to the divine rather than accept praise for his own accomplishments.

Haecker's greatest argument hits the reader forcibly. The highest honor in the ancient world was not to be a Caesar but to be a poet. "To be a great classical poet requires no small measure of good fortune — more even than to be a Caesar" (27). After all, there were many, many Caesars, but only one Virgil. And what was it that Virgil, high Roman pagan and poet that he was, proclaimed? "Love conquers all, and all things yield to love" (*Eclogue* 10).

Would anyone dispute that this is the greatest truth ever revealed to humanity? I certainly would not.

10

The Inklings and J.R.R. Tolkien

THE WHITE CITY, IN ITS PRIDE AND PRESUMP-
tion, lay under siege.

Having gathered "his most cunning smiths and sorcer-
ers," Melko, the twisted one, had directed the creation of organic
machines, through "iron and flame," to attack. Led by Gothmog,
leader of the demonic balrogs, and armed with these unholy
weapons, Melko's forces breached the walls of the city. Troops of
scimitar-wielding Orcs slaughtered spitefully as they entered the
city. Prophets had warned of this, and one of the citizens of the city,
Meglin, had betrayed his family and friends to Melko.

The city burned.

As one of the earliest parts of what was to become a life-long
lengendarium, a vast and at times overwhelming mythology, Lieu-
tenant John Ronald Reuel Tolkien wrote "The Fall of Gondolin,"
one of his "lost tales." Tolkien wrote this tale after his participation
in the horrendous Battle of the Somme and throughout his con-
valescence in an English hospital in December of 1916. It would
prove to be the first element of the entire mythology's two major
repositories: *The Lord of the Rings* and *The Silmarillion.*

Indeed, 1916 changed many things in the young man's life.
Prior to the war, Tolkien had shared an incredible and meaningful
friendship with three others in his public school, King Edward's:
Christopher Wiseman, Geoffrey Smith, and Rob Gilson. The best of
friends, they called themselves the TCBS, the Tea Club and Barro-
vian Society. They stayed close after graduation, holding periodic
"Councils" to share poetry and ideas.

Gilson died on July 1, 1916, at the Somme. Shaken, Tolkien wrote
that the three remaining had a duty to achieve greatness — not for

personal glory, but for God's glory, to be a "great instrument in God's hands." Just as Gilson had achieved greatness through his sacrifice for something beyond himself, so the three remaining friends must be "steeped with the same holiness of courage, suffering, and sacrifice." Tolkien considered July 1 a holy day, one that must be remembered for the rest of their lives. So he wrote Geoffrey Smith on August 12. Sometime in the week before Christmas, Tolkien received a letter from Wiseman. German shrapnel had taken the life of G.B. Smith. Now, only two remained. "Of course the TCBS may have been all we dreamt," Tolkien had written in that letter to Smith, "and its work in the end to be done by three or two or one survivor and the part of the others be trusted by God to that of the inspiration which we do know we all got and get from one another." These words must have echoed in Tolkien's mind and soul as he pondered the death of Smith.

By no means did the deaths of these two close friends provide Tolkien with his only glimpse of brutality in the war. Having served at the Somme from July through November, Tolkien witnessed the destruction of almost an entire battalion at Chemin des Dames. "He saw, and was opposed to, the horrors of war, but was never a pacifist, as wars made him angry and bitter," two of Tolkien's children explained in 1974. "He was never a soldier, but went to war out of a sense of duty."

The enemy had breached the walls of the White City, flame engulfing nearly everything.

The sheer scale of the violence overwhelmed many after the First World War. Indeed, for most literati, World War I destroyed their innocence. "The Great War," Cecil Day Lewis wrote, "tore away our youth from its roots."

But for Tolkien, after every battle, remembrance and repairs must come as well. The White City must be rebuilt, ready to fight a new evil coming in a new and more powerful guise. For it was in the trenches that Tolkien realized the significance of faerie and myth. "The war made me poignantly aware of the beauty of the world I remember," Tolkien said in 1968. "I remember miles and miles of seething, tortured earth, perhaps best described in the chapters about the approaches to Mordor. It was a searing experience." For men such as Tolkien, World War I only increased their belief that England must save Western civilization. For Tolkien, remembrance of beauty undid much of the horror and terror of the world. "A real taste for fairy-stories was wakened by philology on the threshold of manhood," Tolkien told an academic audience in 1936, "and quickened to full by war."

Modernity: the White City betrayed

Tolkien understood that World War I embodied a symptom of a deeper problem for Western civilization. By focusing on the particular, modernity removes a thing from its (or his) relationship to another thing (or person). Modernity divorces the fact from its context through excessive emphasis on the fact. In intellectual life, as discussed twice already in this book, three figures no less important than Charles Darwin, Karl Marx, and Sigmund Freud had contributed to this intellectual narrowing. By focusing on a particular aspect of the human person, each of these figures either ignored the whole of the human person, or worse, exaggerated a particular aspect by claiming it to define the whole person. For Marx, man is at heart economic. For Darwin, man is biological. For Freud, man is psychological. Each of these things is true. But man — a complexity and mystery even unto himself — is all of these things and so much more.

In his own life, Tolkien experienced the loss of community. With the deaths of his parents and friends, his relationships withered one by one. While the loss of his mother and father cannot be blamed on modernity, the results remain the same. Tolkien knew first-hand what it meant to be removed from his context. Much of the rest of his life saw his search for order and friendship.

The White City remembered: myth

As he had in the TCBS, Tolkien hoped to fight the trends of the modern world with poetry, imagination, myth, Christian romance, and Christian friendship. Tolkien lectured to an academic audience at the University of St Andrews in the late 1930s:

> We may indeed be older now, in so far as we are heirs in enjoyment or in practice of many generations of ancestors in the arts. In this inheritance of wealth there may be a danger of boredom or of anxiety to be original, and that may lead to a distaste for fine drawing, delicate pattern, and "pretty" colours, or else to mere manipulation and over-elaboration of old material, clever and heartless. We should look at green again, and be startled anew (but not blinded) by blue and yellow and red. We should meet the centaur and the dragon, and then perhaps suddenly behold, like ancient shepherds, sheep, dogs, and horses — and wolves.

Further, Tolkien asked in that same 1939 lecture, why should one protest the so-called "escape" that literature and mythology provide?

> For it is after all possible for a rational man, after reflection (quite unconnected with fairy-story or romance), to arrive at the condemnation, implicit at least in the mere silence of "escapist" literature, of progressive things like factories, or the machine-guns and bombs that appear to be their most natural and inevitable, dare we say "inexorable," products.

One also thinks of Tolkien's description of Gandalf in *The Silmarillion*. Gandalf, known as Olorin in the True West, was the least of the Istari sent to Middle-earth to aid Men and Elves in their war against Sauron. Though the least powerful, he was the wisest, and he spent many of his days walking among the Elves "unseen, or in a form as one of them, and they did not know whence came the fair visions or the promptings of wisdom that he put into their hearts." *The Silmarillion* records that "those who listened to him awoke from despair and put away the imaginations of darkness."

Tolkien's closest adult friend, C. S. Lewis, also admired the art of escape through poetry, literature, and the imagination. "The Fantastic or Mythical is a Mode available at all ages for some readers; for others, at none. At all ages, if it is well used by the author and meets the right reader, it has the same power," Lewis wrote for the *New York Times* in 1956, "to generalise while remaining concrete, to present in palpable form not concepts or even experiences but whole classes of experience, and to throw off irrelevancies." In its best form, the fantastic can "add to" life, not just "comment on" it.

In his 1928 book, *Poetic Diction*, Owen Barfield wrote: "A civilization ... must look more and more to art — to the individualized poet — as the very source and fountain-head of *all* meaning." In a 1984 interview, Barfield neatly summarized the thinking of Lewis and Tolkien on art and literature: all "felt that literature shouldn't be used as a means of propagating a message." Further, he noted, "the thing that mattered was that it was a good work of art, and that had its own value, which in the long run was a Christian value. I think that that would perhaps be as fair a way as I could imagine of stating both Tolkien's and Lewis's attitude."

By and large, one could correctly describe the friends of Lewis and Tolkien, the Inklings, as conservative, traditionalist, Platonic, Augustinian, Stoic, anti-ideological, Christian poets and mythmakers. They believed in the True, the Good, and the Beautiful, and especially in the One behind all things. They recognized that their position in society was to counter the trends of modernity, not through reaction, but through remembrance. As Lewis's successor at Cambridge, Jack Bennett, wrote: "The stance of a last survivor always attracted him [Lewis]; it is one of the likings he shared with William Morris, and it early drew him to the sagas and the doomed Eddaic gods." The same could be said of Tolkien. Lewis, in his Cambridge Inaugural Address of 1954, described himself as a dinosaur, one of the last "Old Western Men."

> It is my settled conviction that in order to read Old Western literature aright you must suspend most of

the responses and unlearn most of the habits you have acquired in reading modern literature. And because this is the judgement of a native, I claim that, even if the defence of my conviction is weak, the fact of my conviction is a historical datum to which you should give full weight. That way, where I fail as a critic, I may yet be useful as a specimen. I would even dare to go further. Speaking not only for myself but for all other Old Western men whom you may meet, I would say, use your specimens while you can. There are not going to be many more dinosaurs.

Tolkien, too, "was an Old Western Man who was staggered at the present direction of civilization," Clyde Kilby, a Wheaton College English professor, recorded after a summer of conversations with Tolkien in 1966. "Even our much vaunted talk of equality he felt debased by our attempts to 'mechanize and formalize it.'" Like many Englishmen, Tolkien feared a world divided in two, in which the smaller peoples would be swallowed whole by the bigger powers.

While Tolkien saw evil in 1916, he also saw it in 1969. "The spirit of wickedness in high places is now so powerful and so many-headed in its incarnations," Tolkien wrote, "that there seems nothing more to do than personally to refuse to worship any of the hydras' heads." The world, he thought, seemed little better than a new Tower of Babel, "all noise and confusion." It would be difficult for a conservative and traditionalist such as Tolkien to have viewed the world in any other way. In addition to recognizing the effects of original sin over all eras and in all humans, Tolkien found the twentieth century especially troubling, even downright horrifying. Tolkien had lamented the rise of what he and his friends called the machine — mechanizing life, dulling and conforming it, draining it of its vitality. The machine had appeared in a variety of forms. Democratic governments had bureaucratized all the beauty out of language, on the more benign end of the continuum. At the other end, fascist and communist ideologues had raped, plundered, murdered, and dehumanized entire populations, massacring upwards of 200,000,000 persons in the century. Additionally, warfare had claimed another forty million soldiers. Tolkien, like most men of his generation, had done his duty in the First World War only to see his sons go off to fight in the Second World War. The machine was everywhere, making its unholy peace with the White City.

The history of the Inklings, thus far

While much has been written about the contributions of the individual members of the Inklings, very little of what has been written about the group as a whole has progressed beyond the basic thesis presented by Humphrey Carpenter in his 1979 book, *The Inklings*. In it, Carpenter asserted rather strongly that "the Inklings owed their existence as a group almost entirely to" C. S. Lewis. That is, the group revolved around the rather charismatic personality of C. S. Lewis. Carpenter presented firm evidence for his nearly absolutist claim. The Inklings first appeared in print, though not by that name, in Chad Walsh's 1949 biography and analysis, *C. S. Lewis: Apostle to the Skeptics*, at roughly the moment Lewis entered the popular consciousness of the American mind. "The stretch of time from 11:00 to 1:00 on Tuesday mornings Lewis ordinarily manages to keep free so that he can join a small circle of close friends at a certain small, sedate pub," Walsh recorded.

> There, in a private parlor, he and the half a dozen others pass an hour or two conversing on everything from the nature of God to the latest University events. This particular group dates back to the war years when the Oxford University Press (whose headquarters are normally in London!) fled from the blitz to Oxford, and one of its staff, Charles Williams, became the center of a little circle which met Tuesday mornings at the pub and Thursday evenings in Lewis's college rooms. Charles Williams died in 1945, but the Tuesday morning meetings continue. The group is a fluctuating one. It is likely to contain a couple of Lewis's colleagues such as

Professor Tolkien, one or two students, sometimes a relative of someone or a distant friend.

The sheer scope and content of the meetings astounded Walsh.

Only in retrospect did I realize how much intellectual ground was covered in these seemingly casual meetings. At the time the constant bustle of Lewis racing his friends to refill empty mugs or pausing to light another cigarette (occasionally a pipe) camouflaged the steady flow of ideas. The flow, I might add, is not a one-way traffic. Lewis is as good a listener as talker.

In 1947, C.S. Lewis described it as a group of "literary friends. [Williams] read us his manuscripts and we read him ours: we smoked, talked, argued, and drank together." John Wain, a student member of the Inklings, described the group in a similar manner, again focusing on Lewis. In his 1962 autobiography, *Sprightly Running*, he wrote of Lewis's "dramatic personality." Wain wrote that they were "a circle of investigators, almost of incendiaries, meeting to urge one another on in the task of redirecting the whole current of contemporary art and life." Further, Wain argued, C.S. Lewis led the group as a pro-Christian political cell, working with "fellow travelers" such as Dorothy Sayers, Roger Lancelyn Green, and Roy Campbell. In his scholarly *The Precincts of Felicity: The Augustinian City of the Oxford Christians*, Charles Moorman gave as much weight to Charles Williams, who was an Inkling from only 1939 to 1945, as he did to Lewis. Further, Moorman sought to identify a corporate mind at work among the Inklings. Yet visitors, too, viewed the Inklings as essentially Lewis's group. The Inklings, Tolkien explained, were "the undetermined and unelected circle of friends who gathered about C.S.L., and met in his rooms in Magdalen." Lewis, especially, "had a passion for hearing things read aloud."

Since Houghton Mifflin first published Carpenter's group biography of the Inklings, an enormous number of primary sources, interviews, and manuscripts have appeared. While no one could or should rightly deny the extraordinary influence of Lewis's personality and charisma on the Inklings, the statement "without Lewis's influence, the Inklings would not have been" is simplistic. Two other major factors (as well as a host of smaller ones) contributed to the makeup, ideas, and purpose of the Inklings. The first (though not necessarily first in importance) was the publication of Owen Barfield's 1928 work, *Poetic Diction*. Written originally as an undergraduate thesis to earn his B.Litt., and defended against Lewis's dramatic intellectual attacks throughout the series of letters known as the "Great War" of the 1920s, Barfield's book exerted a profound influence on the Inklings. In it, Barfield pursued Plato's idea of "divine madness," arguing that not only does imagination allow us to understand sense data, but also that men "do not *invent* those mysterious relations between separate external objects, and between objects and feelings, which it is the function of poetry to reveal." Instead, Barfield continued, "these relations exist independently, not indeed of Thought, but of any individual thinker."

Barfield, therefore, holds the poet's as one of the most important offices in Western civilization. Without the development of poetry and the recognition of the necessity of the poet, the Western world will become lost in scientific or scientistic nominalism and pragmatism, and the organic unity of the West will be lost, perhaps permanently. While brilliantly argued, Barfield's work here falls neatly into the work of a number of important Christian humanist thinkers of the 1920s: Nicolas Berdyaev, T. S. Eliot, Christopher Dawson, and Paul Elmer More.

As mentioned above, the influence of Barfield's thought and works upon the various members of the Inklings cannot be exaggerated. In many ways, *Poetic Diction* set the tone for the Inklings, as they saw themselves, as Wain best put it, "redirecting the whole current of contemporary life and art," and they believed that myth, metaphor, and poetry would lead the revival. Tolkien may have been the most profoundly influenced, though he had already arrived at the same conclusions as Barfield. *Poetic Diction* allowed Tolkien to order and shape his own not-yet-fully-formed thoughts. In a letter to Barfield, Lewis wrote: "You might like to know that when Tolkien dined with me the other night he said *a propos* of something quite different that your conception of the ancient semantic unity had modified his whole outlook and that he was always just going to say something in a lecture when your conception stopped him in time." Barfield held a strong affinity for Tolkien's notions of myth as well. And though the atheist Lewis of the 1920s had fought vehemently against Barfield's Platonic metaphysical ideas, as a Christian, Lewis embraced them, at least in part. In his learned study of the Barfield-Lewis "Great War," writer and scholar Lionel Adey concludes that Lewis "could not, however, have developed as a religious apologist, novelist or literary historian and expounder of the medieval *Weltanschauung* but for the stimulus of his controversies with Barfield." One can readily see the influence of Barfield on Lewis in his space trilogy, especially in the first book, *Out of the Silent Planet*.

The other major influence on the group came from Tolkien's legendarium. Though already fellow members of Tolkien's academic group the Koalbiters, dedicated to reading Icelandic and northern myth in the original languages, Lewis and Tolkien first discovered their profound kinship in 1929 after a long discussion about their mutual love of the northern giants and gods. Tolkien first presented the minor manifestations of the mythology — *The Hobbit*, written in the early to mid-1930s, and *The Lord of the Rings*, written between 1938 and 1949 — to the Inklings, reading them aloud chapter by chapter. While each of the following facts may be a mere temporal coincidence, the coincidences collectively are too strong to be dismissed: Tolkien met Lewis when he had completed the first major outline of the *Silmarillion*; he served as a member of the Koalbiters, which evolved, for the most part, into the Inklings; finally, the Inklings met less and less after 1949, when Tolkien completed *The Lord of the Rings*. Indeed, Tolkien's mythology served as both a backdrop and as a centerpiece for the Inklings.

Differences aside, friendship truly mattered to the Inklings. Throughout Tolkien's legendarium, friends gather around fires, around food, and around drink. Around each, they tell tales. The tales inspire, serving almost as prayer, just as Aragorn's Tale of Beren and Lúthien prepares the Hobbits for their first battle against the

Ring Wraiths upon Weather Top. As Lewis wrote: "Friendship is the greatest of worldly goods. Certainly to me it is the chief happiness of life. If I had to give a piece of advice to a young man about a place to live, I think I should say, 'sacrifice almost everything to live where you can be near your friends.'"

The White Cities: England and Christendom

In 1950, Tolkien admitted that he originally conceived what would become his Middle-earth mythology, the "Lost Tales" of World War I, as a mythology specifically for England. "I was from early days grieved by the poverty of my own beloved country: it had no stories of its own (bound up with tongue and soil), not of the quality that I sought, and found (as an ingredient) in legends of other lands." Even *Beowulf*, the greatest of Anglo-Saxon poems, dealt with Scandinavians. Tolkien told Clyde Kilby that the seed of the mythology came from the Anglo-Saxon poet Cynewulf and his poem "Crist": "Lux fulgebat super nos. Eala Earendel engla beorhtast ofer middangeard monnum sended." These are "rapturous words from which ultimately sprang the whole of my mythology," Tolkien admitted. Kilby asked Tolkien in person to translate the Anglo-Saxon. "Here Earendel brightest of angels, sent from God to men," Tolkien replied.

Entitled *The Book of Lost Tales*, Tolkien's original mythological stories follow a mariner by the name of Eriol, Angol, Waefre, or Aelfwine. Eriol means "one who dreams alone," Angol is obviously Angle, Waefre is Anglo-Saxon for "restless," and Aelfwine is a character who appears in the Old English poem, "The Battle of Maldon." Perhaps much like Tolkien himself, Eriol is a restless, wandering Anglo-Saxon in search of legend and truth. As Christopher Tolkien noted in his commentaries in the *History of Middle-earth*, "Thus it is through Eriol and his sons that the Engle (i.e. the English) have the true tradition of the fairies, of whom the Iras and Wealas (the Irish and Welsh) tell garbled things." With these stories, Christopher continued, "a specifically English fairy-lore is born, and one more true than anything to be found in Celtic lands."

Though Tolkien eventually abandoned much of his material from "The Book of Lost Tales," his love of—and inspiration from—Anglo-Saxon culture and literature continued. Tolkien's hobbits represented the best of the pre-Norman invasion Anglo-Saxons. Like the English (made up of Jutes, Angles, and Saxons), the hobbits (made up of Harfoots, Stoors, and Fallohides) migrated from the east. Additionally, the hobbits lived on land that was originally not theirs but had once belonged to a greater, and now long-gone, power. There were other specifically Anglo-Saxon elements as well. Tom Shippey speculates that the Rohirrim are Anglo-Saxons as they might have developed had they had a mounted horse culture. For example, much of the ceremony of Gandalf entering the Golden Hall mirrors Beowulf's entrance into the Great Hall. Additionally, the Riders call their own land "The Mark." The old translation for Mercia (an Anglo-Saxon medieval kingdom) was "The Mark." Indeed, Shippey believes that Tolkien mingled his affection for the Anglo-Saxons with his regard for the warrior culture of North American Indians found in James Fenimore Cooper's *Leatherstocking Tales*. Tolkien mentioned in "On Fairy-Stories" that he liked "Red Indians" better than *Alice in Wonderland* or *Treasure Island*, as they offered him "glimpses of an archaic mode of life, and, above all, forests."

Though Tolkien had originally envisioned his myth as a specifically English myth, in his re-conception after *The Book of Lost Tales*, the Anglo-Saxon and northern languages, cultures and mythologies became a means by which to re-energize the world. The myth became one of universal, rather than national, significance. The Christian should embrace and sanctify the most noble virtues to come out of the northern pagan mind: courage and raw will. "It is the strength of the northern mythological imagination that it faced this problem, put the monsters in the centre, gave them victory but no honour, and found a potent but terrible solution in naked will and courage," Tolkien wrote. "The northern [imagination] has power, as it were, to revive its spirit even in our own times." Tolkien thought that a vigorous Christianity needed that northern pagan myth spirit to make it stronger. The German-Italian theologian

Romano Guardini would argue along the same lines in his stunning 1956 book, *The End of the Modern World*:

> Deeply significant for the new religious outlook of medieval man was the influx of the Germanic spirit. The religious bent of the Nordic myths, the restlessness of the migrating peoples and the armed marches of the Germanic tribes revealed a new spirit which burst everywhere into history like a spear thrust into the infinite. This mobile and nervous soul worked itself into the Christian affirmation. There it grew mightily. In its fullness it produced that immense medieval drive which aimed at cracking the boundaries of the world.

From its original formulation as a myth for England, first conceived in muck and blood-filled trenches in northern France, Tolkien's legendarium grew much larger in scope and significance. The story, especially *The Lord of the Rings*, became much more than a myth for any one people or any one nation. It became instead a myth for the restoration of Christendom itself. The intrepid Anglo-Saxon missionaries (in particular St Boniface of Crediton) created medieval, Christian Europe by carrying classical and Christian traditions into the heart of pagan, barbarian Europe. St Boniface converted innumerable barbarians to Christianity, unifying them under Rome. St Boniface even crowned Pepin, son of Charles Martel — an action that would eventually lead to the papal recognition of Charlemagne as the revived Holy Roman Emperor in 800 A D. With the return of the king Aragorn to his rightful throne, Tolkien argued, the "progress of the tales ends in what is far more like the re-establishment of an effective Holy Roman Empire with its seat in Rome." In his own private writings, Tolkien equated numerous parts of Italy with various geographical aspects of Gondor. In his diary, for example, Tolkien recorded that with his trip to Italy, he had "come to the head of Christendom: an exile from the borders and far provinces returning home, or at least to the home of his fathers." In a letter to a friend, Tolkien stated that he had holidayed "in Gondor, or in modern parlance, Venice." That Tolkien should place a mythologized Italy, and ultimately Rome, at the center of his legendarium is not surprising, as he viewed the Reformation as ultimately responsible for the modern, secularized world.

Tolkien believed the Anglo-Saxon world might offer us strength to redeem Christendom. The hero of *The Lord of the Rings*, is, after all, an Anglo-Saxon farmer turned citizen-warrior. Even as an uneducated gardener, this most loyal of companions recognized hope, deep in the heart of Mordor.

> Sam saw a white star twinkle for a while. The beauty of it smote his heart, as he looked up out of the forsaken land, and hope returned to him that in the end the Shadow was only a small and passing thing: there was light and high beauty forever beyond its reach.

Only through myth could the White City be remembered and seen. Only through friendship could the White City be rebuilt. Only through heroism and sacrifice could the White City be defended.

Two Tolkiens, Not One

I've read *The Silmarillion* so many times since the fall of 1977, I have no idea what number of readings I'm actually on. Eight times? Nine? Ten? It was the first Tolkien I'd ever encountered, even before *The Hobbit* or *The Lord of the Rings*. I can still see myself sitting on the floor of my maternal grandparents' family room in Hays, Kansas, trying to read the story of Creation, the "Ainulindalë," over and over again. At age ten, I'm not quite sure how much of it I actually understood, but to this day, I can't read or teach the first three chapters of Genesis without imagining Ilúvatar and the Powers. Tolkien's mythological version of Creation is one of the most beautiful things I've ever read, and I think it does mighty justice to the Hebraic account. Regardless, Tolkien's version is indelibly imprinted on my soul and mind.

This most recent reading of *The Silmarillion* is the first time, however, that I've mapped out the entire book — not just in marginalia but on paper and in document format. I've kept track of characters, plots, empty spaces, ideas, etc. As always and with each reading, I've come to the same conclusion: this is one of the richest stories ever imagined and recorded. Whether I've read it ten times or a hundred times, I will always be amazed by its depth and by the intensity of its beauty.

This time, two new thoughts hit me. Or, if they're not new, they're not ones I remember having had before.

First, if every college student had to read *The Silmarillion*, the world would be a much better place. Indeed, as I finished the book yesterday, I couldn't help but think that almost all of the wisdom found in the collected works of Voegelin, Strauss, Dawson, and Kirk finds its place in this book. Of course, the story of *The Silmarillion* is timeless. It is the story of pride against love, of love against pride. It is the story of preferring self to other, or other to self. It is the story of choosing art over dominion, or dominion over art. In *The Silmarillion*, there are terrible beauties and horrific tragedies. In everything I've encountered, I've never read a non-explicitly-religious book that is as rich with wisdom as is *The Silmarillion*. It is frankly better than anything Hayek, Dawson, or Voegelin ever wrote. And like the Greeks of antiquity, Tolkien tells this timeless tale through myth, dialogue, and parable (though never allegory!). Tolkien's *Silmarillion* does for modernity what Dante did for the Middle Ages and what Virgil did for the Roman age of transition from republic to empire. I firmly believe that Tolkien will someday be understood as the best representative of this epoch of human existence (not that I'll be around to confirm this).

Second, I also have come to realize over the last several years how important Christopher Tolkien is to the entire mythology. At the beginning of this version of *The Silmarillion* (the second edition), Tolkien's son and literary heir, Christopher, reprints a letter his father wrote to a friend and would-be publisher in 1951. It's a long letter and often quoted. Here is just one significant section of it:

> But once upon a time (my crest has long since fallen) I
> had a mind to make a body of more or less connected

legend, ranging from the large and cosmogonic, to the level of romantic fairy-story — the larger founded on the lesser in contact with the earth, the lesser drawing splendour from the vast backcloths — which I could dedicate simply to: to England; to my country. It should possess the tone and quality that I desired, somewhat cool and clear, be redolent of our 'air' (the clime and soil of the North West, meaning Britain and the hither parts of Europe: not Italy or the Aegean, still less the East), and, while possessing (if I could achieve it) the fair elusive beauty that some call Celtic (though it is rarely found in genuine ancient Celtic things), it should be 'high', purged of the gross, and fit for the more adult mind of a land long now steeped in poetry. I would draw some of the great tales in fullness, and leave many only placed in the scheme, and sketched. The cycles should be linked to a majestic whole, and yet leave scope for other minds and hands, wielding paint and music and drama. Absurd.

And yet, it's not absurd at all. In fact, it's exactly what happened. No one knows for certain when Tolkien began his mythology (the "legendarium," as he would come to call it) that encompasses *The Hobbit* and *The Lord of the Rings*, as well as a myriad other stories. In the same letter quoted above, Tolkien claimed that this myth — in some form or another — had always been with him: "I do not remember a time when I was not building it." As mentioned previously, Clyde S. Kilby believed Tolkien had formally begun the planning and writing of the mythology around 1913, while Tolkien gave specific dates ranging from 1915 through 1917. We do know for certain that some of Tolkien's first writings were made in the trenches in World War I, and actually appear on the back of official military orders and messages.

Scholars such as Carl Hostettler and Verlyn Flieger have done much to identify the exact moments of creation in Tolkien's mythology, and I will only refer you to their work rather than go through it now. This much, though, is certain. J.R.R. Tolkien never completed *The Silmarillion*. It took Christopher four more years after his father's death before *The Silmarillion* saw the light of day or an actual bookstore shelf. In 1980, Christopher released yet another compilation of his father's stories, *Unfinished Tales*. Between 1983 and 1996, Christopher published the twelve volumes of *The History of Middle-earth*. Since then, he has edited and released his father's work on the Volsunga, the Finnish *Kalevala*, the Arthurian legends, *Beowulf,* and *The Children of Húrin, Beren and Lúthien,* and *The Fall of Gondolin* (stories set in Middle-earth and taken from *The Silmarillion*).

There was a time when I would have criticized Christopher for this or that choice made in the publishing of his father's work. No more. I realize now how vital Christopher has been to the entire process. He has been absolutely essential, frankly, in getting his father's work out.

And the dates matter. For the sake of argument, let me claim that Tolkien began the formal writing of his mythology in 1915, a date generally accepted by Tolkien scholars. Yet J.R.R. Tolkien passed away in September 1973. His works have continued to be released more than four decades after he left this mortal realm. Christopher is now in his mid-nineties. In other words, the mythology is so profound, dense, and wide that it's taken the lives of two men to bring it to the public. And not everything has been published yet. A few things still remain.

So, a huge thank you to J.R.R. Tolkien, and an equally huge thanks to Christopher Tolkien, RAF pilot, Oxford University professor, and keeper of the flame of the legendarium.

If there has been a greater Christian humanist work than the entirety of Tolkien's mythology in the last one hundred years, I have yet to see it. Only T.S. Eliot's *Four Quartets* rivals it.

11

Sister Madeleva Wolff

Accidents are so often God's way of being doubly good
to us.

Sister Madeleva

ONE OF THE MOST UNSUNG HEROINES OF
an almost unsung movement, Sister Madeleva desperately
needs an Ode or Sonnet (or even a rock ballad) written
in her honor. Sister Madeleva Wolff (1887–1964), if remembered at
all, is remembered for her presidency of St Mary's College, Notre
Dame, Indiana, over an astoundingly long tenure, 1934–1961. Born
to a Lutheran father and Roman Catholic mother in Wisconsin,
Mary Evaline Wolff attended St Mary's College as an undergraduate and entered the Sisters of the Congregation of the Holy Cross
in 1908, taking the name Madeleva. A renowned medievalist who
earned her Ph.D. at Berkeley in 1925 and did her postdoctoral work
at Oxford under such luminaries as J.R.R. Tolkien, C.S. Lewis, and
Father Martin D'Arcy, Sister Madeleva wrote poetry as beautifully
as she could handle expertly all the chores of a Wisconsin farmer.
She was, by all accounts, an absolutely extraordinary person.

As much as Wolff appreciated Tolkien and D'Arcy, it was C.S.
Lewis who intrigued her most. In her sadly out-of-print autobiography, *My First Seventy Years* (Macmillan, 1959), she proudly remembers
her relationship to him, eleven years her junior.

> Oxford that Trinity term meant and continues to mean
> for me Mr C.S. Lewis. After attending his second lecture
> to the Prolegomena to the Study of Medieval Poetry I
> said to some of the students at Cherwell Edge, "Mr Lewis

is the one person at Oxford with whom I should like to tutor." "But," they exclaimed in amazement at my temerity, "Mr Lewis refuses to tutor a woman." "That," I replied stoutly, "does not change my statement in the least."

Lewis, she noted with obvious glee, "dug up medieval poetry by the roots and planted it in our minds, there to grow and flower as it might."

Whether Lewis thought as highly of Wolff as she did of him remains unclear. She appears several times in his collected letters, but the last one written in 1934 ends with this somewhat ominous, if unsurprising, statement (Lewis never felt comfortable around female students): "If I am ever in those parts (which is unlikely) I will certainly brave the 'terrors of convents' and accept your kind hospitality." Certainly, Lewis never did venture to Notre Dame, Indiana. The two did not correspond again until 1951, when she sent him a copy of her work *Lost Language.* Lewis pronounced it "wholly delightful." The two continued to correspond until Lewis's death in 1963. Unexpectedly, he revealed a number of personal thoughts to Madeleva regarding his wife, Joy, and the sacraments. Lewis was not the only one to "confess" to her. The famed historian Bernard DeVoto did as well.

Wolff's connections, however, extended well beyond the Inklings and Father D'Arcy. Indeed, she served as both a critical Christian humanist and a vital nexus between European and American Christian humanists. As an intellectual and poet in her own right, she interacted with, influenced, and was influenced by R.H. Benson, Christopher Dawson, Stringfellow Barr, Clare Booth Luce, Helen Hayes, Robert Speaight, Frank Sheed, Barbara Ward, Arnold Lunn, Josef Pieper, Mortimer Adler, E.I. Watkin, and Jacques and Raïssa Maritain. The list of her friends and allies reads like a who's who of the liberal arts and Christian humanism.

Through these connections, Wolff made St Mary's a vital center of Christian humanism throughout the thirties, forties, and fifties. It was she as president who initiated the Program of Christian Culture, based on the pioneering work of Dawson. Though she held the "Great Books" (as understood by the University of Chicago and St John's College) with deep admiration, she also believed that liberal education should be directed toward a larger truth than our own perception of texts. "The liberal arts are most liberal, most liberating when they rest on complete rather than on partial truth." This was true philosophically as well as empirically. "Here the Catholic college is the authentic exponent for the first sixteen centuries of Christian arts and sciences." The same, she noted, was true for the fine arts. Given her own background as a poetess, a farmer, a nun, and a university president, she often answered the question as to what her favorite books were with these three: the Bible, the Oxford English Dictionary, and various seed catalogues. Books, she noted more seriously and with love, "are my friends. Here they are again, shelf upon shelf, the poets from Beowulf and Langland to Eliot and Millay and Daniel Berrigan on the left of the fireplace, the mystics on the right. Lead me not into digression or we shall never emerge from this room."

It was also President Wolff who racially integrated St Mary's, having no patience for bigotry based on the accidents of birth. As she said when she first accepted a black student: if the school empties in response, St Mary's would simply continue as a college for black women! "I knew only one answer," she wrote, "the right one."

A scholar of Chaucer and of the literature of the high and late Middle Ages in particular, Wolff published well over twenty books during her lifetime. Nearly half of these were collections of her poetic verse. While she wrote poetry in a variety of styles, most of it reads (at least to my untrained if appreciative eyes and ears) as Eliot-esque and quite modern. Imagism especially abounds.

Two examples reveal much.

Wind Wraith

A shy ghost of a wind was out
Tiptoeing through the air
At dawn, and though I could not see
Nor hear her anywhere,
I felt her lips just brush my cheek,
Her fingers touch my hair.

Ultimates

Although you know, you cannot end my quest,
Nor ever, ever compass my desire;
That were to burn me with divinest fire;
That were to fill me with divinest rest,
To lift me, living, to God's living breast
I should not dare this thing, nor you aspire
To it, who no less passionately require
Love ultimate, possessor and possessed.

You who are everything and are not this,
Be but its dream, its utter, sweet surmise
Which waking makes the more intensely true
With every exquisite, wistful part of you;
My own, the depths of your untroubled eyes,
Your quiet hands, and your most quiet kiss.

As one recent writer has noted, the themes of Wolff's poetry are as much those of Emily Dickinson as of Roman Catholicism. Whatever one might label them, these two sample poems reveal the depths of Wolff's soul and artistic ability.

At the end of her page-turning and captivating autobiography, Sister Madeleva reflects on a life well lived, wondering about the culture of modern America and its obsessions with the ownership of "stuff." After a trip to Marshall Field's in Chicago, she concluded, she was happy to "see how many things there are in the world that I do not want."

A fine human being, a devout Catholic, and a poetic Christian humanist, Sister Madeleva Wolff gave every talent she had to the Church, to St Mary's, and to the very fortunate students who attended that college under her leadership. "Someday," she wrote, "I shall have only One, Infinite, Absolute want." That she now possesses, and He possesses her.

12

Peacenik Prophet: Russell Kirk

WHILE VERY FEW MODERN CONSERVA-
tives—especially those who sell conservatism as a
consumer product—even remember Russell Kirk, the
movement's founder, those who do remember him often envision
him as an antiquated relic, having passed from this world long after
he had contributed much to it. At best, Kirk might well represent
a pre-radicalized Western world, and at worst, he was probably
stuck in some early romantic nineteenth century longing for an
aristocratic world.

In fact, those who fail to remember him and those who think
him irrelevant are equally foolish. Kirk's views on the world are
as relevant now as—if not more so than—they have ever been.

Even on his angriest days, Kirk was never what one would call a
hawk, at least not in foreign policy. Holding traditional Washing-
tonian republicanism in deepest respect, Kirk knew that the most
stable societies promoted and encouraged the order of their own
before interfering in the affairs of others. As the first president of the
United States declaimed in his farewell address: "The great rule of
conduct for us in regard to foreign nations is in extending our commercial relations, to have with them as little political connection as
possible." By the end of his life, Kirk had decided that not a single war
in which America had participated had been either just or necessary.

If nothing else, it's worth remembering that the pre-Nixon
Republican Party (at least since the end of Teddy Roosevelt's presidency) was the party of peace, the anti-war party. Kirk came solidly
out of that tradition.

From the days of Reagan's election in 1980 to his leaving office in 1989, Kirk believed the Californian to be an excellent president — a man endowed with intelligence, imagination, and especially audacity. The presidency of Ronald Reagan and the papacy of John Paul II in the 1980s gave Kirk more hope for the world than he had experienced at any other comparable length of time in his life. For an all-too brief moment, Kirk held hope that the world had not only halted the terrors of progressivism, but might have actually reversed them. In 1988, Kirk even willingly trusted that George Bush would quietly carry on the legacy of Reagan's foreign policy. Throughout the first years of the 1990s, however, it became quite clear to everyone that Bush had reverted to the Nixonian neo-conservatism of his CIA days.

Kirk saw Bush's misuse of Reagan's Cold War military apparatus as nothing other than a sheer betrayal of Reaganite, republican, and American principles. In private, Kirk joked that the American people should publicly execute President Bush on the White House lawn. In public, Kirk railed against what he knew to be the beginning of an American empire and a never-ending war. Far from emulating the righteous Reagan, Bush had taken the racist and authoritarian progressives Woodrow Wilson, Franklin Roosevelt, and Lyndon B. Johnson as his exemplars. Thus not only did he derail the Reagan agenda and legacy, but, even more significantly, he undid the true progress in American foreign policy and will-power made in the 1980s. Far from naïve, Kirk knew that American desires for world domination had existed since the rise of democracy in the nineteenth century, but he also knew that countervailing forces remained and arose from time to time as well. As Kirk argued, one might reasonably identify this American tension by dividing it into its arrogant and anxious Puritan side and its confident, inward-looking, republican side. If the former side prevailed, it would consume the world in pure ecstasy, never imagining what the consequences of such actions might be. The Puritan was ruled by his own passions and his own righteous desires, willing to ride roughshod over not only his fellow citizens but all of the citizens of the world as well. What he had once done happily to the Anglicans of the British Isles in the seventeenth century, the Puritan would now do to the peoples of the earth in the twentieth and twenty-first centuries.

Of all of the years of his life, Kirk viewed 1991 as the watershed year, a year of immense sorrow. "Decisions are being made nowadays, in public policies and abroad and at home, that may be irrevocable," he told an audience at the Heritage Foundation in Washington, DC, on February 27, 1991. This was, it should be remembered, the day before President Bush declared Desert Storm a success. This, Kirk told his audience, was the most un-Reagan-like action imaginable. Kirk noted that "the Republican Party, which achieved its greatest vigor in this century during the presidential terms of Ronald Reagan, now seems in the sere and yellow leaf." For the sake of the "oilcan," Kirk lamented, echoing Edmund Burke's words in 1796, President Bush had committed a vain crime against humanity itself. "After carpet-bombing the Cradle of Civilization as no country ever had done before," Kirk continued at the Heritage Foundation, "Mr. Bush sent in hundreds of thousands of soldiers to overrun the Iraqi bunkers — that were garrisoned by dead men, asphyxiated." Not only had we violated the ethical rules of warfare, we had also bribed innumerable corrupt allies to support our cause against another corrupt power. At what point, Kirk wondered, could the use of evil against evil produce good? 1991, Kirk argued, would most likely prove as momentous for the twenty-first century as 1914 had for the twentieth century. The year 1991 marked the beginning of a new period and phase of warfare, a progressive step back toward barbarism. Though undoubtedly a decent man of good intentions, Bush had nonetheless allowed his own failure of imagination and his cravings for power to corrupt himself, his nation, and his civilization. Only in dystopian fiction could there be a "Perpetual War for Perpetual Peace" or a "New World Order," Kirk concluded.

Only a few months later, Kirk further complained that not only had a new American empire arisen on the ashes of Iraq, but it had also adopted an ideology to justify its birth: that of "democratic capitalism." Such a new empire would be built not by the bureaucrats alone, but by corporations, enriching themselves by conforming the world to the mass standardization of the American model. Now that the Russian communists were failing, Kirk noted with irony, "American planners might out-materialize the Soviet materialists." The result of all of this, Kirk predicted, would be a return to fundamentalism as the peoples of the world resist Americanization. "Every living thing prefers even death, as an individual, to extinction as a distinct species," he claimed. "There exists one sure way to make a deadly enemy, and that is to propose to anyone" that they should "submit" to being remade in "my image."

When Russell Kirk passed from this earth in April of 1994, he feared all of the great victories of the 1980s had been not only squandered, but perverted and lost. A quarter of a century later, we must finally recognize the powerful Jeremiad of Russell Kirk. Not only are U.S. forces still in the Near East, but we have radically destabilized the entire region. We even war with our own creations, our very own Frankensteins.

Russell Kirk is not outdated. He's more relevant today than he has ever been.

13

St Russell of Mecosta?

WHEN I FIRST STARTED READING THE WORKS of Russell Amos Augustine Kirk in the fall of 1989, that most joyously fateful of seasons, I had no idea I would wind up three decades later having spent much of my adult life reading him, writing about him, and holding a position named in his honor. Now in my early 50s, I stand happily and proudly in his shadow.

Of all the things I have learned about him, though, nothing has impressed me more than the man's charity, his saint-like dedication to all around him: the poor, the lonely, the disabled, the cranky, the abused, the oppressed, the bizarrely eccentric, the forgotten, and of course, the seekers of truth. At first, the stories of his outreach overwhelmed me. I wondered how I would ever convey them in my own writings. If I began my 2015 biography of him with the all-too-true stories of his saintliness, most readers would understandably see nothing more than my not atypical Birzerian hyperbole. Yet to me, this charity was and still remains the most important aspect of a truly great and brilliant man. For strategic reasons, I decided to make the argument at the end of the book, having by that point—I hope—earned the right to speak about him so effusively.

Growing up in abject poverty profoundly informed his own understanding of money and material wealth as things ephemeral and untrustworthy, and his innate stoicism allowed him to see those around him not as "other," but as fellow persons struggling against the odds so seemingly stacked against them. He housed and fed refugees from the far reaches of the world; he funded pregnant single mothers so they could have their babies; he gave his time and thoughts to any student (or journalist) who asked; he networked those who should know one another; he sent money to those who requested it. Finally, he promoted the works of scholarship and art that he deemed crucial to the defense of a humane civilization.

His beloved grandfather—his true father-figure—Frank Pierce, a man of immense dignity, gave everything of his soul and intellect to the young Russell. His mother gave her entire self to him as well, though Kirk found it painful to reveal his gratitude to her, something he regretted the rest of his life. Later his spouse, Annette, would become his charitable comrade-in-arms, the energetic planner and do-gooder alongside Kirk's more quiet charity.

Far from living out the stereotype of the American conservative as a wealthy, conformist, selfish businessman, plotting the oppression of those around him, Kirk believed conservatism existed to conserve, preserve, and disseminate the good, the true, and the beautiful of this world—however fleeting those things might seem. Indeed, though money was fleeting, it was fleeting in a material world. The good works we do now stay with us in eternity, perhaps even defining our role in the next life. One of Kirk's most interesting (and recurrent) fictional characters, Ralph Bain, might very well spend the next life saving women in danger of being abused. He would do this not just once, but for times uncounted and uncountable. Some might see this as purgatorial, yet Kirk believed that if a man found happiness in what seems to be laborious or tedious, he is most likely fulfilling a purpose that God gave to him. What better way to spend your eternity than in perpetually doing the right thing, doing what God created you to do best?

Most obviously, Kirk's ancestral home, Piety Hill, became a refuge to all who sought it. As Kirk noted, it was a sanctuary from Progress, the "last homely house" of the West.

When one visits Kirk's grave in St Michael's cemetery between Mecosta and Remus, Michigan, he sees a tangible marker to Kirk's charity—the grave of the hobo ex-con, Clinton Wallace, whom the Kirks adopted as a part of the family while he was on parole from the New York prison system. His grave reads, romantically, "A Knight of the Road." He accidentally burned down the Kirk home on Ash Wednesday, 1975, but still Kirk saw only the best in him. Kirk viewed Wallace not merely as the sum of his poor choices, but as the person God had made him, "A Knight of the Road." Wallace appears not once but twice in Kirk's fictional world, as the Viking berserker, Francis Xavier "Frank" Sarsfield, protector of the innocent. Sarsfield, so real in Kirk's short story, "There's A Long, Long Trail A-Winding," impressed even one of the most curmudgeonly of American writers, Harlan Ellison, as a work of genius. High praise, indeed.

In the last several years, movements have begun that seek to advance figures such as J.R.R. Tolkien and Romano Guardini toward canonization. As surprising as it might sound to those who knew Kirk as a bad Catholic (in terms of practice), he deserves sainthood. I don't mean to claim expertise on the canonization process, and I certainly don't believe myself to have God-like knowledge of who resides in heaven and who doesn't. Yet all of the evidence points toward Kirk as a man of deep and abiding charity. This charity was never contrived. It was fundamentally rooted in the man.

In his own life, Kirk took the motto of the Christophers, influenced by Franciscan spirituality: "it is better to light one candle than it is to curse the darkness." In his writings Kirk would often phrase this as "brightening the corner where one finds himself." Sadly, to a generation raised on activist and political conservatism, this advice sounds not merely antiquated but even downright subversive. Yet if we are honest with ourselves, this is probably the best advice for any good person in this rather fallen world. Honest and also humble. It is also, not shockingly, deeply Christian humanist.

It is also a tradition in the Catholic Church to prove three miracles associated with the possible saint. I actually believe there were three such miracles in Kirk's own life. First, his awareness of God — however cloudy — in the lonely desert of Utah in the fall of 1942. Second, his obsession with and understanding of the Shroud of Turin as a physical manifestation of Christ's virtue. And third, his "visits" with St Padre Pio regarding the history and sanctity of a Middle-eastern Christian icon in the days before Kirk's death.

Now, I suppose, we only need to find someone who has been influenced toward the good, the true, and the beautiful since Russell Kirk's passing from this vale of tears in 1994.

Any takers?

14

Eric Voegelin

On my religious position, I have been classified as a Protestant, a Catholic, an anti-semitic, and as a typical Jew; politically, as a Liberal, a Fascist, a National Socialist, and a Conservative; and on my theoretical position, as a Platonist, a Neo-Augustinian, a Thomist, a disciple of Hegel, an existentialist, a historical relativist, and an empirical skeptic; in recent years the suspicion has frequently been voiced that I am a Christian. All these classifications have been made by university professors and people with academic degrees. They give ample food for thought regarding the state of our universities.[1]

O F ALL THE MAJOR NON-LEFTIST THINKERS of the twentieth century, Eric Voegelin (1901–1985) remains perhaps the most difficult to understand. While some of his ideas simply pop off the page, most of them linger in some kind of morass of stumped curiosity, even within the brains of the most willing. Indeed, even the most dedicated conservative scholars find themselves slogging through much of Voegelin's thought. Several conservatives have indeed produced brilliant analyses of Voegelin. In particular, one should begin any study of Voegelin with the works of Ted McAllister and Michael Federici. Though one should perhaps read them in the opposite order. Federici's book on Voegelin offers one of the best introductions ever written to *any* figure, while McAllister's explores the depths of Voegelin's most complicated thoughts.

---

1   Eric Voegelin, quoted in Kirk, *Enemies of the Permanent Things* [1969] (Peru, IL: Sherwood Sugden, 1988), 254.

Born in Cologne, Germany on January 3, 1901, Voegelin moved with his family to Vienna when he was nine years old. There, under the frequent guidance of Ludwig von Mises and the Mises Circle, Voegelin revealed his stunning intelligence. Earning a degree in political science from the University of Vienna in 1922, he then studied at Oxford with Gilbert Murray and in the United States with John Dewey, John Commons (an economist), and Alfred North Whitehead. Armed with these advanced degrees from the most prestigious institutions in the English-speaking world, Voegelin returned to Germany and found himself confronting the terrors of the National Socialists. In his attempt to combat their racism and superstition, he wrote four books: *Race and State*; *History of the Race Idea*; *The Authoritarian State*; and *The Political Religions*. The Nazis confiscated the last of these works, *The Political Religions*, just as it was about to go to press. Though they attempted to arrest Voegelin, he ably escaped to the West in a rather heroic fashion, as he describes in his autobiography.

After arriving in the United States, he taught at Louisiana State University, Bennington College, and the University of Alabama. In 1958, he returned to Germany, taking a position at the University of Munich. There, however, he raised the ire of his colleagues and of the German people by explaining to them that the Nazis, though long gone, had dramatically altered the German conception of life and had woven Gnosticism and authoritarianism into the very fabric of German democracy. Asked to leave because of his views, Voegelin returned to the United States, teaching at Stanford, the University of Dallas, and the University of Notre Dame. He passed away on January 19, 1985.

Probably his best-known works among conservatives are his *The New Science of Politics* (1952), *Order and History* (1956–1987; four volumes, the fifth never completed), and his inaugural lectures at the University of Munich, *Science, Politics, and Gnosticism* (1968). Since his death, a huge series of his unpublished books has appeared under the title *History of Political Ideas* (1997–).

Beginning with his University of Chicago Lectures, the *New Science of Politics*, Voegelin built upon an idea that he had first taken from a footnote in a work written by the famous theologian Hans Urs von Balthasar. This was the idea that symbols matter. Not only how we define symbols, but how we remember them, how we appropriate them, and how we manipulate them. One might think of the Roman *fasces* — a bundle of sticks, wrapped around an axe, tied together by leather straps. As its origin, the *fasces* was the perfect symbol of a republic. All organic — the straps as well as the sticks — the community forms one man, ready to defend itself. Not made for aggression (hence, the axe at the center of the group), a republic does ably defend itself against all aggressors. In the 1910s, Mussolini deeply perverted that symbol.

This is an obvious example, of course. When it comes to words as symbols — words such as "order" or "freedom" — the manipulations become much more complicated. When the president behaves as a tyrant rather than an executive, but he does so "in the name of American democracy" or "on behalf of the American people," a clear response to him becomes confusing and difficult to find. Voegelin labeled this manipulation of symbols a form of Gnosticism, taking the name from the ancient Christian heresy. Those who manipulate, he argued, know exactly what they are doing. They are master actors and masters of deception. They call "evil" good and then ignore the word "evil." Often, though, their motives are well-intentioned, as they desire to flee from the ills and disorders of this world. It confuses and befuddles them.

Gnostics appear under many different labels, all branches rooted in the same mistakes. They can call themselves fascists, communists, National Socialists, progressives, Marxists, positivists, or psychoanalysts, but they are all the same, only varied in appearance. In one of his most famous passages, written for his University of Munich lectures, Voegelin claimed:

> The attempt at world destruction will not destroy the world, but will only increase the disorder of society. The gnostic's flight from a truly dreadful, confusing, and oppressive state of the world is understandable. But the order of the ancient world was renewed by that

movement which strove through loving action to revive
the practice of the "serious play" (to use Plato's expression) — that is, by Christianity.[2]

In essence, Voegelin believed, each of these Gnostics wanted
to murder God. The death of the spirit is the price of progress.
Nietzsche revealed this mystery of the Western apocalypse when
he announced that God was dead and that he had been murdered.
This Gnostic murder is constantly committed by the men who
sacrifice God to civilization. The more fervently all human energies are thrown into the great enterprise of salvation through
world-immanent action, the farther the human being who engages
in this enterprise moves away from the life of the spirit. And since
the life of the spirit is the source of order in man and society, the
very success of a Gnostic civilization is the cause of its decline. A
civilization can indeed advance and decline at the same time — but
not forever. There is a limit toward which this ambiguous process
moves; the limit is reached when an activist sect which represents
the Gnostic truth organizes civilization in an empire under its rule.
Totalitarianism, defined as the existential rule of Gnostic activists,
is the end form of progressive civilization.[3]

None of this should suggest that Voegelin saw only decline in
the world. He actually held out much hope for the world. The way
to combat the evils of the world is to remember. Truly, it is simply
to remember. To remember the beginning of a thing, the truth of
a thing, and the beauty and goodness of a thing. "Don't let them
immanentize the eschaton," pro-Voegelin buttons read in the 1970s.

Voegelin's Gnosticism

Voegelin believed that the ancient heresy of Gnosticism pervades
the modern world, perverting our understanding not only of

---

2   Voegelin, *Science, Politics, and Gnosticism* (Washington, DC: Regnery Gateway, 1968), 12.

3   Voegelin, *New Science of Politics* (Chicago: University of Chicago Press, 1952),
131–32.

time and history, but also of the very nature of the human person. Though we associate Gnosticism with early Christianity, especially with the warnings against the "anti-Christ" in the writings of St John the Beloved, Gnosticism first emerged in the Near East and Asian subcontinent roughly 600 years before Jesus lived. Once Jesus lived and died, however, the Gnostics saw him as the perfect vehicle to promote their own vision of the world. They didn't necessarily love Jesus, but they did see him as a popular figure whose memory and image could be manipulated for their own purposes. The Gnostic hates this world, seeing it as a trap, a means by which our soul becomes imprisoned and lost in the desires and limitations of flesh. As such, Gnosticism is inherently dualistic and anti-Incarnational. Indeed, the very idea that the flesh and the spirit could become one is the antithesis of Gnosticism, which sees the relationship of spirit and flesh as one of tyranny, mistrust, and even hatred.

As Voegelin rightly notes, for the Gnostic, man will always be an alien in this world, and he must always seek a way out. Voegelin quotes a number of ancient writings to support this: "Who has cast me into the suffering of this world?" asked the 'Great Life' — who is considered the "first, alien Life from the worlds of light."

> This world was not made according to the desire of the Life.
>> Not by the will of the Great Life art thou come hither.
>> Who conveyed me into the evil darkness?
>> Deliver us from the darkness of this world into which we are flung.
>> The wretched soul has strayed into a labyrinth of torment and wanders around without a way out....
>> It seeks to escape from the bitter chaos, but knows not how to get out.
>> Why didst thou create this world, why didst thou order the tribes here from thy midst?

As Voegelin saw it, Clement of Alexandria grasped the heresy's essence and dangers best. It is "the knowledge of who we were and what we became, of where we were and where into we have been flung, of whereto we are hastening and wherefrom we are redeemed, of what birth is and rebirth." Consequently, all Gnostic myth—and the Gnostics were, unfortunately, incredible myth-makers— revolves around stories of exile and return. In Gnostic belief, therefore, the Judeo-Christian God (not Jesus, but God the Father) is the evil one. Why? Because he delights in trapping souls in the prison of a human body, suffocating them in a physical world. The "true God," according to the Gnostics, has become hidden and alien to us. He yearns for us to love him, but we must spend our existence finding him. Thus salvation arrives in the form of ecstasies and enthusiasms, in magic, in terrorism, and in mystery cults. The true Gnostic must either embrace total sensuality, thus mocking the norms of puritanism, or he must embrace an ascetic puritan-ism, thus cleansing himself from flesh and matter. Terrorism for the Gnostic is also good, as it is simply violence against the evils of the material.

Those who discover the means of salvation—through secret words, symbol-covered garments, or a sequence of words—share these secrets, these keys to heaven, only with the few, the elect.

The goal of the Gnostic in this world becomes one of re-ordering, of remaking the world according to his own vision that the material is evil and the spirit is good. Gnostics of whatever variety desire to reorder man, history, and society, all of which have been tradi-tionally unjust. Through Gnostic man's creative power, he has the ability and the duty to recreate the world as just and perfect. Nearly any inhumane means becomes justifiable to the Gnostic, since the flesh is evil. Killing, for example, becomes perfectly acceptable for the Gnostic. It releases not only the individual soul trapped in the body, but also reminds the remaining population of the dangers and limitations of the flesh.

Most importantly, Voegelin notes, all Gnostics must murder God, whether symbolically or actually. Of modern Gnostic prophets (not actors), Voegelin argued, the most important by far was Friedrich Nietzsche. As usual, Voegelin supports this contention with a series of quotations from the German philosopher:

> To rule, and to be no longer a servant of a god: this
> means was left behind to ennoble man.
>
> Alas, my brothers, that God whom I created was
> human world and human madness, like all gods.
>
> What you called "the world" shall be created only
> by you: it shall be your reason, your image, your will,
> your love.
>
> If there were gods, how could I endure not being a
> god! Therefore, there are no gods.

Just as Paul Elmer More and Christopher Dawson had argued,
Voegelin saw Nietzsche as the most important figure for modern
Gnosticism. While some scholars have blamed Nietzsche for the
rise of modern German nationalism, National Socialism, and other
evils, Voegelin argued that this analysis entirely misses the fact of
Nietzsche's Gnosticism. We must dismiss, he argues, the notion that
Nietzsche in some way caused the problems of modernity — "the
very popular magical belief, of which Nietzsche like many other
political thinkers has been a victim, that the political analyst who
predicts an event is the cause of the event."[4]

Instead, Nietzsche is simply the greatest prophet of the modern
world. In 1886, Friedrich Nietzsche wrote: "The greatest event of
recent times — that 'God is Dead,' that the belief in the Christian
God is no longer tenable — is beginning to cast its first shadows
over Europe."[5] Despiritualized, Nietzsche continued, "our whole
European civilization is moving with a torture of tension, which
increases from decade to decade, toward a catastrophe." Nietzsche
wrote this three decades before World War I. Strangely enough,
considering the de-spiritualization of Europe, the mad philosopher
argued that the coming destruction would result from a "war of
the spirits."[6]

---

4   Eric Voegelin, "Nietzsche, The Crisis and War," *Journal of Politics* 6 (May
1944): 177.
5   Quoted in Voegelin, *New Science of Politics.*
6   Quoted in Voegelin, "Nietzsche, The Crisis and War," 180–81.

To confront the Gnostic idea, now deeply ingrained in all of modern and postmodern society, man must rediscover and reembrace the ancient verities of Socrates and Dante and the American founders.

Voegelin's order

No creature in all of creation has it as hard as do we humans. Being flesh as well as spirit, humans share in the natures of both the animals and of the angels. Unlike either, however, the human has free will in time. We choose good or ill at every moment of our lives. Animals, merely creatures of instinct, react to pleasure, pain, and the call of the herd. Angels, beings purely of the spirit, make one initial choice, knowing that that one choice predetermines all the others.

Physically incarnate souls, humans exist within the Great Chain of Being — the hierarchy connecting all things from God to the lowest aspect of creation — as the *metaxy*, the in-between. Because of these two vital aspects of the human person, and because of the glorious burden of free will, we humans often make horrible mistakes. That is, we get the balance of flesh and spirit wrong. We tend — individually and as a group — to veer toward one aspect of our being while ignoring the other. In some ages, we focus too much on the material aspect of things. In other times, we place inordinate emphasis on the spiritual aspect. At this moment in history, we are clearly in a phase of extreme materialism. The goal of all aspects of human life — from procreation and the family to economics and government — should be to find the balance of spirit and flesh and to live according to that balance.

Given this thought, Voegelin served as one of the single most important defenders of the Heraclitan ideal of the Logos as that which brings harmony and order to all things. In this defense he shares much in common with many others, ranging from T.S. Eliot to Russell Kirk to Pope Benedict (who greatly admired Voegelin and as a young man met with him).

Raised a Christian, Voegelin's personal faith shifted radically in and out of existence, drifted near and around orthodoxy, and ended (so it seemed) in some extreme heterodoxy. At best, we can state that Voegelin's Logos was certainly Heraclitus' Logos. Whether it was also St John's Logos is a matter of debate. Though nominally Lutheran as a young man, Voegelin continued to reject aspects of orthodoxy toward his later years, even dismissing many of St Paul's writings as Manichean and thus illegitimate.

To return to the point made previously — that humans must balance spirit and flesh — Voegelin believed that humans must intentionally search for a proper, cosmic, and earthly understanding of order as Natural Law. Once they have rediscovered such understandings as far as humanly possible, they must order their own communities at whatever level based on the order they perceive to be true.

For better or worse, Voegelin frequently discussed such ideas either by employing archaic language or by inventing neoterisms, so great was his dislike of the corruptions of modern language. On government, he writes:

> To set up a government is an essay in world creation. Out of a shapeless vastness of conflicting human desires rises a little world of order, a cosmic analogy, a cosmion, leading a precarious life under the pressure of destructive forces from within and without, and maintaining its existence by the ultimate threat and application of violence against the internal breaker of its law as well as the external aggressor. The application of violence, though, is the ultimate means only of creating and preserving a political order, it is not its ultimate reason: the function proper of order is the creation of a shelter in which man may give to his life a semblance of meaning.[7]

For such a government to be something more than a mechanism

---

7 Voegelin, *History of Political Ideas*, vol. 1 (Baton Rouge, LA: University of Louisiana Press, 1989), 225. Brackets appear in original as means to illustrate Voegelin's own edits.

or means to fulfill human desire, it must function as something
organic and meaningful rather than as merely utilitarian.

> But the utilitarian argument, while not being without
> sense in justifying a political order, does not reach the
> emotional center of the [cosmion], this center being the
> desire to create a world of meaning out of these human
> [emotions/aspirations/appetites] and desires, such as the
> desire for procreation and to outlive the fragmentary
> personal life by a projection into the life of [emotion and
> character] or of a more comprehensive tribal or national
> group; the desire to give the questionable achievements
> of an individual life an added meaning by weaving it into
> the texture of group achievement.[8]

Fearful that such a government—working for the common good
rather than the greater good of the people—will acquiesce to the
problems of this world without necessarily trying to solve them
(think, in particular, of an issue such as war: why can't we all just get
along?), opposition will certainly arise in any society. The radicals
(really Gnostics who might or might not realize they are Gnostics)
will demand the perfection of society even at the cost of order and
harmony, which they now see as "privilege" for the few—an excuse
for authority to have authority.

> When the evocative power of an idea has been seriously
> shattered under the pressure of disenchanting analysis
> it may shade off into the twilight of an ideology. A fur-
> ther class of ideas are the utopian dreams. They occur
> frequently in history since there are always men who
> wish to overcome the misery of the finite imperfection
> of the political cosmion by the invention of an order of
> intrinsic value that would settle definitely the struggle
> of the evocative forces. Dreams of this kind, openly or

---

8 Voegelin, *History of Political Ideas*, 1:226.

silently, that one or the other of the essentials of human nature [with need for] change can eliminate from a social order. The elimination of an essential feature of human nature may be said to define technically a utopia. And, finally, men have cherished the idea of abolishing political order altogether and [living] in an anarchic community.... The problem of politics has to be considered in the larger setting of an interpretation of human nature. [9]

Voegelin considers all descent of a properly ordered society as an aspect of misremembering (whether by ignorance or intentional misdirection) and as a form of Gnosticism. That is, man decides that the order he can imagine is greater and more important than the one that nature has given us.

The solution for Voegelin? Anamnesis. To remember. To wash away the corruption that has adhered to words and meanings and to return — through great difficulty, as always — to first principles, right order, and the natural law. The historical success of such endeavors, however, has proven suspect at best. When the Athenians collapsed, Socrates tried to remind them of first principles. They killed him. When Western Europe collapsed during the Reformation, Luther tried to prevent it while Calvin revolutionized its collapse. When Britain began to collapse in the eighteenth century, George Washington led the most successful return to right order in the modern world.

Yet since the French Revolution, Voegelin believed, the Gnostics have grown even more cunning, more hateful and more willing to try anything in order to destroy natural law and right reason. They assassinate leaders, kill civilians in terrorist attacks, and undermine thought in the academy. There's no conspiracy, but there has been a groundswell.

And yet, despite serious losses over the last two centuries to those who desire disorder, man is never powerless. After all, Voegelin argued in his magisterial four-and-a-half volume history of

---

9 Voegelin, *History of Political Ideas*, 1:231.

Western civilization, *Order and History*, participation of being — that is, embracing full humanity, spirit and flesh — is vital to our entire existence. Therefore, our search for order must always exist on the "edge of freedom and necessity."[10] Man, Voegelin reminds us so beautifully, is never blind to the highest things of life. Indeed, it is this very sight and remembrance of the highest things that is the fundamental truth of being human.

---

10   Voegelin, *Order and History*, 1.

15

Flannery O'Connor

MOST CATHOLICS PROBABLY KNOW A great deal about Flannery O'Connor. They know she wrote southern gothic fiction, including several brilliant short stories and a few excellent novels. They know she suffered from a debilitating disease and died far too young. They might even know that she and Russell Kirk deeply admired one another. Almost certainly, they know that she was a devout and practicing Catholic.

What many may not realize, though, is that she was also profoundly conversant in the Christian humanism of her day. She not only analyzed and commented on it but promoted it wherever she could, particularly in her diocesan newspapers, *The Bulletin* and *The Southern Cross*. In 1983, the University of Georgia published a collection of her 1956–1964 reviews under the title *The Presence of Grace*. This might very well be the least known of O'Connor's books. Thankfully though, the press keeps it in print. If you're reading this book, I suggest you stop and order this gem immediately. Then, of course, return to your reading.

During her reviewing years from 1956 to 1964, she reviewed over 140 separate titles in roughly 120 articles. She reviewed everything from hagiography to philosophy to theology to biography to fiction. Each review is short, ranging from a mere paragraph (say 100 words), to several paragraphs for a total of nearly 300 words. Not surprisingly, O'Connor excelled at writing about profound things with much precision. The authors she reviewed serve as a "who's who" of the Christian (and of course, Jewish) humanism of the mid-twentieth century: Etienne Gilson, Romano Guardini, Baron von Hügel, Russell Kirk, Ronald Knox, Evelyn Waugh, François

Mauriac, Wyndam Lewis, Karl Adam, Louis Bouyer, Edith Stein, Frank Sheed, Henri De Lubac, Martin D'Arcy, Maisie Ward, and Charles Péguy. Not surprisingly, she favored the most Catholic and conservative of presses in her reviews: Regnery, Sheed and Ward, and Newman Club. She reviewed some non-Judeo-Christian allies and fellow travelers, too, including Eric Voegelin. One can only imagine what her fellow parishioners must have thought of her. Had they taken her suggestions to heart, Georgian Catholics might very well have been the most educated Americans of the late 1950s and early 1960s. Indeed, any enterprising bookseller should explore the used book stores of Georgia today. She or he will most likely find a number of well-preserved treasures.

As she reviewed, O'Connor personally built up a solid base and understanding of the Christian humanist movement. This is clear from her later reviews, many of which follow threads and continuities of the previous works and authors considered. Her reviews — quite naturally, given her character — are as witty as they are insightful. At times she could be outright brilliant; at other times, mischievous; and, every once in a while, humorous.

In her review of Russell Kirk's most Christian humanist book, *Beyond the Dreams of Avarice* from 1956, O'Connor admitted that even Samuel Johnson — from whom the title is derived — would recognize himself in Kirk, resurrected for the twentieth century. He would also admire the man and his works "for their thought and the vigor with which [the ideas are] expressed." More than any other figure of her day, O'Connor wrote, "Mr Kirk has managed in a succession of books which have proved both scholarly and popular to do both [sc., to accept divine truth and to rethink human truth] and to make the voice of an intelligent and vigorous conservative thought respected in this country." Kirk, of course, received such praise with great delight.

O'Connor found Romano Guardini more perplexing. Though devoid of ridiculous and tapioca pieties, the great German-Italian thinker and priest plodded along in his writing as if he had all the time in the world. She never stopped reading him, however, finding that if one is willing to be patient with the scholar, he reveals much of real piety and Christian intelligence. She reviewed his books more than those of any other author during this period.

It was Father Louis Bouyer, she believed, who had succeeded in writing properly and perceptively about Protestantism with his 1956 *Spirit and Forms of Protestantism.* Too many Catholics, O'Connor lamented, wrote narrowly about Protestantism, always devolving into polemic. Not Father Bouyer, though.

O'Connor gushes over Eric Voegelin, claiming his first three volumes of *Order and History* to be superior to all other attempts to write a philosophy of history. His vision, she argues, is not one of cycles, but one of true progress — the progress of humanity toward an acceptance of God. Thus real history does not seek civilization but faith. Acceptance of faith allowed man to finally become fully human, "a leap in being." The reviewer does caution her readers, however, that Voegelin's works contain long passages that will be of interest only to the most specialized scholars. Still, one has to wonder — how many Georgian Catholics had Voegelin on their bookshelves?

Charles Péguy, she argues, not only reconciled liberty and order for a generation of confused and conflicted French, but also served as one of the most important twentieth-century figures responsible for the current Christian humanist revival in arts and letters.

Perhaps O'Connor's most moving review is that of St Edith Stein's *The Science of the Cross.* Stein, a Carmelite nun who converted from Judaism, best embodied the spirit of St John of the Cross for the twentieth century. Perhaps she even bested John himself. As a highly trained philosopher, Stein combined intense piety with intense intellect, aware that her life under the Nazis led inevitably toward martyrdom. Given her own abilities and physical debilities, O'Connor must have identified strongly with the German-Catholic-Jewess.

O'Connor's *Presence of Grace* is, simply put, a delight and a treasure. It is the kind of book you can read not just once, but over and over. It is truly a work of Christian meditations, of prayers of the intellect.

Not only was O'Connor one of the single most important Christian humanists of the twentieth century — the century of Hell

incarnate — but she also understood what defined Christian humanism. While Christian humanism might very well be conservative,
it was always imaginative, allowing one to imagine what must be
conserved. Like all Christian humanists, O'Connor embraced intellect, piety, and, when necessary, suffering.

16

Clyde Kilby

*U*NLESS YOU'RE FAMILIAR WITH THE EXCEL-
lent Wade Center, chances are good you've never heard
of Clyde S. Kilby (1902–1986), a professor of English at
Wheaton College from 1935 until his retirement in 1981. We should
possess nothing short of piety for Kilby. While he did not make
C.S. Lewis or J.R.R. Tolkien household names, he was arguably the
first American scholar to recognize the literary merit of both men
when popular culture had claimed them exclusively as its own.
Kilby read and analyzed their works, taught courses on them, and
visited them rather frequently in England. A decade younger than
Tolkien but only three years younger than Lewis, he was, for all
intents and purposes, of their generation. He was also a practicing
Christian and a conservative — both things rare in academia, even
in the 1950s and 1960s.

Equally of note, Kilby was rather openly a Christian humanist.
While this might not seem strange to those of us who are reading
this book, it was very strange for a man teaching at Wheaton in the
1950s and 1960s. Why? Because almost every prominent Christian
humanist — from Jacques Maritain to T.S. Eliot — was very high
church and almost always some form of Catholic. Kilby was an
evangelical Protestant.

I first read his 1976 book, *Tolkien and the Silmarillion*, in the late
summer of 1988, preparing for my first ever academic writing on
Tolkien. I was 20, a junior at Notre Dame, and just beginning one
of the best classes I ever took, "Science Fiction and Philosophy." It
was taught by a rather famous Platonist who just also happened
to love Lewis and Tolkien. Though I read anything and everything
like a fiend as a young boy and young man (and still do), literary

criticism was foreign to me in 1988. From an autobiographical standpoint, Kilby's book hit me because it was my first encounter with any form of real criticism. It also hit me because I realized that Kilby really understood Tolkien. He knew him. And when he didn't understand some aspect of Tolkien, he admitted it. I loved Kilby for these qualities — his humility, his honesty, and his enthusiasm. For what it's worth, I've tried very hard to emulate these qualities in everything I've read and taught.

After rereading Kilby's *Tolkien and the Silmarillion*, I looked up several reviews of the book. As I feared, if it hasn't been entirely forgotten, it has been dismissed as dated. True, hundreds of books and thousands of articles about Tolkien have come out since Kilby published the book in 1976. Only a year after the release of *Tolkien and the Silmarillion*, *The Silmarillion* (the actual one) appeared for the first time in print. Since then, *Unfinished Tales* and twelve volumes of the *History of Middle-earth* have been published, as well as a number of Tolkien's longer pieces on Beowulf, the Volsunga, and King Arthur. In other words, in the first third of the twenty-first century, we have so much literary archeology to dig through that we Tolkien lovers are simply overwhelmed.

Yet Kilby understood Tolkien, and just as importantly, he appreciated him. In the early 1960s, after he had come to know Tolkien and Lewis, Kilby offered his services as a fan and as a literary critic to help Tolkien get *The Silmarillion* into publishable shape.

> But for the encouragement of C. S. Lewis I do not think that I should ever have completed or offered for publication *The Lord of the Rings*. *The Silmarillion* is quite different, and if good at all, good in quite another way, and I do not really know what to make of it. It began in hospital and sick-leave (1916–1917) and has been with me ever since, and is now in a confused state, having been altered, enlarged, and worked out, at intervals between then and now. If I had the assistance of a scholar at once sympathetic and yet critical, such as yourself, I feel I might make some of it publishable. It

needs the actual presence of a friend and advisor at one's side, which is just what you offer.[1]

When Tolkien gladly accepted Kilby's offer, the Wheaton professor departed for Oxford, spending the summer of 1966 reading through the mass of stories that make up the first and second ages of Middle-earth. Kilby stayed just a few blocks away from the Tolkien home, walking there daily for the entire summer to work on the manuscripts. Often he would talk with Tolkien and his wife, but more often, he dug through the mass of manuscripts. Outside of Tolkien's closest friends and family, Kilby was the first person to see any part of *The Silmarillion,* which serves as the entire basis and background for the better-known *The Hobbit* and *The Lord of the Rings.*

Tolkien and the Silmarillion is a memoir of Kilby's work in 1966. Far from outdated (though I wasn't even born when it was written), the book offers incredible insight into Tolkien the man and Tolkien the myth-maker. Kilby realized immediately that Tolkien was not only utterly brilliant, but also equally and utterly disorganized. Tolkien's life, the life of an academic, was a good and happy one, but his scholarship and fiction were in complete disarray. Manuscripts abounded, all in various stages of completion or incompletion. Rather than edit his original manuscripts, thus marking and editing a single document, Tolkien began every creative work anew, taking the best of what he'd already written but beginning again from scratch. Often, manuscripts would conflict, with some parts from manuscript A appearing in C, but not in B. Additionally — and I think this is a critical point about Tolkien — he mixed all of his work together. Academic articles and research, fictional manuscripts from Middle-earth, poetry (original and otherwise), bestiaries, illustrations, maps, and translations of great works by ancient authors freely mixed with one another. When Kilby offered to archive the material in a proper and organized fashion, Tolkien balked! Never again would he find anything, should Kilby do such a thing.

---

1   Tolkien to Clyde Kilby, dated December 1965, and reprinted/transcribed in *Tolkien and the Silmarillion,* 17.

In between his descriptions of what was then unpublished in Tolkien's mythology, Kilby reveals much about Tolkien's personality. He was hilarious, fast-talking, fastidious in dress, emotional, devoted to his wife, children, and grandchildren, animated, and passionate. He was also opinionated, mocking poor scholarship and those who pretended to know him and his work. Yet he did even these uncharitable things with a twinkle in his eye and a mischievous manner. In no particular order, he loved gardening, found trees to have distinct personalities, and devoured everything he could find in the field of science fiction and mysteries. At times during conversation, he would break into Elvish song. He despised modern technology and the swarms of bureaucrats who never diminished in size while seeking to conform all things to their own image — especially in education. He despised no academic field more than psychology, and he blamed its rise in the 1920s for the current destruction of Western civilization.

Tolkien and the Silmarillion is far from outdated, and it should never have been forgotten. Unfortunately, the published version (the only published version) from 1976 is only 89 pages long. Happily, however, the Wade Center at Wheaton and the archives at Marquette University have the unpublished chapters from the book. These chapters are every bit as good as those actually published. One chapter describes Tolkien and Lewis as the last true men of the West.

Here's one representative and fascinating passage not published:

> Worst of all briar patches was what he persistently regarded as the spiritual decay of our times and particularly of his own Roman Catholic church, of which he was a longtime and devout member. The Church, he said, "which once felt like a refuge now feels like a trap." He was appalled that even the sacred Eucharist might be attended by "dirty youths, women in trousers and often with their hair unkempt and uncovered" and, what was worse, the grievous suffering given by "stupid, tired, dimmed, and even bad priests." An anecdote I have heard

involved his attendance at mass not long after Vatican II. An expert in Latin, he had reluctantly composed himself to its abolishment in favor of English. But when he arrived next time at services and seated himself in the middle of a bench, he began to notice other changes than the language, one a diminution of genuflection. His disappointment was such that he rose up and made his way awkwardly to the aisle and there made three very low bows, then stomped out of the church.[2]

At Christopher Tolkien's request, Kilby also omitted his chapter that summed up the story of *The Silmarillion*. Christopher's request is understandable given that Tolkien's reputation had not yet emerged in proper academic circles, and no one quite knew how a book as dense as *The Silmarillion* might do. It was also then only a year away from publication in its full and official form. It seems ridiculous to imagine in the first third of the twenty-first century, but there was a long period during which Tolkien's reputation remained in doubt.

Kilby's summation of the story offers some fascinating insights into Tolkien's world. In particular, Kilby focused on a discussion between an Elf and a human wise woman. The conversation deals with the possible Incarnation of Eru (God the Father) in the world. How could an author enter into his book without exploding it? How could God enter into His creation without destroying it? Tolkien had written a note on the manuscript of the conversation stating — in no uncertain terms — that this conversation must serve as a central part of the final, published version of *The Silmarillion*. I can state without exaggeration that this conversation explains and describes the Incarnation more expertly and with more beauty than anything I've ever read (with the important exception of T.S. Eliot's "Little Gidding"). And yet, pick up your copy of *The Silmarillion*. Thumb through it, and you'll see no such conversation. As

2 Unpublished parts of *Tolkien and the Silmarillion*, Wade Center, Wheaton College.

literary heir, Christopher chose to exclude all explicit theological and philosophical discussions, focusing instead on the mythological narrative of the story. This vital conversation that reveals so much about Tolkien and his mythology did not see print until volume 10 of the *History of Middle-earth: Morgoth's Ring*.

Most importantly, though, Kilby's *Tolkien and the Silmarillion* reveals the depth of Christianity found in Tolkien's mythology. I will make two points here, each vital to understanding Tolkien's theological convictions. First, Tolkien admitted to Kilby in conversation that summer that the "Secret Fire" was, indeed, the Holy Spirit. Thus, when Gandalf confronts the Balrog in Moria, his "I am a servant of the Secret Fire," is no more and no less than an invocation of the Third Person of the Most Blessed Trinity. Additionally, Kilby asked Tolkien about the role of Christ in *The Lord of the Rings*, to which the author admitted that the offices of Christ appear as symbol but not allegory: Frodo is priest; Gandalf is prophet; and Aragorn is king. This, of course, stands in great contrast to Lewis's Aslan.

Kilby must have been a rather humorous person, and one finds little treasures in his memoirs from that summer as well. Little treasures that make his visit seem very real. As one example, Kilby received letters of encouragement from the States, as revealed in his personal letters, collected at Wheaton College. "A letter received today (July 30) from one of my friends in New York says: 'We're all saying prayers and lighting votive candles for the early appearance of the SILMARILLION. Tell JRRT his following is no longer a cult. It is a zeitgeist. He is determining the frame of mind of a whole university generation.'" As many saw it, Kilby's work would make or break Tolkien's reputation.

Kilby even saw *The Sound of Music* in the movie theater during that summer. His ticket stub is still stuck in his notes on *The Silmarillion*.

17

Friedrich Hayek's Intellectual Lineage

W HEN FRIEDRICH HAYEK ANNOUNCED HIS personal political philosophy as an "unrepentant Old Whig" in his magnum opus *Constitution of Liberty*, he was reaching deep into the well of the Greco-Roman and Judeo-Christian traditions. This despite the fact that he had originally spoken these words against his friend, Russell Kirk, in their famous Mont Pelerin debate of 1957.[1] While the Old Whigs founded themselves rather spontaneously as a coherent movement during the 1680s in England, they drew their inheritance and patrimony from the great republican and Stoic thinkers of the Occident. As did other liberally-educated persons of his generation, Hayek frequently referenced the great thinkers of the ancient world, especially Aristotle and Cicero, in his own works. Of course, he also cited a number of other thinkers who helped develop the Whig and republican movements during the Glorious Revolution of 1688, including James Harrington, Algernon Sidney, and John Locke. Finally, he discussed later intellectuals, including Commonwealth men such as John Trenchard and Thomas Gordon, Edmund Burke, Adam Smith, James Madison, Alexis de Tocqueville, and Lord Acton. Hayek rightfully viewed himself as in a line of succession with these profound social critics and philosophers.[2]

1   On their relationship, see Birzer, "More Than 'Irritable Mental Gestures': Russell Kirk's Challenge to Liberalism, 1950–1960," *Humanitas* (2008): 64–86.

2   This is not to imply that Hayek accepted the complete corpus of each thinker's beliefs, of course. He took issue, for example, with Aristotle several times. See Friedrich A. Hayek, "The Results of Human Action but Not of Human Design," chapter in Richard M. Ebeling, ed., *Austrian Economics: A Reader* (Hillsdale,

While Hayek openly rejected the label "conservative," he did find and identify with many of the same heroes of the past as did self-professed conservatives such as Kirk and R. A. Nisbet. Indeed, with the very important exceptions of Locke, Mill, and Acton, the primary influences on all three men were nearly identical. That Hayek came from Central Europe and Kirk and Nisbet from America probably helps explain, in many ways, the desire on Hayek's part to avoid the label of "conservatism." Its American (and English) manifestation was quite different from the continental variety. Hayek, of course, knew its twentieth-century English and American types, but he had seen much in Europe that almost certainly shaped his distaste for the term "conservative."

Regardless, I think it's critically important that those of us not on the ideological left give Hayek his due as a thinker and as a man. While Hayek has much to tell us about many things (he was, after all, accomplished in philosophy, economics, law, and psychology), I'll offer just two of his most important ideas: the necessity of voluntary community, and the fatal conceit.

Hayek argued that while "each man knows his interests best," one's gifts should be used in community, where reason is "tested and corrected by others."[3] Daniel Rush Finn has done an excellent job of contrasting Hayek's and John Paul II's economics in his 1999 article, "The Economic Personalism of John Paul II: Neither Right nor Left," so I won't try to rehash that or make the attempt to claim that Hayek's understanding is fully commensurate with Catholic social teaching.[4] It's clearly not, though John Paul II held Hayek in great respect. John Paul even consulted Hayek on some issues in 1980.

Hayek's views on community and the role of the individual within community are very Western, if not completely Catholic. What follows is a very long passage from Hayek, but I think it's worth quoting all of it:

MI: Hillsdale College Press, 1991), 134; and Hayek, *The Fatal Conceit* (Chicago: University of Chicago Press, 1988), 48.

3   Hayek, "Individualism: True and False," 15.

4   Daniel Rush Finn, "The Economic Personalism of John Paul II: Neither Right nor Left," *Journal of Markets and Morality* 2 (Spring 1999): 74–87.

This entails certain corollaries on which true individualism once more stands in sharp opposition to the false individualism of the rationalistic type.

The first is that the deliberately organized state on the one side, and the individual on the other, far from being regarded as the only realities, which all the intermediate formations and associations are to be deliberately suppressed, as was the aim of the French Revolution, the noncompulsory conventions of social intercourse are considered as essential factors in preserving the orderly working of human society. The second is that the individual, in participating in the social processes, must be ready and willing to adjust himself to changes and to submit to conventions which are not the result of intelligent design, whose justification in the particular instance may not be recognizable, and which to him will often appear unintelligible and irrational.

I need not say much on the first point. That true individualism affirms the value of the family and all the common efforts of the small community and group, that it believes in local autonomy and voluntary associations, and that indeed its case rests largely on the contention that much for which the coercive action of the state is usually invoked can be done better by voluntary collaboration need not be stressed further. There can be no greater contrast to this than the false individualism which wants to dissolve all these smaller groups into atoms which have no cohesion other than the coercive rules imposed by the state, and which tries to make all social ties prescriptive, instead of using the state mainly as a protection of the individual against the arrogation of coercive powers by the small groups.

Quite as important for the functioning of an individualist society as these smaller groupings of men are the traditions and conventions which evolve in a free society and which, without being enforceable, establish

flexible but normally observed rules that make the
behavior of other people predictable in a high degree.
The willingness to submit to such rules, not merely so
long as one understands the reason for them but so
long as one has no definite reasons to the contrary, is
an essential condition for the gradual evolution and
improvement of the rules of social intercourse; and
the readiness ordinarily to submit to the products of
a social process which nobody may understand is also
an indispensable condition if it is to be possible to dis-
pense with compulsion. That the existence of common
conventions and traditions among a group of people will
enable them to work together smoothly and efficiently
with much less formal organization and compulsion
than a group without such common background, is, of
course, a commonplace. But the reverse of this, while
less familiar, is probably not less true: that coercion can
probably only be kept to a minimum in a society where
conventions and traditions have made the behavior of
man to a large extent predictable.[5]

Hayek's understanding, after all, agrees with Aristotle's (and
St Paul's and Marcus Aurelius's) belief that "man is by nature an
animal intended to live in a polis." That is, man must employ his
particular gifts within community to make and render them meaningful.[6] Hayek was anti-utopian regarding this, however. Man is a
"very irrational and fallible being," Hayek wrote, "whose individual
errors are corrected only in the course of the social process."[7] The
market process, and consequently the social process, help attenuate the problems of man's inherent flaws, but they do not erase
them or make man somehow good. The system of private property
rewards virtue and punishes vice (at least to a great extent), and

    5 Hayek, "Individualism: True and False," chapter in *Individualism and Economic
Order* (Chicago: University of Chicago Press, 1948), 22–24.
    6 Aristotle, *The Politics*, Book I.
    7 Hayek, "Individualism: True and False," 8–9.

allows entrepreneurs to try and fail and try again. As an additional advantage, private property also brings a considerable amount of harmony to a community. In this, Hayek sounds as much like Adam Smith as he does like Burke. As the great Anglo-Irish statesman had argued, commerce reconciled "conflicting interests without giving one group power to make their views and interests always prevail over those of others."[8] But it was more to Bernard Mandeville and Adam Smith that Hayek turned, arguing that commerce and virtue were not incompatible. Certainly, Mandeville and Smith each recognized that man is fallible. One can neither reshape nor redesign the human person.

One significant difference between Hayek and his republican and Whig ancestors is that the Nobel-prize winning economist believed democracy to be a strong safeguard against tyranny.[9] Most seventeenth- and eighteenth-century republican and Old Whig thinkers abhorred democracy as nothing more than mob rule. Certainly Plato challenged the concept in *The Republic*, arguing that democracy always devolves into the leadership of a morally suspect tyrant, because this tyrant represents the lowest common denominator. The people are too easily swayed by their emotions and passions, foregoing their rationality for the sake of the moment.[10] As with most of those in the Whig tradition, though, Hayek did call for balance within government, as well as argue for strict limitations on the actual functions of government.[11]

We should return to Hayek's relationship with Tocqueville. Hayek, as noted above, saw himself as a de Tocquevillian, and he especially advanced Tocqueville's arguments regarding the voluntary association. It is only through voluntary association, whether in the private (that is, market) or the independent sector, that society experiences true progress. As Hayek wrote, paraphrasing the

---

8   Hayek, "Individualism: True and False," 13.

9   Hayek, *The Constitution of Liberty* [1960] (Chicago: University of Chicago Press, 1978), 403.

10   Plato, *The Republic* (New York: Oxford University Press, 1993), 293–302.

11   See, for example, Hayek, *Law, Liberty, and Legislation*, vol. 3: *The Political Order of a Free People* (Chicago: University of Chicago, 1979), especially chapter 13.

eighteenth-century Scot Adam Ferguson, society develops not by human design, but rather by human action.[12] When man acts alone, he acts with only limited knowledge. This natural restriction applies equally to the entrepreneur and the politician. Hayek explained:

> This is the constitutional limitation of man's knowledge and interests, the fact that he *cannot* know more than a tiny part of the whole of society and that therefore all that can enter into his motives are the immediate effects which his actions will have in the sphere he knows.[13]

Because the world is so complex, it is only through human action, rather than human design, that societies grow, evolve, and truly progress.[14] Indeed, Hayek concluded, it is the knowledge problem and the price system that allow for a division of labor, and hence a civilization, to occur.[15]

Hayek's second great contribution to the understanding of republicanism and Whiggery is his argument that, by trying to create heaven on earth, man will instead create a hell. Hayek called this the "Fatal Conceit" — the belief that an individual can reshape the world in his own image, overturning centuries of finely-evolved history, morality, and philosophy.

In the modern world, one may trace the origins of the "Fatal Conceit" and its resulting widespread destruction of lives to the French Revolution. Burke described it well: "Have we not produced it ready made and ready armed, mature in its birth, a perfect goddess of wisdom and of war, hammered by our blacksmith midwives out of the brain of Jupiter itself?"[16] In turn, the goddess will devour its creators.

---

12   Hayek, "The Meaning of Competition," in Ebeling, ed., *Austrian Economics: A Reader*, 264–80.

13   Hayek, "Individualism: True and False," 14.

14   Hayek, "The Use of Knowledge in Society," *American Economic Review* 35 (September 1945): 519–30; and Hayek, "The Results of Human Action but Not of Human Design" chapter in Ebeling, ed., *Austrian Economics: A Reader*, 134–49.

15   Hayek, "Use of Knowledge in Society," 528–29.

16   Burke, "An Appeal from the New to the Old Whigs," in *Reflections on the Revolution*, 92.

At the end of the nineteenth century, many thinkers in the Whig tradition feared the twin intellectual evils of their time, nationalism and socialism. They rightly feared that these evils, either individually or intertwined, would wreak widespread destruction upon the world of the twentieth century. Whig historian Lord Acton stressed that the end of Christendom and Western ideals would mean the rise of nationalism. "Christianity rejoices at the mixture of races," he wrote in his famed essay, "Nationalism." Paganism, however, "identifies itself with their differences, because truth is universal, errors various and particular." Though he wrote in 1862, Acton seems to have understood that a Nietzsche would soon arise "by making the State and the nation commensurate with each other in theory." Those deemed inferior, the historian argued, will be "exterminated, or reduced to servitude, or outlawed, or put in a condition of dependence."[17] Hayek made a similar point in his December 1945 lecture in Dublin:

> Whether even the small countries will escape will depend on whether they keep free from the poison of nationalism, which is both an inducement to, and a result of, that same striving for a society which is consciously organized from the top.... Nationalism ... is but a twin brother of socialism.[18]

The twentieth century — whether described as fatally conceited or Nietzschean — has witnessed the greatest shedding of blood of any century in world history. The sheer numbers of those killed by their own governments are simply mind-boggling. According to demographer and political scientist R.J. Rummel, governments murdered nearly 170 million citizens between 1901 and 1987. The Soviet Union slaughtered 62 million; China nearly 45 million (Mao and Chang Kai Check taken together); and National Socialist

---

17 John Emerich Edward Dalberg-Acton, *Essays in the History of Liberty* (Indianapolis: Liberty Fund, 1986), 409–33.

18 Hayek, *Individualism and Economic Order*, 28.

Germany 21 million. By contrast, war took the lives of "only" 35 million between 1901 and 1987.[19] More recent estimates show these figures to be much higher — roughly 205 million executed by their own states, another 50 million killed in war.

Progressives, Hayek argued, hate the natural order and the natural law. They demand that "everything must be tidily planned" by an "all-powerful central government."[20] Ironically, their attempt to create order only begets severe and violent disorder, the shattering of the soul and of the world.

Hayek was not a conservative, though. "Conservatism is bound by the stock of ideas inherited at a given time," Hayek feared. "And since it does not really believe in the power of argument, its last resort is generally a claim to superior wisdom, based on some self-arrogated superior quality." Hayek did praise conservatives for their ability to create and defend "spontaneously grown institutions such as language, law, morals, and conventions." But their victories lay in the past, he believed. Today's conservatives, Hayek argued, "lack the courage to welcome the same undesigned change from which new tools of human endeavors will emerge."

As anti-ideologues, we take the good — that which is timeless — from each man. Hayek had more than most to offer us, and his words will certainly continue to shape, limit, and inspire throughout the twenty-first century. If we want to change our society, our laws, our culture, and our government; if we want to prevent the big government conservatives, the neo-conservatives, and the militaristic liberals from continuing to shape the world according to their unholy wills, then we probably don't have the right to dismiss an ally such as Hayek.

I'll give Hayek the last words:

> To the accepted Christian tradition that man must be
> free to follow his conscience in moral matters if *his*

---

19   R.J. Rummel, *Death by Government* (New Brunswick, NJ: Transaction Press, 1994). See also Stephane Courtois, et al., *The Black Book of Communism: Crimes, Terror, Repression* (Cambridge, MA: Harvard University Press, 1999).
20   Hayek, "Individualism: True and False," 27.

actions are to be of any merit, the economists added the further argument that *he* should be free to make full use of his knowledge and skill, that *he* must be allowed to be guided by *his* concern for the particular things of which *he* knows and for which *he* cares, if *he* is to make as great a contribution to the common purposes of society as he is capable of making.[21]

---

21 Hayek, *Individualism and Economic Order*, 14.

18

Ray Bradbury at His End

ONE OF THE HARDEST THINGS I'VE HAD TO assess in my professional life as a historian and a biographer is just how much to take seriously in a person's life. I consider, pass, and render judgments on a moment-by-moment basis! Judge not, lest you be judged. Oh boy. I'm in trouble. I must always ask: how much do I credit something said on day X versus something said on day Y? I can assure you, it's not easy. One of the many things I love about biographers such as Joseph Pearce and Steve Hayward and David McCullough is that they take chances. The biographer is not a mere antiquarian, but an observer, one who must place his own being within the soul, eyes, and brain of his subject. It was very difficult with Kirk. He had a great fondness for self-proclaimed individualists such as Albert Jay Nock and Isabel Paterson, but he despised individualism as an ideology. How does one take all of this in? Additionally, Kirk was much more skeptical of government in his younger years than in his later years. As a biographer and scholar, do I claim the later attitude destroys the younger? Surely, there must be a continuity rather than a breach?

And then, sometimes, we can only go on what evidence we have. We barely know person A, but she left a diary that covered three months of her life in 1778. Do we extrapolate a life from three months of intimate revelations? Sometimes it is all we can do, and we have to make the best of it.

With Ray Bradbury, the problem is not too little information, but too much. And not just "too much," but an avalanche, a tidal wave, a flood, an F5 tornado just having passed through the feed lot...well, you get the idea. And yet, with Bradbury, more is never enough. Amazing that God makes a few of those in His image so endlessly fascinating. Bradbury is one of those few. What was God thinking when he made Ray Bradbury? The man overflowed with creativity, life, imagination, and everything else that matters in our whirligig of existence.

Melville House, a publisher on the move, has recently published a series of "Last Interviews" with great authors. Thus far, the series includes Kurt Vonnegut, Jacques Derrida, Hannah Arendt, and a few others. Sam Weller, who spent the last dozen years with Bradbury, put together *Ray Bradbury: The Last Interview.* Weller, it should be noted, does incredible work, and he does not take the trust that Bradbury showed in him lightly. At the very end of his life, Bradbury admitted that Weller probably understood him better than he himself did. And, very touchingly, during their last meeting, Bradbury admitted that he considered Weller the son he'd never had.

On the secret of life:

> The secret of life is being in love. By being in love, you predict yourself. Whatever you want is whatever you get. You don't predict things. You make them. You've gotta be a Zen Buddhist like me. Don't think about things. Just do them. Don't predict them. Just make them. (4)

On comic strips and books:

> Because I've been collecting comic strips all of my life. I have all of Prince Valiant put away. I have thirty years of Prince Valiant Sunday illustrations put away. I have all of Buck Rogers put away, too. I put those away starting when I was nineteen years old. So my background in becoming a writer was falling in love with comic strips. (8)

On the moment:

> Every single moment. Every single moment of my life has been incredible. I've loved it. I've savored it. It was beautiful. Because I've remained a boy. The man you

see here tonight is not a man, he's a twelve-year-old boy, and this boy is still having fun. And I will remain a boy forever. (10)

On science fiction versus fantasy:

I had a hell of a lot of fun writing [*Fahrenheit 451*]. It just came with its own spirit. But now that it's everywhere, I'm so happy that so many people love it. I love that book too. Remember this — I am not a science fiction writer. All of my books are fantasy writings. All my books are fantasies. But the one book that I've written that is pure science fiction is *Fahrenheit 451*. So I'm glad that I wrote it, and I'm glad that you feel that way about it, too. (20)

Let me also state — especially in this world of intangibles and ebooks and other bizarrenesses — this is a beautiful book. A nice cardboard-ish cover with fine paper, *Ray Bradbury: The Last Interview* is a joy to hold. It's also delightfully short. I mean this in the best way. It's the kind of book you can spend a later afternoon and evening enjoying. Frankly, serious publishers need to offer such diversity in length and topic more often. There are nights that demand serious reading and full immersion. Other nights call out for a sprinkling and for thoughts of goodness but not of life-or-death import. Bradbury was a truly wise man, a gifted artist, and Weller perfectly captures and conveys that Bradbury that we all want to know and love.

Ray Bradbury was a national treasure — indeed a treasure of Western civilization — and Weller's work on and with the great author is a Godsend. There is not a paragraph, let alone a page, in which Bradbury does not share a thought worthy of reflection and meditation.

Like Russell Kirk, Bradbury despised modern technology, especially automobiles. Unlike Kirk, however, Bradbury got to pilot the Mars rover from the Jet Propulsion Laboratories. "So while he hasn't driven on the 405 Freeway, he's driven across the sand dunes of Mars — and they actually gave him a little Mars driver's license" (19). How fitting.

19

Shirley Jackson's Haunting

THOUGH SHE NEVER MADE IT PAST THE young age of 48, Shirley Jackson was known for two important things during her lifetime: her perceptive anti-democratic short story, "The Lottery," and her humorous "Family Circle"-like anecdotes about her own four kids, husband, and household. Her most famous novel, *The Haunting of Hill House* — ostensibly about the occult and occult occurrences — has been made into a movie twice since the book was first published. Neither instance did justice to the depths and complexities of Jackson's fine psychological novel.

Though Russell Kirk never cited *The Haunting of Hill House* or the author, it is rather clear to anyone who has read his *Old House of Fear* or his *Lord of the Hollow Dark* that Jackson must have had a substantial influence on him. She lingers over the entire atmosphere of these two Kirk novels. Willing to cite the inspiration directly, Stephen King describes her importance explicitly in his own history of horror in novels and movies, *Danse Macabre*. As King sees it, Jackson has reached the "quiet epiphany that every writer hopes for." In some mysterious way, he continues, Jackson has written "words that somehow transcend words, words which add up to a total greater than the sum of the parts." Additionally, King frequently openly borrows two elements from Jackson's novel: the repeated line, "Whatever walks in Hill House, walks alone," as well as the incident of stones falling from a clear sky on a house. The same incident is central to King's first novel, *Carrie*, and it is mentioned in several of his other novels.

Jackson's writing style far surpasses anything produced by her better-known contemporaries and near-contemporaries, such as

John Updike and Philip Roth. Indeed, Jackson's writing in *The Haunting of Hill House* is as strong as anything produced by any revered American writer from the past one hundred years or so. King, as noted above, saw art surpassing art in *The Haunting of Hill House*, and it would be the cynic indeed who would readily disagree with this sentiment. Take, for instance, the words that moved King so much, the opening paragraph to the novel:

> No live organism can continue for long to exist sanely under conditions of absolute reality; even larks and katydids are supposed, by some, to dream. Hill House, not sane, stood by itself against its hills, holding a darkness within; it had stood for eighty years and might stand for eighty more. Within, walls continued upright, bricks met neatly, floors were firm, and doors were sensibly shut; silence lay steadily against the wood and stone of Hill House, and whatever walked there, walked alone.

Hill House, not sane, stood by itself.

While Jackson offered the history of the house, the gossip that surrounded many of its scandals, and the emotions (often quite angry, though rarely bloody) let loose in the house, she never fully explained — much to her credit and to the lasting depths of the story — why exactly the house was "haunted." When the question of haunting naturally occurs in the story, the lead anthropologist, John Montague (a rather Kirkian scholar who hopes to offer some rational explanation for the obviously irrational) explains that certain structures throughout human history have always seemed disturbed, sick, diseased, leprous, vile, unclean, forbidden. "Certainly there are spots which inevitably attach to themselves an atmosphere of holiness and goodness; it might not then be too fanciful to say that some houses are born bad," Montague claims.

> Hill House, whatever the cause, has been unfit for human habitation for upwards of twenty years. What it was like before then, whether its personality was molded

by the people who lived here, or the things they did, or whether it was evil from its start are all questions I cannot answer. Naturally I hope that we will all know a good deal more about Hill House before we leave. No one knows, even, why some houses are called haunted.

And, while there may exist scientific and observable reasons as to why a house continues to be discomforting, it is most likely out of the realm of the visible to understand why it began that way.

In his own praise of Jackson's work, critic and journalist John J. Miller explains why the haunted house has such power to move and unsettle us:

> The novel's power draws straight from the disturbing likelihood that the house itself is the antagonist. This possibility violates the very essence of what a home should be: a place of safety, nurture and comfort. The living can choose to avoid graveyards, where apparitions may rule at night. Shelter, however, is not optional — and so haunted houses pose a special threat to our collective sense of security.[1]

The Haunting of Hill House revolves around three intrepid explorers who accept Professor Montague's invitation to spend a summer living there, getting to know one another and getting to know — intimately — the workings of the house. While one of the invitees, Luke Sanderson, is a member of the extended family that legally owns the house, the other two had been invited by the professor because they had each experienced paranormal activity during their life. Of these two, the more interesting is known only as Theodora. Bohemian and cynical, but still quite kind and empathetic, she is almost certainly a lesbian. That Jackson only hints at this possibility makes Theodora an absolutely fascinating character. Truly, she's one of the most intriguing characters I've encountered

1   John J. Miller, "Chilling Fiction . . .," *Wall Street Journal* (October 29, 2009).

in modern literature. Had her lesbianism become obvious, Theodora would never have leapt off the pages in the manner she does throughout the book.

The protagonist is a lonely and somewhat disturbed thirty-two-year-old named Eleanor Vance. From the first chapter to the last, it is unclear if the book is really about a haunted house or if it's about Eleanor descending into madness. Of course, the answer to this question might very well be a "both/and" rather than an "either/or." A liar and a romantic, Eleanor has spent her entire life in the shadow of her domineering mother. Free of her mother for only two months — after her mother succumbed to death, possibly due to Eleanor's neglect of her health — Eleanor has moved in with a hated sister and her family when we first meet her in the novel. When the invitation arrives from Dr. Montague, Eleanor readily and gladly accepts, viewing it as a chance not only to escape her familial imprisonment but also to find her own individuality and personality. As Eleanor departs from her sister's family and interacts with the other three in Hill House, she reveals her strong loves and hatreds, often confusing one for the other and sometimes unable to separate herself from those around her. She even begins to doubt her very existence. "I could say all three of you are in my imagination; none of this is real."

While Hill House harasses Eleanor, she also finds herself in sympathy with it and its anger. Each resents its past, it seems, and each wrestles with its contradictory desire for solitude and company. At one critical moment, she realizes that should the house and Montague's explorers find one another in opposition, she would side with the house. Though I will not spoil the ending — a rather shocking one — I will state that Eleanor finds herself in much deeper trouble than she could possibly have imagined.

Whatever her own views on life, Jackson presented a fully Christian humanist view of trauma, fear, and life in her strange and macabre tale of a corrupt house.

20

Wendelin E Basgall

LIFE WASN'T EASY FOR MY GRANDPA AND grandma. My grandfather was born Wendelin Basgall on December 3, 1907, in Pfeifer, Kansas. He later adopted the letter "E" without the period as his middle name, thinking "Wendelin E Basgall" seemed somehow more dignified than "Wendelin Basgall" or "Wendelin E. Basgall." It certainly had an air of mystery, that single letter "E." With or without the mysterious "E," my grandpa was one of the most dignified, determined, intelligent, and stoic men I have ever met, or, I'm sure, ever will meet. He was also devoutly Catholic in all aspects of his life and being. Born into poverty, my grandpa lost his own father, Martin Basgall, in 1918, when he was just a young boy. He had an older sister and three younger brothers, and his mother supported the impoverished family by bootlegging. Kansas had been dry long before the Prohibition insanity hit the nation and seriously tarnished the dignity of the U.S. Constitution. Roman Catholics, not shy when it comes to alcohol, made up the bulk of the population of Ellis County, and the county sheriff would make his monthly visits to the Basgall house and quietly and mercifully look right over the still. Everyone in town, however, pitied and mocked the Basgalls, proclaiming that they "would never amount to anything." More often than not, at least according to the recollections of my grandfather, these words were openly spoken in town. Determined to undermine this wicked prophecy, my grandpa as a young boy did everything possible to earn good grades and support his family, even though two of his younger brothers always resented him for this. Nuns from the motherhouse in Concordia, Kansas, recognized Wendelin's intellectual gifts and sent him to school in Salina, where he studied to become a teacher. From all accounts, he was a stern but good and effective schoolmaster.

Still, tragedy seemed to follow the family. Shortly after my grandfather's father passed away, my grandfather, then aged 11, was asked to watch his youngest brother, aged 2 or 3. Wendelin turned away for a moment, distracted by some fleeting thing. In that moment, the littlest brother, over whom my grandfather had charge, got into some detergents, drank them, and died. My grandfather never forgot this, and he most likely never forgave himself.

In the 1920s, Wendelin's sister, Cecelia, contracted tetanus. The entire community came together to collect the $200, a huge sum of money, necessary to purchase the shot that should save her life. Some men then drove over four hours to Kansas City to get the shot. When they returned, the shot was administered to my aunt, but she died a few days later, on May 19, 1927, just four months shy of her twenty-first birthday. One can only wonder what influence her death had on my grandfather, with whom she had been very close. She had also been seriously involved with a local boy, who later became a Catholic priest after her death. I never asked my grandfather about her, and my grandmother never knew her. The events of her life are now completely lost, outside of her tragic death which seems to have defined her life. I have visited Cecelia's grave many times in my life; she rests under a gravestone with her oval picture embedded in it. Though the porcelain containing the picture is cracked and chipped, the image intrigues me. My great aunt looks intelligent and more than a bit mischievous. She's visited me a time or two in my dreams, but she was merely playful, and I never heard her speak. Her grave faces east in the windswept and dramatic valley of Pfeifer, under the shadow of the gothic church, Holy Cross. In some way I could never explain rationally, I love my great aunt, and I'm eager to meet her someday. I think of my grandfather and how close he was to her, and I think she must have been a truly fascinating woman. From dreams to visits to the Pfeifer cemetery, she has always been a presence in my life, though hers had been so brief and had ended over forty years before mine began. My wife and I named our fifth daughter after her, slightly changing the spelling. Like her name sake's, our Cecilia Rose's life ended all too tragically and all too soon.

Teaching during the Great Depression barely kept a person out of poverty. A teacher received pay only during the months he taught, usually eight months out of the year. During the other four months, the teacher would have to find extra sources of income. My grandpa did odd jobs here and there, including work as a short-order cook. One of the more interesting and intense (in terms of sheer back-breaking labor) was his job picking beets in eastern Colorado. This one has always humbled me, as I think about what it must have been like for a very upstanding, intellectual man to perform such labor during his summers, taking my grandmother with him and living out of the back of his car. One must remember that these people were suffering not just through the Great Depression but through the horrors of the Dust Bowl as well. Would I have had the stamina to do such a thing? I ask myself this question, amazed at my grandfather's fortitude and willingness to do what was right for his family.

My grandfather went on to become a prominent banker in his local community (offering and approving loans to the very people who had once said he and his family would amount to nothing), the Ellis County clerk (working closely with Bob Dole, serving in offices the next county over), an Army intelligence officer in World War II, and a representative in the Kansas State Legislature. All of this impressed me, of course, but I especially remember a Saturday morning visit with my grandfather to the world-famous Sternberg Museum (famous for its fossil, a "fish within a fish") in Hays. As the two of us approached the parking lot on the university campus, an open parking space stated, "Reserved for Professor XXXX." My grandfather, in his calm, stoic manner, turned to me and said, "Bradley, I think I'll be a professor today." We then spent the day among the remains of the dinosaurs.

My grandfather died in 1982, finally succumbing to heart failure (after rheumatic fever as a child and three heart attacks as an adult). I cannot help but recognize that without the kinds of sacrifices my grandparents were willing to make, I would not be where I am now, able to provide for my own family in the manner and fashion that I do. Knowing my grandfather as I did, and thinking of him and my grandmother picking the beets, only increases the wondrous mystique around my grandfather. He was truly a great man, and his sacrifices serve to remind me of what is necessary for family to survive and thrive, generation after generation, if a true and meaningful Christian humanism is to survive the ephemera of our own era.

Since 1982, he's visited me once or twice in my dreams. In the most vivid one, he was about the age I am now, and we were walking together along railroad tracks in western Kansas. We talked about many things on that walk, all things that matter: family, books, ideas, politics. But in the dream I remember most him turning to me, still smoking a filterless Camel, the Kansas wind blowing his thin hair, looking rather glorious with the setting sun behind him, telling me how proud he is of me — now, I get to park in a space reserved for a professor, and not just on Saturdays.

One of the best stories I ever heard about my maternal grandfather came from my mother, just a few summers ago. We were walking through her town of Ellinwood, Kansas, and I asked her about a number of specific memories from her childhood. I asked in particular for stories about World War II.

During the Second World War, my grandfather worked for Army intelligence at the Walker Air Force Base near Hays, Kansas. My mom still remembers the day an officer came to the front door of their very humble house and knocked. In a dignified manner (at least to my mother's ears) he asked to see my grandfather. The two walked into their tiny living room, and sitting down on the sofa, the officer asked my grandfather how much money he would like to earn, and whether he would be willing to work for government intelligence to help wage the war against the Axis powers.

For a young man who had once been deemed unworthy by his community (because of a restless father, soon deceased, and a bootlegging mother), he must have been elated at the promise, not only of a meaningful career, but also of a job that would allow him to serve his country in a fundamental and tangible way. As had the good nuns out of Concordia, Kansas, someone had recognized my grandfather's immense talents, not wanting to see them go to waste.

My grandfather was so loyal and so secretive about his government job — as he had been commanded to be — that my grandmother feared for their marriage. She was never quite sure why he was gone or what he was doing at any one time during the war. Amazingly enough, she even began to suspect her husband of having an affair (he wasn't!). As my mother tells the story, my grandfather worked with officers and draftees, preparing them for an invasion of the Japanese islands and mainland. Knowing my grandfather as I did for a mere fourteen years of my life, I'm sure he dedicated himself completely and utterly to his task.

When President Truman decided to drop the atomic bombs on two Japanese cities, the news reached America almost immediately after the first bomb detonated. To celebrate this victory, my then nine-year-old mother approached my grandfather. In her youthful vigor, she performed a victory dance for him. With great love but also with humane sternness, my grandfather tempered my mother's enthusiasm. "Rita, don't you understand, America did what was necessary, but it was not good. The bomb didn't just kill soldiers, it leveled entire cities, killing women like your mother and little girls like you," teaching my mother to love the humane above the jingoistic, human beings above the nation.

21

Julitta Kuhn Basgall

P

ROBABLY FEW WHO PASSED MY GRAND-
mother on the street would have thought of her as a "great
woman." She had led a long life, 1911–2003. It was also, I
believe, a rather meaningful and humane life.

She was the best cook and baker I've ever encountered, and I've
met quite a few. I've done everything I can to live up to her cooking
and baking skills, but I'm afraid I'm not the perfect heir.

Born in August 1911 in Ellis, Kansas, the oldest girl of seventeen
children, Julitta Kuhn found herself not just the oldest sister but the
unofficial second mom of the family. With seventeen kids, it really
couldn't be otherwise. Though she helped with all things on the
farm, she helped more in the house, more in the cooking and baking,
and more in the kid-rearing than her brothers who spent their days
in the field. When she was old enough, her parents hired her out as
a cleaning woman and "babysitter," though this latter term is far too
tame to describe the kind of care she gave. Because of her familial
duties, she dropped out of school quite young. Though incredibly
wise, she would never have been considered "learned" in any sense
of the term. Her own mother tongue, a 1763 form of Swabian, was
her only language until she was in her late 20s when she learned to
speak English. She regarded any person who didn't speak her form
of German as "English" — even the female black entrepreneur who
owned the local merchandise, retail, and grocery store.

My grandmother, certainly never wealthy, would only every
once in a while have a penny to her name. After Julitta placed the
copper coin on the glass counter of the candy display, the owner
would offer a certain number of pieces. The owner couldn't speak
any form of German, and my grandmother couldn't speak English.

Julitta would hold tight to her penny until satisfied the woman had offered her enough candy. She would then let go of the money, scoop up the candy, nod a thanks and leave. To my very central European grandmother, the black entrepreneur was always that "English" lady. Until the end of her days in the world, she spoke very heavily accented English, and every sentence ended with a "nun" or a "gella," the Swabian equivalents of "right?"

Devoted to the Roman Catholic Church her entire life, Julitta was also the very first person baptized in the newly built St Fidelis in Victoria (Herzog, as the Germans called its southern part), Kansas. Within a year of Julitta's baptism, William Jennings Bryan visited St Fidelis and christened that church "The Cathedral of the Plains," a name that has stuck with tourist brochures, though the church never rose to the level of basilica. Today, however, the U.S. and Kansas governments have also recognized its rather stunning architectural qualities, and tourists, nearly bored to death on I-70, often stop to visit it. Though my grandmother's body now rests in a cemetery in Hays, Kansas, I certainly feel her presence every time I'm near St Fidelis.[1]

In addition to her profound and deep faith in the Church, Julitta also kept a cedar chest of treasures her whole life. That chest, a hand-made gift from her father, always rested at the foot of her bed. In it, she kept photos, handkerchiefs from dances (which she would drop in front of a boy if she wanted to dance with him), her wedding dress and veil, prayer cards, and a number of other wonders. Whether I simply didn't care that much about the chest as a child or whether my grandmother kept it private, never thinking to show me its secrets, I'm not quite sure.

I do clearly remember finally getting to look through it all when she was a year or so away from death. Everything in the chest came with a story, and I'll never forget that day with her, exploring the parts of her life I had never known. Every person should have at

---

1   As an aside, one should never regard Kansas or any part of it as "fly over country." It is deeply mysterious and gorgeous in its own right — at least for those who have eyes to see and an ounce of imagination in the soul.

least one such day in his or her life. It was one of the best days in my life, and I'm pretty sure she felt the same. The items in that chest weren't knick-knacks or odds-and-ends. They were precious things, each with its own essence and its own teleology. Taken together, they told the story of a life well lived and never taken for granted.

When asked, however, Julitta never shied away from telling stories. Whenever I asked, she told story after story about her parents, their rented farm, her work as a house keeper, my grandfather, my mom, her church, the nuns, her neighbors, and everything else that mattered to her. Though she possessed unquantifiable amounts of common sense, she also had a mystical streak all of her life. Sometimes, she just "knew" things, and she fondly remembered watching the "faeries dance across the wheat fields at dusk" as a child. Every night after evening prayers (she prayed throughout the day, every day), she and my grandfather would sprinkle holy water in each room of their modest house, driving away any lurking evil spirits.

Toward the last decade of her life, her health declined rapidly. During one Thanksgiving celebrated in Boise, Idaho, she began to yell things out rather spontaneously. At one point, in the middle of an intense conversation between my mom, my great friend Joel, my brother, my sister-in-law, and me, grandma suddenly screamed out, "Pass the PEPPER!!!!" We all paused, stunned, handed her the pepper jar, and then all burst into laughter — including my grandmother.

On a sadder note, I was the one visiting her in her kitchen when we realized that her eyesight had almost completely failed. Not only was she cutting up tin foil — assuming it to be onions — but red ants were swarming all over her food preparation area. My grandmother was not only an amazing cook throughout her life, she was as neat as possibly imaginable. Always, her home was spotless. Her blindness came as a huge blow to all of us.

I must also mention one other thing about my grandmother. She wielded her stoicism as an article of faith. It never failed to impress me. Things happened, she reasoned, and they happened according to God's will. Our life, set in His hand, was what it was, and we were to accept it completely. For almost the last decade of her life, she sat in near blindness and deafness saying her prayers ceaselessly. She knew of no other reason why God kept her on this earth. Obviously, she lived to pray. When she had said all of her prayers, God would take her. And take her he did. The evening before her death, my wife, my mom, and my three oldest children (then very young) sat with grandma. She, frankly, looked like hell, but my daughter, two-year-old Gretchen, kept saying to her, "Grandma, you are so beautiful." When I asked Gretchen about it later, she said that colored lights and angels were dancing all around grandma. Perhaps the wheat field faeries had come to pay their last respects.

The next day, a priest and my mom in deep conversation next to her, my grandmother reached up, grabbed the priest's hand, and told him it was time. They said the Lord's Prayer, and my grandmother died peacefully at the words "Thy will be done." A life well lived in service to God and family and a good death are the essence of Christian humanism.

22

Ronald Reagan

The West will not contain communism, it will transcend communism.

OR TWO FULL MINUTES, THE ATTENDEES OF the graduation ceremonies at the University of Notre Dame offered President Ronald Reagan a standing ovation.[1] He entered the ACC—Notre Dame's basket-ball and hockey arena— accompanied by priests, professors, and diplomats. Throughout his time on the stage, the crowd cheered "wildly."[2] Only those who are a part—even in the most limited of ways—of the Notre Dame or Texas A&M families understand such heartfelt but gushing and over-the-top enthusiasm. To be welcomed by either community is more akin to baptism by full immersion than baptism by mere sprinkling.

"Knute, Knute," the 12,500 graduates and their families and guests chanted, honoring Reagan's friend, Pat O'Brien, who had played Rockne to his George Gipp, "The Gipper," in the famed 1940 movie *Knute Rockne: All American.*

In his first appearance outside of Washington, D.C. since John Hinckley Jr. had nearly assassinated him, Reagan, the talking heads and pundits had reported, would be delivering a major foreign policy address to the graduates.[3] Four years earlier, President Jimmy Carter had given his famous talk to the Notre Dame graduates of that year

---

1   James Gerstenzang, "'The Gipper' Returns to Notre Dame as President," AP (May 18, 1981).

2   Dean Reynolds, "A Sad, Bizarre Chapter in Human History," UPI (May 17, 1981).

3   Bill Roeder, "The Gipper Will Hit the Line Hard," *Newsweek* (May 11, 1981), pg. 21; and William Safire, "The Notre Dame Shift," *New York Times* (May 4, 1981), pg. A23.

on why America had unhealthily acquired an "inordinate fear of communism."[4] In contrast, and to some of the loudest applause yet, Reagan began his speech claiming he most certainly would "not talk about the great issues of the day."[5] Instead, he noted, he wanted to offer those graduating something more of "inspiration" and "appropriate to the occasion."[6]

The response of Notre Dame overwhelmed Reagan. Not only did he cry when his friend Pat O'Brien received an award, but he redis-covered — probably for the first time in almost two months — the confidence he'd lost after his all-too-close brush with death.

> The president drew strength and vigor from the sus-tained standing ovation. As he stood in front of the crowd, donning cap and gown, I could tell he was happy to be there ... [in original] to be anywhere.[7]

No fan of Reagan, ABC's Sam Donaldson understood, at least in part, just how important the visit to the University of Notre Dame had been. "By most accounts, the President's speech was not one which will be long remembered, but no matter, more important than anything he said was the fact that he had come here today to say it," he calmly reported. "Mr. Reagan has resumed the public life of his presidency."[8] Donaldson's assessment of the speech was not unique. The UPI as well as *The New York Times* also dismissed the speech as unimportant, a mere excursion into nostalgia for Reagan, taking him back forty-one years to his pre-war movie career.[9]

4   Roeder, "The Gipper Will Hit the Line Hard," 21.

5   Diane Curtis, "Washington News," UPI, May 18, 1981.

6   Howell Raines, "Reagan is Welcomed on Notre Dame Trip, First Since Shoot-ing," *New York Times* (May 18, 1981), pg. A1; and Helen Thomas, "Reagan Prepares for Sentimental Journey to Notre Dame," UPI (May 16, 1981).

7   Michael K. Deaver, *A Different Drummer: My Thirty Years with Ronald Reagan* (2001), 147.

8   Sam Donaldson, "Reagan Gets Honorary Degree from Notre Dame Along with Pat O'Brien," ABC News Transcripts (May 17, 1981).

9   "Domestic News," UPI (May 18, 1981); and "News Summary," *New York Times* (May 18, 1981), pg. B1.

Oddly enough, no American press organ with the exception of *The Christian Science Monitor* understood the vital importance of the speech.[10] Somehow, nearly every American news agency missed ten important words, ten words that changed the entire course of American foreign policy since Truman implemented it in the mid-1940s. "The West will not contain communism, it will transcend it."[11] With understandable irony, only the official Soviet news agencies, TASS and Pravda, recognized what the speech meant.

> These statements are made at a time when, according to the President himself, the United States is going through both a moral and an economic crisis. Reagan expressed concern over economic stagnation, born of inflation, "burdensome and unnecessary regulations and … a punitive tax policy." The crime rate and violence, whose victim the President himself was recently, is speedily growing in the country. Even before President Reagan's visit to Notre Dame University a movement of protest against his appearance started there. The newspaper *National Catholic Reporter* strongly criticized the administration for taking billions of dollars from social programmes and giving away those billions, and many others, to military programmes. The White House, the newspaper said, crudely flouts human rights, which is seen particularly vividly from the example of El Salvador.[12]

Pravda argued that the Catholic Crusades of the Middle Ages inspired the radical and outmoded fortieth president of the United States, Ronald Reagan.

> This is not the first time that prophets foretelling the imminent death of communism emerge in the West.

10   "America as a Beacon," *Christian Science Monitor* (May 18, 1981), pg. 24.
11   Wilson Miscamble, ed., *Go Forth and Do Good: Memorable Notre Dame Commencement Addresses* (Notre Dame, IN: University of Notre Dame Press, 2003), 211.
12   TASS Report, as reported in "President Reagan's Speech in Indiana," BBC (May 20, 1981).

> The anti-communist crusade which began in 1917 has
> always featured fanaticism characteristic of medieval
> crusaders rather than rational thinking. The Reagan
> administration also bears the mark of such fanaticism.[13]

Pravda, perhaps for the first time in its existence, fully grasped America's resolve.

The first words he had spoken publicly outside of D.C., and the first public words at all dealing with foreign policy or the Soviet Union in his presidency, Reagan's address at the University of Notre Dame, far from being an "amiably rah-rah speech" as reported by *Newsweek*, set the stage for the rest of his presidency. It also set the stage for the beginning of the end of the Soviet Union's totalitarian grip on Eastern Europe, its expansionism abroad, and its control over its own citizens.[14] Words matter. Ideas matter. Reagan understood this, and so did his enemies.

Yet, these ten words that changed the world were not as new or as baseless as many thought them. Lost in the call for a coherent and sustained foreign policy statement concerning the Reagan Administration's first term agenda, reporters at home who even noticed the anti-communist words assumed that the president had thrown these in as a simple act of patriotism. In fact, these ten words reflected almost twenty years of intense thought on the president's part. Since roughly 1963, Ronald Reagan had been rigorously imagining what it would take to bring down the Soviet Union and the communists. Now, as president, he had the power to do it. And after surviving the assassin's bullet, he had the will.

Reagan's optimism

While every person on every side of the spectrum would like to discover — or rediscover — the secret of Ronald Reagan's success,

---

13   "Pravda Likens Reagan to Medieval Crusaders," UPI (June 3, 1981).
14   Tom Morganthau, et al., "The Gipper Loses One," *Newsweek* (June 1, 1981), pg. 22.

many on the conservative side of things have readily dismissed him as a rarely closeted progressive who blithely saw the good in all. They believe the fortieth president to be a high priest of the American civil religion. After all, it is always morning in America.

While one might readily prove that Reagan was an optimist a little bit in excess of Pollyanna herself, optimism does not equate with progressivism. Rather, it would be fair to label Reagan as a grand proponent of the ingenuity and potential of each individual person. Yet in his very reliance on the individual, Reagan could not have the same faith in history itself. After all, history was merely the culmination of billions of decisions made every single second by the billions of persons running around on the world. Just as the actions of each creative person could prove unpredictable — hence, the creativity — so, too, would the sum of their decisions and experiences. Thus, in ignorance of what is to come, one has to possess faith in the individuals of the world in order to have faith in the future of the world. This is not the same thing as progressivism, which demands a confidence in the very direction of history toward some inevitable and purposeful end. Reagan had faith, but his understanding of time and history and the future also demanded a proper ignorance and humility.

It should and must be noted that Reagan read constantly. As Dick Allen noted, Reagan "read everything." Though certainly no conservative, journalist David Gergen remembered:

> Working for him, I saw he was no dullard, as his critics claimed. From his eight years as governor and his many other years of writing and speaking out, he had thought his way through most domestic issues and knew how to make a complex governmental structure work in his favor. In the first year of his presidency, I also saw him dive into the details of the federal revenue code and become an authority as he negotiated with Congress. When he wanted to focus, he had keen powers of concentration and could digest large bodies of information. He was also one of the most disciplined men I

have seen in the presidency (much more so than Clinton, for example), so that he worked straight through the day, reading papers and checking off meetings on his list. At day's end, he headed off for a workout and would plow through more papers in the evening in the upstairs residence. He made the presidency look easy in part by keeping a strict regimen. He also had a retentive mind. After years of memorizing scripts in Hollywood, he would recall verbatim a lot of what he had read. He recited Robert Service poems as well as he did jokes.[15]

Martin Anderson remembered something quite similar:

Working for him, one of the first things that struck me about him was his high intelligence. I can recall many times sitting or traveling with him, introducing an idea or essay or memorandum. He would grasp its essence almost immediately; then, sometimes weeks or months later, he would interpret it and weave the relevant material into a speech or statement of his own.[16]

Russell Kirk, though, argued that Reagan's sharp intelligence wasn't sufficient to make him the leader he was. Honing his keen intellect, Reagan added a profound confidence, "audacity, and again audacity, and always audacity."[17]

One vital contemporary of Reagan was Whittaker Chambers. As is well known in conservative and libertarian circles, Chambers left communism not because Marxism was doomed to failure, but because it was morally and ethically wrong. Even after leaving that foul ideology behind, Chambers continued to believe and fear

---

15   David Gergen, *Eyewitness to Power* (New York: Simon and Schuster, 2001), 197.

16   Martin Anderson in Peter Hannaford, ed., *Recollections of Reagan* (New York: William Morrow, 1997), 11.

17   Russell Kirk, *Reclaiming a Patrimony* (Washington, DC: Heritage Foundation, 1982), 115.

that he had chosen the losing side. While we know that Whittaker Chambers fundamentally affected and shaped Reagan, we do not know to what degree. Still, we can state with some confidence that Reagan's vision of history, and his essential faith in the future, came from a rejection of Chambers' philosophy — from an inversion of it.

As mentioned previously, Reagan offered his clearest statement of the imminent Soviet collapse in his speech at the University of Notre Dame on May 17, 1981:

> The years ahead are great ones for this country, for the cause of freedom and the spread of civilization. The West won't contain communism, it will transcend communism. It won't bother to denounce it, it will dismiss it as some bizarre chapter in human history whose last pages are even now being written.

Yet Reagan's belief that the Soviets were doomed had nothing to do with the laws of history, of progress or of regress. There were no "forces" at work in history in Reagan's understanding. Instead, the Soviets ignored an essential fact about humans: their individual and unpredictable creativity. The Soviets had therefore doomed themselves, whatever the fates or gods or forces might rule.

In 1968, in a book all too easily forgotten by friend and foe alike, Reagan outlined his very Burkean and Smithian vision of spontaneous order. The book, *The Creative Society* — a somewhat obvious jab at and humorous take on Lyndon Johnson's "Great Society" — was published by the relatively obscure firm of Devin-Adair and sold relatively well. In this book, Reagan brought together the contemporary work of Robert Nisbet, Friedrich Hayek, and Russell Kirk, arguing not only for allowing the creative energies of the individual to flourish, but the creative energies of the individual to flourish within community. Governmental laws, he argued, served only to diminish the good of the whole. A government *of* laws, however, allowed society to grow exponentially, as it turned over the most important functions to individuals and communities:

The Creative Society, in other words, is simply a return to the people of the privilege of self-government, as well as a pledge for more efficient representative government—citizens of proven ability in their fields, serving where their experience qualifies them, proposing common sense answers for California's problems, reviewing governmental structure itself and bringing it into line with the most advanced, modern business practices. Those who talk of complex problems, requiring more government planning and more control, in reality are taking us back in time to the acceptance of rule of the many by the few. Time to look to the future. We've had enough talk—disruptive talk—in America of left and right, dividing us down the center. There is really no such choice facing us. The only choice we have is up or down—up, to the ultimate in individual freedom consistent with law and order, or down, to the deadly dullness of totalitarianism.

If Reagan's vision of a Creative Society is progressive, it is no more so than Burke's, Tocqueville's, or Kirk's. In other words, it's not progressive in the least. It is a vision of a decentralized society—a society of associations, a society of charity, and a society of entrepreneurship. Like the man himself, Reagan's vision was at once humble and humane.

23

Walter Miller's Augustinian Wasteland

There was objective meaning in the world, to be sure: the nonmoral *logos* or design of the Creator; but such meanings were God's and not Man's, until they found an imperfect incarnation, a dark reflection, within the mind and speech and culture of a given human society, which might ascribe values to the meanings so that they became valid in a human sense within the culture. For Man was a culture-bearer as well as a soul-bearer, but his cultures were not immortal and they could die with a race or an age, and then human reflections of meaning and human portrayals of truth receded, and truth and meaning resided, unseen, only in the objective *logos* of Nature and the ineffable *Logos* of God. Truth could be crucified; but soon, perhaps, a resurrection.[1]

A CANTICLE FOR LEIBOWITZ HAS BEEN ONE OF my favorite books for most of my adult life. I have read it and reread it many times. In fact, I have read it and perused it too many times to count. I find the work as compelling as the best of Eliot. But, while Eliot always uplifts, Miller always sobers. In *Canticle*, one discovers some of Eliot's thought, but also

1   Walter M. Miller, Jr., *A Canticle for Leibowitz* [1959] (New York: Bantam/ Spectra, 1997), 145–46. Unless otherwise noted, quotations are taken from this book. Much of the content of this chapter comes from a discussion of the book with the students/scholars affiliated with the McConnell Center, led by Dr. Gary Gregg, at the University of Louisville.

some of Christopher Dawson's, Jacques Maritain's, and especially St Augustine's thought. Much like his fifth-century forebear, Miller places a variety of anthropologies and humanisms before the reader, as well as competing visions of history. Unlike his North African counterpart, though, Miller never answers his own questions and puzzles definitively. The reader remains restless, for he never rests in Thee.

I also have taught the book several times in various classroom settings. With only a few exceptions, bright college students find it intriguing and thought-provoking, even if the theology confuses them (Catholic students as well as Protestant). The characters of Mrs. Grales and Rachel tend to cause much wonder and concern among students.

Walter Miller served as a tail gunner on a bomber during the Italian campaign in World War II. His bombing group, in part, aided in the destruction of Monte Cassino, the oldest monastery in the Western world. The destruction of this Benedictine institution haunted Miller, and after the war, he found himself drawn not only to the study of Western civilization and its preservation, but, more importantly, to the endurance and significance of the Roman Catholic Church as a protective institution. Probably to the chagrin of many of those around him, Miller converted in 1947, shortly after his marriage. He explored Roman Catholic theology in his many short stories written during the 1950s. As it turned out, this decade proved to be Miller's Golden Age, an age that he spent much of his remaining adult life trying to recapture, but unsuccessfully. In 1996, frustrated with God knows what and taunted by who knows what, Miller took his own life. Another author completed Miller's unfinished sequel, *St Leibowitz and the Wild Horse Woman*. This second book takes place during the second of the three eras featured in *Canticle*, roughly 1,200 years after the atomic war of 1960.

Numerous readings of *Canticle for Leibowitz* have left me with this conclusion: it is a complicated, nuanced, and perplexing novel, a mystery to be enjoyed, time and again, but never to be solved. Set in the Intermountain Desert West in the futureless United States of America, *A Canticle for Leibowitz* offers a vibrant image of a desiccated human culture and desiccated human politics, an irradiated landscape, and an inevitably dark and shameful future. As with some of its contemporaneous fiction such as Ayn Rand's much less earnest *Atlas Shrugged*, *Canticle for Leibowitz* offers great insight into the nature and power of ideas while set in a dystopian world. While Rand, better known by far in popular culture and in book sales, possesses a stunning power to devise an intricate plot, she cannot match Miller in character development or writing style. As an example, take this beautiful sentence: "The water was clouded and live with creeping uncertainties as was the Old Jew's stream of memory" (167).

Certainly I am not alone in my appreciation of this novel. Edmund Fuller, one of the best literary critics of the 20th century, called *Canticle* a "memorable fantasia" (*New York Times*, January 12, 1964), and Martin Levin called it "ingenious" (*New York Times*, March 27, 1960). Many, though, have thought it a waste of paper. An anonymous reviewer in *Time* magazine, for example, wrote of Miller: "His faith in religious faith is commendable but not compelling," claiming the book to be intellectually vacuous (*Time*, February 22, 1960).

In the beginning of *Canticle*, set roughly five and a half centuries from now, a wandering Jew throws pebbles at a confused and seemingly not-so-bright monk, Brother Francis. When the confused Catholic, led by the hand of the perturbed Jew, discovers an underground tavern, office, and bunker, he finds what he considers holy relics — a shopping list, some blueprints, and the body of a dead woman. This encounter, shaped from its beginning by the will and observation of the Jew, starts the cycle of civilization, corruption, decay, and death all over again. Throughout the novel, the cycles of civilization revolve around two points: the wandering Jew and the monastery.

The question Miller asks the reader and himself is this: can man escape original sin? Or will man, doomed, carry it wherever he goes, whether it be into the American West or into the new frontier of space? And if so, can man do anything by his own will to attenuate these great evils, of which he is not only so capable but seemingly so desirous?

Throughout the novel, Miller asks us and himself some of the most important questions to be asked by any person at any time. What is the human person? How does one man recognize the dignity of another man?

> Few theologians whose belief in Hell had never failed them would deprive their God of recourse to *any* form of temporal punishment, but for men to take it upon themselves to judge any creature born of woman to be lacking in the divine image was to usurp the privilege of Heaven. Even the idiot which seems less gifted than a dog, or a pig, or a goat, shall, if born of woman, be called an immortal soul, thundered the *magisterium*, and thundered it again and again. (98)

In the long run, can man use his technological prowess for the good of society and the good of his fellows?

> They belonged to a race quite capable of admiring their own image in a mirror, and equally capable of cutting its own throat before the altar of some tribal god, such as the deity of Daily Shaving. It was a species which often considered itself to be basically a race of divinely inspired toolmakers. (245)

Homo faber, indeed.

By what means and by what authority do political bodies govern? In what ways can and does the power of political bodies ignore, mock, or usurp cultural and religious bodies and authorities?

> *That's where all of us are standing now,* he thought. On the fat kindling of past sins. And some of them are mine. Mine, Adam's, Herod's, Judas's, Hannegan's, mine. Everybody's. Always culminates in the colossus of the State, somehow, drawing about itself the mantle of godhood, being struck down by wrath of Heaven. (282)

Throughout all three parts of the novel, Miller presents rather complicated characters, witty dialogue, and never-ending questions about the most important things. It is not without reason, then, that some aficionados of the novel consider it not only a classic of the science fiction genre, but also a classic of American and Western civilizations.

I would place myself in this latter category. While I write only from opinion and certainly not from expertise, I do believe Miller to be one of the great authors — not only one of the great science-fiction authors and Catholic authors — of the 20th century. Horribly, Miller ended his own life in tragedy. I do not know, nor do I ever expect to know, what demons haunted this brilliant artist. Clearly, he failed to resist them in the end. But of course, each one of us is deeply flawed. Perhaps we are deeply flawed in different ways than Miller, but we remain flawed nonetheless.

Along with many others, I will continue to teach this novel as a great work of imagination. I do hope, however, that Miller was wrong not only about his own personal understanding of hope, but also about the bleak, decaying future of Western civilization and its citizens. Depending on what day, and sometimes on what hour, I agree and/or disagree with Miller. The novel means different things to me at different times, but I always recognize its profundity. As the last line of the novel reads, "the shark swam out to his deepest waters and brooded in the old clean currents. He was very hungry that season" (338). The reader also broods and hungers at the end of the novel. Miller never lets us rest, making us uncomfortable on purpose. Christian humanism is as much a challenge as it is a comfort.

But I do pray — may Walter Miller finally rest in Him.

24

Alexander Solzhenitsyn as Prophet

Shut your eyes, reader. Do you hear the thundering of
wheels? Those are the Stolypin cars rolling on and on.
Those are the red cows rolling. Every minute of the
day. And every day of the year. And you can hear the
water gurgling — those are prisoners' barges moving on
and on. And the motors of the Black Marias roar. They
are arresting someone all the time, cramming him in
somewhere, moving him about. And what is that hum
you hear? The overcrowded cells of the transit prisons.
And that cry? The complaints of those who have been
plundered, raped, beaten to with an inch of their lives.
We have reviewed and considered all the methods of
delivering prisoners, and we have found that they are
all...worse. We have examined the transit prisons, but
we have not found any that were good. And even the
last human hope that there is something better ahead,
that it will be better in camp, is a false hope. In camp it
will be...worse.[1]

THOUGH FACED WITH SEVERE REPRISALS
from the state, his being betrayed to the Soviet government
by his first wife, and eventual exile from his beloved though
tortured homeland, Solzhenitsyn recorded the tyranny perpetuated by the Soviet ideologues in a number of deeply meaningful

---

1 End of Volume 1 of the *Gulag.*

works, including most famously *The Gulag Archipelago*. Some of this massive work he wrote on scraps of paper; some he memorized on the rosary beads given to him by Catholic prisoners.

Solzhenitsyn knew firsthand of that of which he wrote in his appropriately subtitled "An Experiment in Literary Investigation."

> And where among all the preceding qualities was there any place left for kindheartedness? How could one possibly preserve one's kindness while pushing away the hands of those who were drowning? Once you have been steeped in blood, you can only become more cruel.... And when you add that kindness was ridiculed, that pity was ridiculed, that mercy was ridiculed — you'd never be able to chain all those who were drunk on blood.

More than any other work, the *Gulag* forced Western journalists and academics to confront the monstrous realities of the Soviet Union — not only under Stalin's cult of personality dictatorship, but under the wretched evil that pervaded the entire system. Indeed, the Soviet Union ran on the blood of those who deviated from its vision of harmony and perfection. From the very beginning of the Soviet takeover of Russia, Solzhenitsyn noted, the revolutionaries established the ideologically-driven police, militia, army, courts, and jails. Even the labor camps — the Gulag — began in embryo form only a month into the revolution. The parasitic Soviets craved blood from 1917 to 1991; such bloodletting was an inherent part of the system. Solzhenitsyn claims that the Gulag state murdered 66 million just between 1917 and 1956.

The ideological system created distrust. "This universal mutual mistrust had the effect of deepening the mass-grave pit of slavery. The moment someone began to speak up frankly, everyone stepped back and shunned him: 'A provocation!' And therefore anyone who burst out with a sincere protest was predestined to loneliness and alienation." The system also, Solzhenitsyn understood, established a permanent lie.

The permanent lie becomes the only safe form of existence, in the same way as betrayal. Every wag of the tongue can be overheard by someone, every facial expression observed by someone. Therefore every word, if it does not have to be a direct lie, is nonetheless obliged not to contradict the general, common lie. There exists a collection of ready-made phrases, of labels, a selection of ready-made lies.

Ultimately, those who died immediately had the best of it, the Russian prophet knew. To survive meant not merely to lose the body at some point, but almost certainly the soul as well.

No mere anti-communist, Solzhenitsyn did not just attack the ideological regimes of Russia and its former communist allies in Eastern Europe, he challenged all of modernity — in the East and in the West. Western consumerism, he warned, will destroy the West by mechanizing its citizens in a more efficient and attractive manner than communism could. "Dragged along the whole of the Western bourgeois-industrial and Marxist path," Solzhenitsyn stated,

a dozen maggots can't go on and on gnawing the same apple *forever*; that if the earth is a *finite* object, then its expanses and resources are finite also, and the *endless, infinite* progress dinned into our heads by the dreamers of the Enlightenment cannot be accomplished on it.... All that "endless progress" turned out to be an insane, ill-considered, furious dash into a blind alley. A civilization greedy for "perpetual progress" has now choked and is on its last legs.

Only by embracing a transcendent order and the true Creator, Solzhenitsyn argued, can mankind save itself from the follies and murders of the ideologues. In his 1983 Templeton address, he took his arguments against modernity even further.

Our life consists not in the pursuit of material success but in the quest of worthy spiritual growth. Our entire earthly existence is but a transition stage in the movement toward something higher, and we must not stumble or fall, nor must we linger fruitless on one rung of the ladder.... The laws of physics and physiology will never reveal the indisputable manner in which the Creator constantly, day in and day out, participates in the life of each of us, unfailingly granting us the energy of existence; when the assistance leaves us, we die. In the life of our entire planet, the Divine Spirit moves with no less force: this we must grasp in our dark and terrible hour.

In his commentary on Solzhenitsyn's address, Russell Kirk argued that the above passage "expressed with high feeling...the conservative impulse." Certainly, Kirk and Solzhenitsyn were kindred spirits.

One should never underestimate the importance of Solzhenitsyn's moral imagination. As one of the leading Solzhenitsyn scholars, Edward E. Ericson Jr., has argued: "I would say that *One Day in the Life of Ivan Denisovich* put the first crack into the Berlin Wall and *The Gulag Archipelago* was an irresistible blow to the very foundations of the Soviet edifice."

Alexander Solzhenitsyn, the prophet, is dead. The priest (John Paul II) and the king (Ronald Reagan) went before him.

25

The Ferocity of Marvin O'Connell

ON AUGUST 19, 2016, FATHER MARVIN R. O'Connell passed away in South Bend, Indiana. Author of a number of critical studies — biographical as well as historical and philosophical — O'Connell taught in the history department of the University of Notre Dame for most of his professional career. He was, strangely enough, not a member of Notre Dame's founding and reigning order, Holy Cross, but was rather a priest in the Diocese of St Paul, Minnesota, "on loan" to Notre Dame.

Not one of Father O'Connell's students would ever accuse him of softness, favoritism, or sloth. He was a fierce man, a fierce priest, and a fierce professor. He possessed perhaps the most penetrating and intelligent eyes and brow I have ever encountered in a teacher. He had a booming voice, and he loved to quote Churchill. Sometimes, he would break into a Churchill speech when trying to explain some complexity of history. Certainly, the most memorable moment in any class I took in college was O'Connell's full recitation of Churchill's speech of May 1940, his first speech — "the finest hour" — as Prime Minister. I was fairly certain that Churchill was, in fact, standing in our classroom in O'Shannessey Hall at Notre Dame in that fall of 1988. It's quite possible that O'Connell was shooting lasers and lightning from his eyes as he delivered this speech. Whatever it was, Father O'Connell cast a spell over the entire classroom. We were ready to go to war against the Nazis, even if it meant our most certain death. Never have I felt a greater call to arms. When O'Connell finished, I looked around the room.

There was nothing but stunned silence and a number of tears flowing from the eyes of his students.

Not surprisingly, O'Connell was a master storyteller. He knew this as well, and he used it to full effect. On the first day of each of his classes, he proudly informed us that he would allow no sleeping in his class. "I once kicked Joe Montana out of class. If I can kick Montana out of class, I can certainly kick you out," he declared. Once, a good friend of mine — the director of the radio station — did actually fall asleep in class. Without breaking his lecture, O'Connell grabbed a number of books, walked to the desk of the sleeping student, and dropped all of the books at once. The noise, of course, startled the student. O'Connell looked at him and said, "get out." The student did, and Father O'Connell kept lecturing as if nothing out of the ordinary had happened.

Father O'Connell also loved telling us about his first assignment as a parish priest. I don't remember all of the details — I think it was in St Paul proper, but I don't remember exactly. His parish was across the street from some evangelical/fundamentalist church. Just to shock the Protestants, Father O'Connell would stand in front of the church in full cassock, smoking his cigarettes like a chimney. He strove, he told us, to be misidentified as a "Jesuit." "Once the Protestants call you that," he said, "you know you've made it."

He was not only a storyteller, however. He was painstakingly rigorous in what and how he taught. His stories always perfectly illustrated a point, but they were never a substitution for the truth — they were an illustration of it. He would usually take the first several days of a semester simply to give us context for the course. Imagine, he told us, what it would've been like to travel from Rome to Wittenberg by foot or horse, or from Hanover to London by aerial bomber. He would then describe such a journey in great detail, noting everything from time consumed to food and calories needed.

I had the great fortune of taking three classes from him, and he was by far the most demanding professor I had in all of my schooling. He had earned his reputation as one of the toughest professors at Notre Dame, and he rather reveled in what he considered a great — perhaps the greatest — accolade. Well, at least almost as great as being wrongly considered a Jesuit.

Earning a "B" from Father O'Connell was equivalent to earning an "A+" in any other class. As to his students, he demanded of us everything we had — not only in the classroom, but outside of it as well. My papers would come back from him dripping in the blood red ink of his marking pen. After waging the slaughter, he would always add an encouraging note. "Birzer, you're getting better. Keep thinking and keep working!"

After spending the entirety of my sophomore year in Innsbruck, Austria, I came back to Notre Dame in the fall of 1988 rather fluent in German but — weirdly enough — rather deficient in English. When I received my first paper back from Father O'Connell, he wrote on the final page: "Are you a native German speaker?" Believe me, this was not a compliment.

That same fall was the first fall I could vote in a presidential election. Father O'Connell was a true, old-fashioned conservative. In a pre-Internet age, I knew that Bush had won, but I had no idea about the fine details of the election. After class, I asked Father O'Connell — then holding a copy of the *New York Times* — about the details of the election. In conversation, he asked me about my own views on politics. When I told him I had voted for Ron Paul, he showed visible disappointment in me. "That's not healthy for the republic," he told me.

Over the three decades since I graduated from Notre Dame, I have kept in contact — though not as steadily as I should have — with Father O'Connell. Again, as I mentioned above, he was never cuddly. He was fierce. Yet I greatly desired his approval of what I've done, as a writer and a scholar. In fact, there's no teacher I've had from whom I've wanted approval more. I have no idea if Father O'Connell ever did approve of my work, but I do know that he established and lived the standards by which I measure myself. His was a taught as well as a lived Christian humanism.

26

The Good Humor of
Ralph McInerny

WHEN I FIRST HEARD THAT RALPH MCIN-
erny had passed away, I smiled. I ran to the top of the
stairs, yelled down to my wife that he had died, and
then smiled again.

I will fully admit, this is not my usual first reaction to hearing of
a death. But McInerny seems a special case. My first image — even
before hollering down to my wife — was that of McInerny meeting
his own wife, and Jacques Maritain, Aquinas, and Dante, beyond
the Gates. I have a feeling the several of them have a lot of catch-
ing up to do; and I'm equally sure that the conversation will continue...eternally.

Though I consider one of McInerny's sons, Dan, a good friend,
I only had the privilege of meeting his father once. Sponsored by our
college Catholic Society, Ralph McInerny came to Hillsdale shortly
after I arrived here (in 1999) and gave an excellent talk to a group
of Catholic faculty. I found him piercingly intelligent and equally
kind. His visit has stayed with me throughout the past decades.

Just writing this quasi-obituary, the smile returns. What more
could a Christian give to the world than what McInerny gave, short
of martyrdom?

Surely, if there is justice, history will remember McInerny as one
of the wittiest Christian thinkers and apologists of his age. McInerny stood as a pillar of all that is good at the University of Notre
Dame. Indeed, he was one of the three men (along with Fathers Bill
Miscamble and Marvin O'Connell) who served as Notre Dame's
conscience for years. A proper critic of the excesses of the culture

surrounding Vatican II (a "Peeping Thomist" as he called himself), and a prose writer of considerable grace and imagination, McInerny offered himself as a citizen of the City of God to this City of Man throughout the entirety of his lifetime.

Now residing in Michigan, my wife (a Texan) and I (a Kansan) frequently and insanely pack six children into our Honda Odyssey (named "Aeneas" just to spite the Greeks) and venture to the middle and southern parts of the country to visit our respective extended families. While the kids spill stuff (stuff which for this quasi-obituary will remain undefined) on the seats and the floor of the van, push one another, and watch the landscape fly by, my wife reads McInerny novels to me. Being more than a bit of an obsessive-compulsive, Germanic control-type of person, I drive. I also listen. McInerny's works have been a central part of our family travels since our wedding. I know his protagonists well — Roger Knight, Father Dowling, and Vincent Traeger. They almost seem like family.

But it's not just McInerny's mysteries. I will never forget one drive when Dedra (my wife) read a particular passage from his 1991 novel, *The Search Committee*. The passage involved a committee discussion about which minority/"outgroup" person would be most qualified to serve as a university chancellor. The answer, stated with complete irreverence, was so funny that at least ten mile markers flew by before we could stop laughing. I'll leave the answer for your own reading pleasure.

I'll also never forget the sobering and emotional (even to the point of gut-wrenching) moments in Professor McInerny's *Connolly's Life*, the story of a "Spirit of Vatican II" priest re-evaluating his life and its meaning.

For years, McInerny served as the Michael P. Grace Professor of Medieval Studies at Notre Dame. A proper and just title, indeed. A professor, a writer, a wit, a father, a husband, a publisher, an editor…

So, Professor McInerny, I continue to smile. You give me great hope in the power of a Christian, a professor, a thinker, and an author to temper, to poke fun of, and even — through the gratuitous gifts of grace — to leaven this City of Man.

Ralph (if I may), enjoy the reunions and the conversations far beyond this world. I look forward to joining you some day. Thank you for your deeply humane Christianity.

27

The Beautiful Mess
That is Margaret Atwood

I F A PERSON WERE MERELY TO GLIMPSE superficially at the life, work, and reputation of Margaret Atwood, he should be not necessarily either condemned or blamed, and easily forgiven, for assuming two things about this Canadian sage.

First, that she's just another radicalized ideologue from the bygone days of the 1960s, predictable and uninteresting — or, if interesting at all, only as one of many typical cookie-cutter feminists who invaded academia in the 1970s. When she published *The Handmaid's Tale* in 1985, professors of women's studies across North America embraced her with a sycophantic love bordering on the occultish, seeing Atwood and her book as little more than vehicles of protest.

Second, that even if she is interesting at some level, she's still very much a part of the typical tapioca-leftist postmodernism of early twenty-first century academe. The sources she employed for her famous six Cambridge University Empson Lectures of 2000, as just one typical example of her academic work, seemingly reek of predictability: Isaiah Berlin, E.L. Doctorow, Peter Gay, John Irving, D.H. Lawrence, Claude Levi-Strauss, Alice Munro, and Sylvia Plath.

Ugh. Utterly boring and disappointingly unoriginal.

A closer look at her Cambridge lecture sources reveals a bit more. In addition to the unenlightened and unimaginative list of scholars just mentioned, there also lurk around and through the pages of the lectures the works and ideas of L. Frank Baum; Lewis Carroll; Graham Greene; Stephen King; and, most wonderfully, Ray

Bradbury and Ursula LeGuin. Atwood just skyrocketed in terms of interest. Peter Gay? Again, ugh. But Peter Gay and Ray Bradbury? Far more interesting.

Reading even the first several pages of the Cambridge first lecture, the reader is struck by a profound truth about Margaret Eleanor Atwood (b. 1939). Whatever poor intellectual company she keeps, she is rather gloriously and absolutely her own person, and she probably always has been.

Physically quite beautiful and striking as a woman in the second half of her seventies, she likes to joke that while she might look like a "kindly granny," she is anything but. Her neighbors even tease her that she looks best with a broom, sweeping the blustery October leaves. "Witch," however, would not be the best word to describe her. These words do work: brilliant, genius, quirky, funny, merciless, odd, gothic, rational, individual, personal, moving, witty, maddening, and eclectic. Whatever one might say or write about her, it is clear that she never is and never was boring. Thinking about her own childhood, moving from place to place in the lesser known reaches of Canada, she explains what she believes to be the source of her own wacky and fertile imagination:

> Because none of my relatives were people I could actu-
> ally see, my own grandmothers were no more and no
> less mythological than Little Red Riding Hood's grand-
> mother, and perhaps this had something to do with
> my eventual writing life — the inability to distinguish
> between the real and the imagined, or rather the attitude
> that what we consider real is also imagined: every life
> lived is also an inner life, a life created.[1]

The dreadfully uptight and haughty Peter Gay does not readily emerge from such a passage, but the irrepressible Ray Bradbury leaps from it in full ecstasy.

---

1   Margaret Atwood, *Negotiating with the Dead: A Writer on Writing* (New York: Anchor Books, 2003), 7.

Yet however interesting her imagination, Atwood never dismisses or downplays her more rigorous and intellectual side, describing herself in interviews as an eighteenth-century rationalist who just happens to have all kinds of voices and persons and stories floating around and interacting with one another in her head. Whatever pretense she has toward the rationalism of several centuries ago, she falls rather clearly into the broad camp of the humanists, Christian and otherwise. As such, she expertly sculpts, caresses, and condemns in her art the horrors and the achievements of the human person. "Why is it that when we grab for heaven — socialist or capitalist or even religious — we so often produce hell?" she plaintively asks. "I'm not sure, but so it is. Maybe it's the lumpiness of human beings."[2] Lumpiness, indeed. Neither Thomas More nor Russell Kirk could have said it better.

To explore the humanist aspect of Atwood, it's worth reconsidering her most famous and well-known work, *The Handmaid's Tale*, a story that has been made into a major motion picture as well as a television series (Hulu, 2017–), and is read throughout high schools and colleges in the English-speaking world as gospel. "Don't let the bastards grind you down," playful faux words that inspire the heroine to resist her enslavement.

When the novel first came out in 1985, *The Handmaid's Tale* was both praised and condemned for being anti-male as well as pro-abortion. Those who loved it and hated it viewed it as an updated, feminist *1984*. Whether it was a poor reflection or a logical extension of Orwell's classic, no one much cared. It was what it was. To this day, however, criticism of *The Handmaid's Tale* has barely moved passed the praise and condemnation it received at its birth. Nearly every public school in the United States offers it as a modern classic, sometimes replacing and sometimes augmenting *Brave New World* and *Lord of the Flies*. Now so pervasive, it's taught in an almost perfunctory way. When pressed, however, those who teach it and those who read it claim to do so for the very same

<hr>

2   Atwood, *In Other Worlds: Science Fiction and the Human Imagination* (New York: Doubleday, 2011), 84.

reasons as those who first adopted the book in the mid-1980s. Regardless, *The Handmaid's Tale* has achieved a rare status in our culture, and has certainly become a significant artifact of North American postmodern culture. It's also hard to imagine, for example, the bestselling books and the myriad of shelves dedicated to Young Adult fiction at your local Barnes and Noble without the influence — however indirect or incorrect — of *The Handmaid's Tale.* After all, in our age of intellectual stagnation, who better to destroy patriarchal oppression than a noble and brave teenage girl, a postmodern Joan of Arc?

This, to be sure, is a most superficial reading of the novel, and the story is as complicated as anything Huxley or Orwell wrote. Indeed, in many ways, *The Handmaid's Tale* is the best dystopian novel written thus far, even better than its predecessors. This is true in part because it builds so effectively on what came before it. As a grand work of art, it is very deep. The story moves rapidly, but the symbolism and nuances of the art take not one but innumerable readings to discover. Without question, it is a work of art far too deep to be categorized in the simplistic terms of left or right.

I read it the first semester of my junior year in college. Not surprisingly, as this was 1988, I had to read it for a course on the history of women in America. Though written by a Canadian, *The Handmaid's Tale* served as an updated *The Scarlet Letter,* as we began the course with colonial women and the plight of those living in New England. Though I had devoured science fiction and dystopian fiction for years at that point — my favorite genres of literature — I then suspected *The Handmaid's Tale* of being some sick joke of a politicized feminist imposition on the sacred realm of intellect and art. I was still proudly wearing my anti-PC button on my buffalo-check denim jean jacket in those days. And yet what I found in the novel, at least at its most fundamental level, had nothing to do with imposing any ideology on the reader. Like all such dystopian fiction, it served as a new type of warning. For those of us who grew up in middle-class pro-Goldwater households in the 1970s and 1980s, *The Handmaid's Tale* describes almost perfectly the two things we were rightly taught to fear: fascist and communist tyrannies that had inflicted so much pain and suffering on the Western world, and the puritanical televangelists then emerging as cultural brokers for and within the New Right. While Pat Roberts might be more attractive than Stalin, each represented forms of control and unjust authority.

In *The Handmaid's Tale*, Atwood imagines just what might happen should a culture on the verge of collapse embrace the very tyranny it had struggled against throughout much of the century. What if, after defeating the Nazis and the Communists, the United States succumbed to a new Cromwell — one who is shiny and glittering even in his despotism? Near the beginning of the novel, the heroine — who has been made a sort of demonic anti-nun through no fault of her own — describes her mistress:

> It's one of the things we fought for, said the Commander's Wife, and suddenly she wasn't looking at me, she was looking down at her knuckled, diamond-studded hands, and I knew where I'd seen her before. The first time was on television, when I was eight or nine. It was when my mother was sleeping in, on Sunday mornings, and I would get up early and go to the television set in my mother's study and flip through the channels, looking for cartoons. Sometimes when I couldn't find any I would watch the Growing Souls Gospel Hour, where they would tell Bible stories for children and sing hymns. One of the women was called Serena Joy. She was the lead soprano. She was ash blond, petite, with a snub nose and huge blue eyes which she'd turn upwards during hymns. She could smile and cry at the same time, one tear or two sliding gracefully down her cheek, as if on cue, as her voice lifted through its highest notes, tremulous, effortless. It was after that she went on to other things. The woman sitting in front of me was Serena Joy. Or had been, once. So it was worse than I thought.

Any reader of my age and background will readily visualize with dread the Commander's Wife as Tammy Faye Bakker. And yet, one cannot stop there. Though Atwood repeatedly read *1984* and *Darkness at Noon* as a high school student, having nearly memorized each, she also earned her PhD under the famous Harvard scholar of the Puritans, Perry Miller. In the early 1980s, Atwood lived and studied in West Berlin, taking a side trip into the communist East. Utterly horrified by the crippling Leviathan of Communism, she found the actual inspiration for her own dystopian novel, set in a new Puritan New England.

None of this should suggest that feminism does not inform Atwood's fiction. It most certainly did and does. But to limit her fiction to a feminist interpretation alone is to denigrate almost beyond recognition Atwood's deep and creative individuality. When asked about her own views of feminism not long after the astounding success of *The Handmaid's Tale*, Atwood answered with her characteristically eccentric caution against all oppressions — left, right, above, or below — rather clearly to the surprise of the interviewer:

> But I'm an artist. That's my affiliation, and in any monolithic regime I would be shot. They always do that to the artists. Why? Because the artists are messy. They don't fit. They make squawking noises. They protest. They insist on some kind of standard of humanity which any such regime is going to violate. They will violate it saying that it's better for the good of all, or the good of the many, or the better this or better that. And the artists will always protest and they'll always get shot. Or go into exile.

If feminism inspires good questions to challenge unjust authority, Atwood supports it. The moment the feminists gain control, however, she knows that she would be the first to lead the rebellion against it.

Just as *The Handmaid's Tale* proved an effective examination of the genre of dystopia, so too have several of her other tales of a horrific and bizarre Moreau-esque future, the MaddAddam (a rather obvious palindrome and a play on Genesis) trilogy, consisting of *Oryx and Crake* (2003); *The Year of the Flood* (2009); and *MaddAddam* (2013). By "flood," Atwood is not referring to the biblical deluge, but rather to the genetic manipulation of the human species into something less than human in the immediate as well as into the far future. Though she does not generally refer to the thought or work of C.S. Lewis, except in derision of his female characters — "fond as he was of creating sweet-talking, good-looking evil queens" — her MaddAddam trilogy most definitely reflects Lewis's *The Abolition of Man* and *That Hideous Strength*. "All long-term exercises of power, especially in breeding, must mean the power of earlier generations over later ones," Lewis wrote in the third part of *The Abolition of Man*. "What we call Man's power over Nature turns out to be a power exercised by some men over other men with Nature as its instrument."

In Atwood's MaddAddam trilogy, one generation of corporations and their government allies play too deeply with the genetic code, thus ending man and beginning him again into something new and rather alien. Though the ghost of Lewis lurks over this trilogy, so do the ghosts of H.G. Wells, Aldous Huxley, and Arthur C. Clarke. When Snowman (aka, Jimmy, the protagonist of *Oryx and Crake*) first describes the children who find his humanity so bizarre, uncomfortable, and simultaneously intriguing, Atwood writes in a vein that would have made Huxley blush: "Still, they're amazingly attractive, these children — each one naked, each one perfect, each one a different skin colour — chocolate, rose, tea, butter, cream, honey — but each with green eyes. Crake's aesthetic."[3] Frankly, that Atwood so readily engages previous writers in the fantasy and science-fiction genres makes her even more interesting, not less. In everything she writes, as the above passage reveals so clearly, there is at once something deeply familiar and disturbingly alien. It is one of her greatest gifts as an artist.

As one of her many lovable quirks, Atwood insists on defining genres differently than do the PR persons for her publishers.

---

3 Atwood, *Oryx and Crake* (New York: Doubleday, 2003), 8.

Though one might readily label much of what she writes as "utopian" or "dystopian," Atwood believes all utopias and dystopias are of a whole, calling them "ustopias." Additionally, she believes her fantastic literature is not "science fiction" but "speculative fiction." She fights vehemently over this last definition, noting that her fiction never involves things that simply could not happen or have not yet been invented. Every aspect of her fiction, she claims, is possible, here and now.

As I mentioned earlier in this piece, photos of Atwood taken over the last several decades reveal what a beautiful and striking woman she is. What is most striking, however, are her eyes. Her eyes radiate intelligence and mischievousness. Truly, they are a gateway to her soul. And very bright indeed must that soul then be.

As she herself has noted, art is messy, and artists are even messier. Somehow, though, this Canadian has managed to fuse and harness the messiness of her mind and her soul in and with her art. Blissfully, in Atwood's humanist (if not Christian) imagination, there is no one way of doing all things, and no one way of thinking about all things. If we conservatives and libertarians cannot embrace the diverse and unique art of Margaret Atwood — whatever way she votes or to whatever charity she gives — we have lost our own ability to be ourselves and to celebrate the good in life.

CONCLUSION
Confusions and Hope

*I*N ONE OF THE MOST SINFULLY FORGOTTEN
novels by one of the most sinfully forgotten authors of the
past century, Willa Cather presented a scene of simultaneous
humanist wonder and bitterness.

> I don't myself think much of science as a phase of human
> development. It has given us a lot of ingenious toys;
> they take our attention away from the real problems, of
> course, and since the problems are insoluble, I suppose
> we ought to be grateful for distraction. But the fact is,
> the human mind, the individual mind, has always been
> made more interesting by dwelling on the old riddles,
> even if it makes nothing of them. Science hasn't given
> us any new amazements, except of the superficial kind
> we get from witnessing dexterity and sleight of-hand.
> It hasn't given us any richer pleasures, as the Renais-
> sance did, nor any new sins — not one! Indeed, it takes
> our old ones away. It's the laboratory, not the Lamb of
> God, that taketh away the sins of the world. You'll agree
> there is not much thrill about a physiological sin. We
> were better off when even the prosaic matter of taking
> nourishment could have the magnificence of a sin. I
> don't think you help people by making their conduct
> of no importance — you impoverish them.[1]

In this novel, so unjustly glanced over by our current crop of
literary theorists, Cather uses the house as a representation of

---

1   Godfrey St Peter in Willa Cather, *The Professor's House* (1925).

the mind and soul of its protagonist. Cluttered and dusty, the memories of and in the house haunt the now retiring academic, Godfrey St Peter. Has he done enough, or has he failed to do what was necessary? His wife and daughters only care about the most superficial aspects of life such as glamour, travel, and luxury, and his one prized student has died in war overseas. What does he have to show for it all? Whatever his many failings, the above passage reveals that he knows what matters most in life: the fact that he is human and that what he studies and loves is humane.

In so many ways, Cather is the true American artist of the twentieth century, resisting modernity and its many progressive temptations and detours. In almost every word she wrote—and no matter how simplistic the style might seem, the depth of meaning is layers upon layers deep—she upheld the artistic and the humane against the sentimental and unmeasured. Whether it's through the buffoonish populists of *O Pioneers* or the intrepid fur trappers of *Shadows Upon the Rock*, Cather always injected truth and beauty into her fiction. Real literature, she claimed, must always reach for the highest level of artistry. Only then, she believed, could it hold deeper meaning.

Over three decades after Willa Cather wrote this beautiful scene, and a decade after its author passed from the earth, a relatively young, upstart man of letters, Russell Amos Kirk, founded the journal *Modern Age*. A title at once mocking and yet respectful of the complexities of an ideological world—a world trapped in the throes of violence and upheaval—Kirk's *Modern Age* appeared for the first time on July 19, 1957. Its purpose? To conserve the best of Western civilization and to enrich the ideas of the world. To bring back, if not the Lamb of God (as even the skeptic Godfrey St Peter recognized), at least the pagan Logos of the Stoics. "We are not ideologists; we do not believe we have all the remedies for all the ills to which the flesh is heir," Kirk assured his readers on page two of the brand-new journal. After the unexpected success of his published dissertation, *The Conservative Mind*, Kirk wondered exactly what it was he hoped to conserve. In his following books—*A Program for Conservatives* (1954), *Academic Freedom* (1955), and *Beyond the Dreams of Avarice* (1956) — as well as in this journal, Kirk believed the only thing worth conserving was the humane or humanist tradition, beginning with Heraclitus and reaching to and through the thought and poetry of T. S. Eliot. It was, Kirk believed, the noblest of traditions, encompassing the greats from Socrates to Cicero, from Augustine to Dante, from Petrarch to More, and from Burke to Tocqueville. After he had successfully become a household name in late 1953, Kirk wanted to make his mark by conserving not merely "conservatism," but also what he referred to as the "humane tradition" of the West. In his own day, thinkers as diverse as Paul Elmer More, Willa Cather, Christopher Dawson, Nicolas Berdyaev, Sister Madeleva Wolff, Gabriel Marcel, Jacques Maritain, Frank Sheed, C. S. Lewis, Flannery O'Connor, Etienne Gilson, Eric Voegelin, Robert Nisbet, Leo Strauss, and Ray Bradbury as fellow travelers embraced various forms of the humanities and humanism. If anything could offer a real alternative to the whirligig of the modern world, the humanities and humanism could. Kirk argued that, for true humanism, the "past and present are one — or, rather, that the 'present,' the evanescent moment, is infinitely trifling in comparison with the well of the past, upon which it lies as a thin film."[2]

In no way does this book suggest that all modern conservatism came from the humanists and their allies. Indeed, when Russell Kirk wrote his magisterial *The Conservative Mind* in 1953, he was openly combining the humanism of Babbitt, More, and Hulme with the polite anarchism of Albert Jay Nock, the fabulism of G. K. Chesterton, C. S. Lewis, and Ray Bradbury, the libertarianism of Isabel Paterson and Friedrich Hayek, and the agrarianism of John Crowe Ransom and Hilaire Belloc. Over the next several years, Kirk would add Leo Strauss, Eric Voegelin, Robert Nisbet, and several others to his list of heroes and exemplars. Strauss, for example, figured so prominently in Kirk's thought that one of the primary purposes of the journal *Modern Age* was to defend Strauss from the myriad of attacks coming from the academy.

---

2 Russell Kirk, *Beyond the Dreams of Avarice* (Chicago: Regnery, 1956), 176.

Kirk wanted Strauss on the editorial board, but Strauss believed Regnery too untrustworthy when it came to Zionism, and thus refused to associate officially with him. In other words, Kirk's vision was not strictly of a Christian humanism, but rather of an ecumenically religious and Socratic humanism. Additionally, it must be noted and noted forcefully that Kirk saw this journal as a bulwark against any form of bigotry — ideological, racial, or religious. With so many errors in the world, Kirk held such prejudices to be not only unethical but practical wastes of time as well. Two of Kirk's greatest political heroes, Barry Goldwater and Ronald Reagan, would feel the same.

Given that Hulme and Babbitt lived through the rise of Marxism and Freudianism, both fanatical ideologies, as well as the wiles of Friedrich Nietzsche, their humanism not only makes perfect sense but also reveals much about the need to transcend any one conflict or division in the world through a belief which transcends time. Their humanism also argues in favor of citizenship in the Ciceronian ideal of the cosmopolis. While soil matters, it is only a thing — at least in terms of the classical virtue of temperance — only something to be used on the way to good. It is material and plastic, a substance created by God to allow us to live and survive in a world of material and time. Our true loyalties, as Cicero and those (like Kirk) who followed him argued, are with all of humanity, from Adam to the last living man. Our real citizenship resides elsewhere, and we are merely sojourners in the here and now. Indeed, it must be stressed vehemently that the very essence of the humanities exists to promote what is essentially human, not accidentally so.

That Kirk created the journal *Modern Age* at the height of the Cold War makes sense as well, given that he believed his humanism could conserve the best of Western civilization against the communists and other ideologues of the world, including democratic ideologues. Modernity itself embraced words and ideas as something separate from their contexts, exaggerating each thing against its relations and fellows. It focused on the specific at the expense of the universal, thus (as Babbitt said) losing any meaningful sense of proportion. The communists had made a religion out of community; the fascists had made a religion out of nation. Neither community nor nation is evil, but in isolation each becomes a grotesque thing of horror. The human person then becomes its material and plastic, thus subverting proper order.

Now that we have witnessed the first two decades of the twenty-first century, however, we must also recognize that our need for a humanism to conserve the dignity of the human person has not lessened in the least. As I write this, the American national security state is the largest and most intrusive in our history. There are so many agencies protecting the American population that no overview or oversight of all of them is actually possible. They have multiplied hideously since 9/11. Despite the rise of Homeland Security, the Transportation Safety Administration, etc., there is no tangible evidence that the American people are any safer than they were prior to 9/11. Given the prevailing and rising attitude that the enforcement of safety depends upon centralized authority, the will of the people to claim its own right to defend itself might very well mean that we are actually less safe than we were prior to the rise of the intrusive national security state.

Over the last several decades, we have also witnessed the rise of angry and manifest emotion as a form of bullying and propaganda. On our radios and televisions and across the internet, people fail to restrain almost any feeling. Instead, the public arena has become a place not for reason and measured tones, but for reaction and justified anger, for soundbites and slogans. Not surprisingly, then, populism has once again become a major force in politics and entertainment, with personality becoming nothing but a grotesque show of horrors.

Racial tensions are as high as they have been since the 1970s. While a person in the 1980s might well have seen Bono's lyric, "in the kingdom come, when all the colors bleed into one," as idealistic, he would not have seen it as unreachable and absurd. In this first third of the twenty-first century, the pleadings of that aged Irishman seem, sadly, somewhat quaint. Our identity politics have unleashed the fury of all, and righteousness — by all races — has become superior to civility. Since race is not even a real category, our civilization will most likely move past this ridiculous stage of bigotry, but there may be significant violence and misunderstanding before the end arrives.

Indeed, we live in a world of confusions. We no longer have the right to pretend the century is young; to believe that we cannot judge it in the way we can judge any previous century. This century demands analysis and criticism. What would we write or say or argue or claim or believe that would make this century any better than the previous one? Whatever the horrors of communism, fascism, nationalism, tribalism, and racism that so often prevailed — to diabolic effect and the slaughter of millions of innocents — the lines of division were relatively clear. All those same deadly ideas linger to this day, but they have become almost relentlessly blurred, one easily bleeding into another. The fascists and the anti-fascists of our day are, of course, both fascist, their tactics of bullying and violence indistinguishable in type or result. The anti-capitalists and capitalists, too, are often just capitalists, universally corrupt and willing to use whatever power exists in whatever form and to whatever degree for their own benefit. Certainly, those who riot against capitalism use the very tools and products of capitalism to challenge it. Perhaps the Apple Watch on the wrist of every protestor in Portland is just the piece of rope the capitalist is willing to sell to hang himself and his fellow profit-seekers.

The racists and the anti-racists of our day are both extremely racist, trading anti-black blusterings for anti-white blusterings. American society evolved (rather positively, overall) toward a neutral position on race in the 1950s and 1960s, only to have the government step in and codify that one moment of success through the federal laws of 1964 and 1965, thus trapping societal norms and derailing future progress. Whatever merits "affirmative action" might have, it is merely "positive discrimination," and those who have benefited from it become suspect by their mere success. Did they succeed because of their excellence or because of their skin tone? Those who were left behind because of affirmative action carry with them — just or not — anger and bitterness. Fewer things could be more dangerous for the common good of a republic (the *res publica*, the good or public thing) than laws that benefit any one segment of the people over another segment. That the Jim Crow laws were heinous is without question. The answer to such historical atrocity is not the same thing done against the abusers, but a level playing field. By almost every measurement, for example, racism is stronger now than it was, say, in 1990. By any just standard, discrimination against anyone because of the accidents of the person's birth is both ethically evil and practically ridiculous. Socrates knew this 24 centuries ago, and our failure to understand this now is a comment on our ignorance and our sinfulness.

We twenty-first-century humans have, seemingly, abolished the sexes, trading what was once male, for example, for what is metrosexual, homosexual, bisexual, omnisexual, and the list of possibilities of variations seems unending. And, when the younger generations of the West are marrying, they do so with a million caveats that generally resolve not in a marriage, but in a temporary civil association and union, a kind of temporary business in which employees come and go, and products become secondary considerations.

In the traditional liberal arts (as understood in the West, but also within many traditional understandings in the East), one understands the incredible and complex diversity not only of all of existence, but of each individual thing within existence. The goal of liberal education, though, is never to celebrate such diversity, balkanizing one aspect of a thing from another, but to find its wholeness and, especially, its connectedness. In understanding its wholeness, a thing becomes no less complex, but it (or he or she) does become more mysterious. And, as opposed to "systems," liberal education recognizes that some things can and never should be known. One might very well have come to understand — at least at a certain moment and place in history — the A, the D, and the E of a thing, knowing that the B and the C exist (indeed, must exist), but cannot or should not be known. Thus, the liberal arts demand a certain humility in both knowledge and wisdom. In a proper understanding, one does not exaggerate the A at the expense of the D and the E, but attempts to unify each with proportionality and balance, with dignity and sense.

It should not go unnoticed that the confusions of the twenty-first century are each and every one of them materialist confusions, with the typical heretical attempts to infuse some of the materialism with religious symbolism and fervor. By focusing only on the material, the material becomes bizarrely spiritual.

One of the many things the conservatives of the twentieth century got right was the need to return not just to first principles but also to proper definitions. They attempted to define such vital terms as academic freedom, liberalism, dignity, freedom, liberty, community, individual, person, etc. If we cannot agree on the meaning of a word, we can have no debate and no serious discussion. Simply put, without defining our terms, we can make no progress in the least. It becomes impossible. And, thus, we find ourselves not only in a society of confusion but in a society that resorts more often than not to personal and community violence.

Those of us who reject ideologies have the supreme duty of bringing the conversation back to the most important things. We can only do that by example — but presenting our best selves. By arguing with depth, not soundbites. By treating our opponents not as opponents, but as human persons who are as flawed (if in different ways) as we ourselves are. We must also be willing to rest our arguments in mystery, offering more than a smattering of humility. None of this will change overnight, and, if it did, we should distrust it. Our current confusions sprang from a century or more of poor and arrogant academic thought and public acceptance of mediocre ideas and crass political solutions. A way out is certainly possible, but, as with all good things, it will take time, immensely hard work, and more patience than most of us currently possess.

Abroad, Islamic fundamentalists slaughter wantonly, and Russia and China are making terribly aggressive moves in their respective regions. Indeed, at this moment in time the world situation looks far more as it would have looked to T.E. Hulme than as it did to Kirk. We fight not against organized ideologies, but against fundamentalist chaos. Perhaps the only real difference between 2019 and 1919 is that the United States now possesses a powerful and widespread, if extremely flabby, empire. We have troops — at various levels — stationed in nearly 150 of the almost 200 countries in existence. We possess the greatest navy the world has ever seen, but we lack direction, focus, and will.

Granted, it's a serious difference, but it does not lessen our duty to conserve the best of what has come before in preparation for what is to come. Perhaps, as Cather's St Peter suggested, we might once again reclaim the Lamb of God and the magnificence of sin. If so, there are no better models in the modern age than Hulme and Babbitt on how to proceed from here.

And, yet, it's always worth remembering. It takes only one candle to push back the darkness, to allow us to move through Tenebrae and to what might lie beyond.

BRADLEY J. BIRZER is Russell Amos Kirk Chair in American Studies and Professor of History, Hillsdale College. Co-founder and senior contributor of *The Imaginative Conservative*, he is also the author of several critically-acclaimed biographies, including those of Russell Kirk, Christopher Dawson, J.R.R. Tolkien, and Charles Carroll of Carrollton. He is also proudly a member of Tom Woods's Liberty Classroom. Birzer and his wife, Dedra (also a professional historian), have seven children and divide their time between Michigan and Colorado.

CPSIA information can be obtained
at www.ICGtesting.com
Printed in the USA
FSHW021330170720
71761FS